The Municipal
Year Book
2014

PRESS

The authoritative source book of local
government data and developments

The Municipal
Year Book
2014

Washington, DC

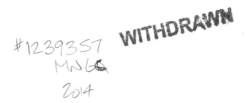
ICMA
PRESS

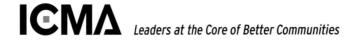

ICMA *Leaders at the Core of Better Communities*

ICMA advances professional local government worldwide. Its mission is to create excellence in local governance by developing and advancing professional management of local government. ICMA, the International City/County Management Association, provides member support; publications, data, and information; peer and results-oriented assistance; and training and professional development to more than 9,000 city, town, and county experts and other individuals and organizations throughout the world. The management decisions made by ICMA's members affect 185 million individuals living in thousands of communities, from small villages and towns to large metropolitan areas.

Volume 81, 2014

ISBN: 978-0-87326-616-1

ISSN: 0077-2186

Item number 43677

Library of Congress Catalog Card Number: 34-27121

The views expressed in this Year Book are those of individual authors and are not necessarily those of ICMA.

Suggested citation for use of material in this Year Book: Jane S. Author [and John N. Other], "Title of Article," in *The Municipal Year Book 2014* (Washington, D.C.: ICMA Press, 2014), 00–000.

Design and composition: Erika Abrams, Charles E. Mountain

Contents

Photo of Kansas City, Missouri, which achieved true professional management beginning in 1940, when L.P. Cookingham was hired by city reformers and became the "dean of the nation's city managers."

Source: "Kansas City History," kcmo.gov/kansas-city-history.

The Legacy of Local Government Professionalism: A 100-Year Perspective

Robert J. O'Neill Jr.
Executive Director, ICMA

The year 2014 represents a number of significant milestones for ICMA: the 100th anniversary of the association and the professionalization of local government management in the United States, the 90th year of the ICMA Code of Ethics, and the 80th hardcopy printing of our best-selling *Municipal Year Book*. Each of these events grew out of the development of the council-manager plan, which Richard Stillman described in his seminal work, *The Rise of the City Manager*, as "a product of the Progressive reform era."[1] This foreword commemorates the rich history of professional management in local government, suggests the challenges and opportunities facing the field, and sets the stage for future generations of professional city, town, and county managers.

Council-Manager Government: A Brief History

As more and more people throughout the United States moved away from an agricultural way of life and poured into burgeoning industrialized urban areas, new burdens were placed upon local governments. By the 1840s, U.S. local governments had expanded their range of services to include such functions as police and fire protection, operation of public schools, basic welfare (i.e., relief), and water provision.[2] In the half-century between 1860 and 1910, these governments experienced unprecedented growth and began to hire full-time employees.[3]

The influence of urbanization and industrialization and the great American corporate trusts changed the way scholars and practitioners thought about the management of their communities.[4] Although growing populations were reflected in the expanded size of local government councils, the increased demand for services—from the construction of roads to the development and enforcement of building codes—gave rise to a need for specialized expertise that council members, who had little time or experience to perform these administrative tasks, could not provide.[5] The result was the election of individuals whose primary objective was short-term, personal economic gain rather than long-term community values and goals.[6] Seemingly overnight, the country saw the sudden rise of partisan "city bosses," politicians who indulged in nepotism, patronage, and the exploitation of the municipal funds over which they were granted control.[7] This decentralization of local government led to increasing citizen dissatisfaction with the quality of municipal services and the inefficient, wasteful administration of local government.[8]

BRIBERY & CORRUPTION

NEW YORK

RIGHT UNDER HER NOSE EVERY DAY IN THE WEEK

"City bosses" and Tammany Hall–type political machines controlled municipal politics in the United States for years. Source: Library of Congress, Prints & Photographs Division [LC-USZ62-13093]

In response to this public discontent, progressive reformers fought for and won a series of local government reforms that spawned several organizational experiments.[9] This was one of only a few times in U.S. history when a transformation occurred that was "so remarkable that a molt seems to take place, and an altered country begins to emerge."[10] And the council-manager system played a major role in this transformation as one of the few original American contributions to political theory.[11] This system provided a structure through which the elected executive, elected council, and a management professional appointed by the entire governing body could work together to provide their communities with strong political leadership, strong policy development, a relentless focus on execution and results, a commitment to transparent and ethical government, and a strategy for representing and engaging every segment of the community.[12]

Contrary to the image of undemocratic "appointed technocrats" who, in their eagerness to wipe out city corruption, were pitted against more democratic chief executives,[13] professional managers did not diminish the role of local elected officials. This was because, unlike government at the federal and state levels, the council-manager form contains no counterproductive separation of powers between an elected executive and the elected governing body; thus, it provides a parliamentary system in which all power is concentrated in the entire elected body.[14] Under this form, a principal elected official such as the mayor assumes a

significant, coordinating, and activist leadership role within an elected board of directors, which develops policies that benefit the community as a whole.

Functioning much like a business organization's chief executive, the appointed professional manager directs the daily operations of the community. Selected by the council on the basis of education, training, and experience, the manager works through a professional staff to ensure the provision of services and enforce the policies adopted by the elected council.[15] Qualifications and performance—and not skillful navigation of the political election process—are the characteristics that make this appointed management professional attractive to a governing body.

Professional local government managers have no guaranteed term of office or tenure. They can be dismissed by the council at any time, for any reason. As a result, they must always be responsive to residents and dedicated to the highest ideals of honesty, integrity, and excellence in the management and delivery of public services—hence, the development of the ICMA Code of Ethics in 1924.

The strengths of the council-manager system include its flexibility to change. A community may require different management skills and talents at different times. Professional managers who have served a number of communities bring a range of fresh, innovative ideas to each new position. At the same time, they can provide critical continuity of experience during times of transition, such as the turnover of elected officials; as a result, a change in political leadership within the community that employs a professional manager does not have to result in wholesale changes in top management.

The Rich Legacy of the Council-Manager Plan and Professional Local Government Management

During the past 100 years, the council-manager structure of government has flourished in U.S. cities, towns, and counties dedicated to improving the quality of life for their residents, and it has become the most popular system of local government for communities with populations of 2,500 or more.[16] In December 1914, when eight city managers met in Springfield, Ohio, "to promote the efficiency of city managers" and formed the City Managers' Association (CMA), there were only 31 cities with city managers.[17] Today, 3,677 U.S. municipalities with populations of 2,500 or more and 819 U.S. counties operate under this system of local government,[18] and more than 150 million Americans—nearly half the U.S. population—live in communities with professional managers in place.[19]

Pictured are the eight city managers who met in Springfield, Ohio, in 1914 to form the City Managers' Association (CMA).

The legacy of success resulting from the professionalization of local government is well documented. Seventy-five percent of communities recognized with the National Civic League's coveted All-America City Award between 2007 and 2013 are run by professional managers.[20] A February 2011 study by IBM Global Business Services found that cities that operate under the council-manager form of government are nearly 10% more efficient than those operating under the mayor-council form,[21] a testament to the fact that "investing executive authority in professional management shielded from direct political interference should yield more efficiently managed cities."[22]

Among the 2013 CNN-*Money Magazine* top 50 small-town "Best Places to Live," 68% operate under the council-manager form of government.[23] The form is also flexible enough to meet the needs of some of the largest U.S. communities, including Phoenix, Arizona (pop. 1,488,750); San Antonio (pop. 1,382,951) and Dallas (pop. 1,241,162), Texas; San José, California (pop. 982,765); Austin (pop. 842,592) and Fort Worth (pop. 777,992), Texas; Charlotte, North Carolina (pop. 775,202); and Kansas City, Missouri (464,310).[24]

The Future of U.S. Local Government: Drivers of Change and Creativity

Despite the professionalization of local government, our communities continue to grapple with myriad changing forces. For example, "the fiscal challenges gripping our federal and state governments will force local governments to fend for themselves for at least the next 10 years. This decade of local government will be a time of 'creative destruction' that will produce an unprecedented amount of innovation."[25]

Reviewing *The Metropolitan Revolution,* a 2013 book by the Brookings Institution's Bruce Katz and Jennifer Bradley, *New York Times* columnist David Brooks discusses the authors' argument that "Washington paralysis is already leading to a power inversion. As the federal government becomes less energetic, city governments become more so."[26] He notes that as U.S. society continues to cluster demographically, the authors "describe a country that is segmenting slightly into divergent city-states"; that economic changes are reinforcing regional concentration; and that local, rather than federal, government will become more dynamic because the latter "have power over the basics, which are the key to promoting growth."[27]

Over the past year or so, ICMA has examined some of the issues that will drive these changes, and the ways in which focused local government leadership can help foster innovation while exercising the discipline to harness it—two decidedly unique but not mutually exclusive concepts. Five significant factors will influence the future roles and strategies of local government in the United States:

1. *The public-sector fiscal crisis.* However Congress chooses to deal (or not deal) with issues surrounding taxes, spending and debt, the federal deficit challenge will not be easily resolved. This means increasingly reduced funding [to local governments] for domestic and local programs and greater reliance on regulation and preemption.

2. *Demographic changes.* In coming decades, the percentage of the country's population that is white will decline, the Latino population will grow and the baby-boomer population will experience some serious aging. The United States is becoming a truly pluralistic, multicultural society.

3. *The impact of technology.* We now have the ability to contact nearly every household multiple times a day to encourage community engagement and help frame conversations around service delivery. At the same time, we no longer can control those conversations. Social media is accessible by people of both good and bad intent, and we ignore it at our peril. Meanwhile, the potential of "big data" is enormous, enabling us to amass large amounts of information that will afford us greater transparency and accountability and give local officials an opportunity to partner with many different stakeholders.

4. *Polarized politics.* The divide in politics has been most evident in Washington, D.C., but it is increasingly filtering to the local level. The challenge is to reach reasoned compromises to move issues forward. What we see in Washington is deadlock: Anyone can say "no" and everyone has a veto. The question [for local officials] is: How do we reach some constructive form of "yes"?

5. *An increasing gap between the haves and the have-nots.* Are we creating a new class of people who will be unable to fully participate in the economy?

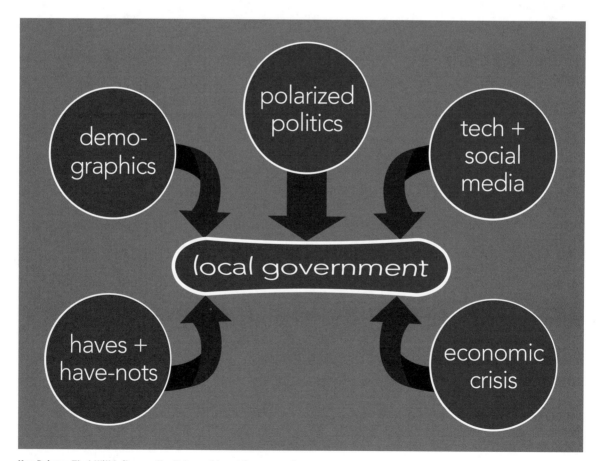

Key Drivers That Will Influence the Future of Local Government

Will work no longer be wholly rewarded—that is, will the American Dream become unattainable—no matter how hard one tries?[28]

Issues That Matter, and Multisectoral/Multidisciplinary Approaches to Service Delivery

Over the past few years, ICMA has examined feedback obtained from resident surveys to identify the issues that matter most to people throughout the United States. The six issues that have predominated in the findings are jobs and the economy, education, safety, health care, the environment, and overall quality of life (including infrastructure and transportation).[29] All six issues require scale and a multisectoral, multidisciplinary, and intergovernmental strategy to produce the outcomes that matter most to our communities.

In contrast to this thinking, as the world has grown more complex, governmental leaders have responded by constructing their organizations to leverage specialization. Today's local governments have separate departments for police, fire, recreation, engineering, public works, social services, and the like. But is this approach consistent with the need for multidisciplinary, multisector strategies to respond to the issues that matter most?[30]

Observations made in a 2011 report issued by the Bureau of Justice Administration (BJA), which examined the leadership issues that police agencies are dealing with, are applicable to local governments in general. Specifically, the "command-and-control structure; territorial, function-based silos; and single-jurisdictional service delivery" approach that characterizes many of today's local governments is being profoundly challenged by "severe economic pressures . . . ; diverse community socioeconomic and demographic complexities . . . ; differing, and often competing, service needs within regions and sub-regions; the increased pace of change, particularly in the areas of technology and communications . . .; and a transforming workforce, including multi-generational staffs with often competing values and expectations."

In response, many local government organizations are using "aggressive cost-cutting strategies" as well

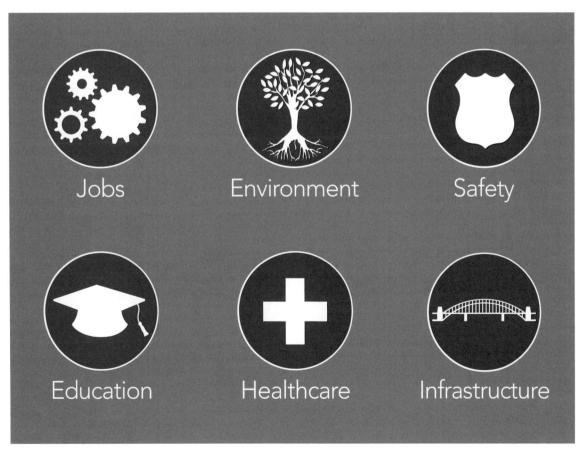

Issues That Matter Most to Residents

as "new ways of collaborating, such as shared services and consolidations. . . . Yet these strategies rely on traditional organizational structures and do not address the reality . . . that a from-scratch approach may be necessary to create and manage" the organization of the future.[31]

From the BJA report, it is easy to conclude that the "stand-alone, single-discipline governmental department may be going the way of the dinosaur." In its place, "an 'integrated partnership organization' in which community goals are achieved within a multi-disciplinary environment that requires [local government employees] to acquire a diverse professional background and skill set as well as the ability to collaborate with other agencies, disciplines and organizations" may be required.[32]

"It is often said that the important work of most organizations is conducted outside the traditional organizational structure, and many local governments adapt their existing structures through the use of multi-disciplinary task forces and interdepartmental teams. Others establish intradepartmental networks, particularly when service needs are too complex to address through a single discipline and require the involvement of several departments or agencies. . . . The question for governmental leaders is this: How do we take advantage of the enormous power of specialization yet organize around the issues that matter most to those we serve" and that, at a minimum, require multidisciplinary and multisectoral approaches to service delivery?[33]

Future Leadership Role of Professional Managers

The discussions above raise some interesting questions for the future of the local government management profession. Among the most important is: Will professional managers be the reformers or are they to be reformed?

To achieve success against the backdrop of these major drivers, complex public policy issues, and a new set of local conditions will test the leadership capacity of elected and appointed local officials. Local government managers will need to view these challenges from a new perspective that enables them to "see more clearly how to manage, use, and optimize resources in a much different way than has been done in the past."[34]

We will need to release "our tightly clenched grasp on some commonly held assumptions" and move toward a new, easily understood transparency around the fiscal health of our communities.[35] We will also need to find creative, nontechnical ways to forecast what our communities will look like in the next 5 to 10 years by "differentiating between one-time and ongoing revenues and expenditures" and, thus, eliminating much of the uncertainty that often surrounds our programs and projects.[36]

Hampton, Virginia's "I Value" campaign, for example, offers residents the opportunity to identify which services they value most and to provide input into the budgeting process. The city learned that offering residents multiple communication channels, such as phone polling, online surveys, and community meetings, encouraged civic engagement. More than 1,000 residents participated in the online survey portion of the "I Value" campaign during its first year, and many also took part in a phone survey or attended community forums. The campaign, according to City Manager Mary Bunting, has enabled the city to build a "larger body of evidence about what the community is thinking" and to acquire valuable data and information for use by city staff as they begin their budget deliberations.[37] The success of the campaign brought Bunting to the White House in September 2012 to be honored as an "Innovation Champion of Change"—an award given to government leaders who make government more transparent, provide new venues for citizens to become involved and foster new methods for the public, private and nonprofit sectors, and citizens to work together.[38]

Finally, the professional local government leaders of the future will need to work collaboratively with elected officials, their staffs, and their communities. Local government organizations have changed in large part because, according to Simon Farbrother, city manager of Edmonton, Alberta, Canada, and ICMA's 100th president, staff expectations concerning their involvement in the decisions that affect them have changed, paving the way for increased innovation and creativity in the workplace. Managers "'are now facilitators or moderators of the community conversation' who . . . hold responsibility for setting the 'tone . . . norms, and standards of behavior' for their organizations."[39]

Welcome to the new era of local government!

Notes

1 Richard J. Stillman II, *The Rise of the City Manager: A Public Professional in Local Government* (Albuquerque, N.M.: University of New Mexico Press, 1974), 1.

2 Charles R. Adrian, "Forms of City Government in American History," in *The Municipal Year Book 1988* (Washington, D.C.: International City Management Association, 1988), 5.

3 Stillman, *Rise of the City Manager*, 6–7.

4 Ibid., 8.

5 Adrian, "Forms of City Government," 5.

6 Ibid., 8.

7 Ibid.

8 Ibid., 7.

9 Stillman, *Rise of the City Manager*, 12.

10 Doris Kearns Goodwin, "Preface," in *The Bully Pulpit: Theodore Roosevelt, William Howard Taft, and the Golden Age of Journalism* (New York: Simon & Schuster, 2013), xii.

11 Roger L. Kemp, "The Council-Manager Form of Government in the United States," in *Current Municipal Problems*, vol. 13 (Callaghan & Company, 1987), 20–29.

12 Robert J. O'Neill, "The Mayor-Manager Conundrum That Wasn't" (unpublished article, 2005), icma.org/en/icma/knowledge_network/documents/kn/Document/9263/The_MayorManager_Conundrum_That_Wasnt.

13 Henry Kippen, "Can Cities Save Us?" *RSA Journal* (Winter 2012), thersa.org/fellowship/journal/archive/winter-2012/features/can-cities-save-us.

14 Chester A. Newland, "Council-Manager Government: Positive Alternative to Separation of Powers," *Public Management (PM)*, July 1985, 7–9.

15 Ibid.

16 ICMA, "Inside the Year Book," in *The Municipal Year Book 2014* (Washington, D.C.: ICMA Press, 2014), xxii and xxv.

17 Stillman, *Rise of the City Manager*, 30.

18 ICMA, "Inside the Year Book," xxii and xxv.

19 From ICMA's local government database with 2012 population estimates from the U.S. Bureau of the Census.

20 Calculated from date obtained from the National Civic League (2013), allamericacityaward.com/about-2/.

21 David Edwards, *Smarter, Faster, Cheaper: An Operations Efficiency Benchmarking Study of 100 American Cities* (Sommers, N.Y.: IBM Global Business Services, February 2011), 8.

22 Ibid.

23 Calculated from material obtained from "Best Places to Live: America's Best Small Towns," *CNNMoney* (2013), money.

cnn.com/magazines/moneymag/best-places/?iid = BPL_sp_header.

24 All populations are 2012 estimates from the U.S. Census Bureau, available at quickfacts.census.gov/qfd/index.html#.

25 Robert J. O'Neill Jr., "Local Government in an Era of Creative Destruction," *Governing.com*, May 1, 2013, governing.com/columns/mgmt-insights/col-local-government-creative-destruction-challenges-leadership.html (accessed February 23, 2014).

26 David Brooks, "The Power Inversion," *New York Times*, June 6, 2013, nytimes.com/2013/06/07/opinion/brooks-the-power-inversion.html?_r = 0 (accessed February 23, 2014).

27 Ibid.

28 O'Neill, "Local Government in an Era of Creative Destruction."

29 Robert J. O'Neill Jr., "Public Services and the Limits of Specialization," *Governing.com*, July 24, 2013, governing.com/columns/mgmt-insights/col-public-services-multi-sector-disciplinary-intergovernmental-management.html (accessed February 23, 2014).

30 Ibid.

31 Ibid.

32 Ibid.

33 Ibid.

34 Jon Johnson, Chris Fabian, and Cheryl Hilvert, "Embracing the 'Decade of Local Government'—How to Face Challenges and Seize Opportunities," *Public Management (PM)*, October 2013, 8, webapps.icma.org/pm/9509/.

35 Ibid.

36 Ibid.

37 Robert Brauchle, "Hampton's Bunting Honored at White House," *Daily Press* (Hampton Roads, Va.), September 26, 2012, articles.dailypress.com/2012-09-26/news/dp-nws-bunting-white-house-award-20120926_1_hampton-city-government-city-manager-community-forums (accessed February 23, 2014).

38 Kellyn Blossom, "White House Honors 'Champions of Change' in City and County Innovation," White House Office of Intergovernmental Affairs, September 25, 2012, whitehouse.gov/blog/2012/09/26/white-house-honors-champions-change-city-and-county-innovation

39 ICMA, "Where Do You See the Future of the Profession?," summary of Simon Farbrother's closing address at ICMA's 99th Annual Conference, Boston, Mass., September 25, 2013, icma.org/en/icma/newsroom/highlights/Article/103811/Where_Do_You_See_the_Future_of_the_Profession.

Acknowledgments

Many of the issues discussed above are explored in this 2014 edition of the *Municipal Year Book*, which focuses on, among other issues, the rich legacy of the professionalization of local government in the United States and the future direction of the field. We thank the authors who contributed to this edition, as well as the thousands of city, town, and county managers; clerks, finance officers; personnel directors; police and fire chiefs; and other officials who patiently and conscientiously responded to ICMA's surveys. Your participation, research, and analysis of the profession have helped us to ensure the ongoing viability of professional local government management.

I would also like to thank all of the ICMA staff who have devoted countless hours to making the *Year Book* such an invaluable resource, particularly, Ann Mahoney, ICMA director of publications, and Jane Cotnoir, the *Year Book* editor. Other ICMA staff members who contributed to this edition are Evelina Moulder, director of survey research; Erik Sundvall, creative director; Sebia Clark, program analyst; Nedra James, editorial and publications assistant; and Michele Frisby, director, communications and public information. Finally, thanks go to Sandra F. Chizinsky, ICMA consulting editor.

Robert J. O'Neill Jr.
Executive Director
ICMA

Inside the *Year Book*

Inside the *Year Book*

Local government concerns are increasingly complex and sophisticated, and the need for familiarity with a broad range of issues is unsurpassed. Furthering the knowledge base needed to better manage local government is one of ICMA's top goals.

Management Trends and Survey Research

1 Upholding and Expanding the Roles of Local Government Managers: State of the Profession 2012

Many changes have occurred in local government since eight city managers from the 31 council-manager cities met in 1914 to establish the City Managers' Association. Nevertheless, the basic advisory role and administrative responsibilities of local government managers have essentially remained the same although managers' interactions with citizens have greatly expanded. Today, with over 8,800 top administrators in municipalities and counties and 100 years of collective experience, it is worth examining how current top administrators view their roles, assess the leadership of elected officials, and rate their own level of satisfaction in their position. Using responses to ICMA's *State of the Profession 2012* survey, this article provides a profile of responding top administrators; reviews their roles with respect to their governing boards, citizens, and elected officials; and considers what the changing conditions in local government management today will mean for professional managers in the future.

2 100 Years of Tackling Societal Changes

Local government managers have been committed to improving life for the people in their communities from the beginning. This article provides a retrospective of the policy issues facing local government professionals over the past century—from the early years, when managers tackled public health and built the basic infrastructure; through the 1920s, when they wrestled with financing long-term water and power needs and debated municipal ownership of public utilities; through the Great Depression, when they struggled to secure a balanced revenue system and find innovative solutions to problems; through the war years and the postwar period, when they rose to meet the demand for labor and the challenges of rebuilding; through the social unrest and urban challenges of the 1960s and 1970s, when they recognized that local governments could not solve the problems of poverty and racial inequality alone and began to push for a national approach to these pressing issues; through the economic boom of the 1980s and 1990s, when technological advances dramatically changed the way they worked and communicated with citizens; and into the 21st century, as they continue to combat the persistent national issues of economic disparity, aging populations, immigration, changing demographics, the federal debt, and sustainability, as well as such global issues as natural and man-made threats and climate change.

3 100 Years . . . and We Are Still Reinventing Government!

From the beginning of the local government profession, managers have been called upon to constantly improve and "reinvent" themselves and the ways in which local government conducts its business. For the current generation of managers, perhaps the most significant call to action was the 1992 book *Reinventing Government: How the Entrepreneurial Spirit Is Transforming the Public Sector,* by David Osborne and Ted Gaebler. Its recommendations formed the basis of the "New Public Administration" movement, which encouraged local governments to be more "entrepreneurial" in their work—more mission driven, customer focused, and results oriented. Since its publication, local governments have been supporting initiatives to improve customer service, contract and partner for service delivery, use enterprise funds, impose fees to generate revenue, and make increased use of technology. This article celebrates the continuing relevance of *Reinventing Government* by reviewing its principles and highlighting the local governments that have adhered to those principles, seeking innovative approaches to reinvent the services and programs they provide and thereby showing that being mission driven, customer focused, and results oriented remain viable goals for local government managers today.

4 ICMA's Evolution as an International Organization

ICMA's vision of an international presence started as early as 1924—when, just 10 years after its founding, the City Managers' Association added "International" to its name. This article traces the development of ICMA's international program, beginning in the mid-1950s when executive director Orin Nolting traveled extensively abroad to promote the council-manager plan and further the exchange of ideas and experiences between U.S. and Canadian managers and their counterparts in other countries. It then continues through the formation of the ICMA Task Force on International Education in 1976; the multimillion-dollar Municipal Development and Management Project awarded by USAID in 1989 to assist local government officials in several developing countries; the establishment of the International Municipal Programs department; ICMA's work in the 1990s with countries facing the challenges of decentralization and democratization; the establishment of CityLinks in 1997, ICMA México-Latinoamérica in 2004, and the ICMA China Center in 2011; and the vital work the program has done to provide stability in such conflict-torn areas as Iraq and Afghanistan.

5 Intermunicipal Cooperation: The Growing Reform

ICMA's ongoing alternative service delivery (ASD) survey, which has been measuring local government use of ASD mechanisms since 1982, provides a way to track experimentation and innovation at the local level. The 2012 ASD survey sought to determine how the declining revenues and increased need for public services brought about by the Great Recession affected local governments in their choice of service delivery mechanisms. This article reports on findings from that survey, which show that intermunicipal contracting is now the most common delivery alternative—more common

even than for-profit contracting—and it explores some of the factors explaining this trend. It also discusses motivators for and obstacles to ASD, and it presents a disturbing fact about local government evaluation of ASD mechanisms: that monitoring and evaluation of contracted services continue to be low.

6 Advancing Sustainable Communities through Civic Engagement and Performance Measurement

The term *sustainability* is understood to have three components: economic growth, environmental protection, and social equality. A sustainable community is defined as one that is able to consistently thrive over time, making decisions to improve the community in ways that will not adversely affect future generations. To derive a national baseline of local sustainability policies and programs, ICMA surveyed local governments in 2010 and found that, for the most part, sustainability at the local level in the United States is still in its infancy. However, among the leading communities that have adopted sustainability as a framework, two main approaches stand out: (1) civic engagement to identify priorities and develop nongovernmental partnerships and (2) indicators and measures to help manage performance. This article looks at specific communities that have used civic engagement to help identify needs and strategies to promote sustainability, with a particular focus on Dubuque, Iowa. It also focuses on efforts in Texas and North Carolina to devise tools and metrics to better understand the results of their sustainability policies and interventions; on the STAR Community Rating System; and on performance measurement in Minneapolis, Minnesota.

7 Spreading Innovation

We apply the term *innovation* to any idea or action that (1) is new to a given organization and, when implemented, (2) produces a better result. Thus, the success of an innovation is reflected not only in the immediate effects on the organization in which it is implemented, but also in the extent to which diffusion occurs. In other words, ideas that are not shared and disseminated for implementation will not amount to an innovation. This article first considers the factors that are required for innovative ideas to spread and the five-stage process through which innovative ideas may be adopted. It then reviews the maturation process through which innovative ideas might begin as emerging practices and then become leading practices and, finally, prevailing practices, and it illustrates this process using case studies from 19 different jurisdictions. Finally, it provides seven "takeaway" lessons that reinforce the key points behind policy innovation diffusion.

8 CAO Salary and Compensation: Stability Continues

There is always interest in the compensation of public employees, whether related to pensions and benefits or to actual salaries. Yet identifying a "typical" salary and benefits for a city or county manager or chief appointed official is difficult because of the many variables that have an impact on the compensation package. According to the "ICMA Guidelines for Compensation," the compensation of local government managers should be "fair, reasonable, transparent, and based on comparable public salaries nationally and regionally." Moreover, "compensation should be based on the position requirements, the complexity of the job reflected in the composition of the organization and community, the leadership needed, labor market conditions, cost of living in the community, and the organization's ability to pay." Examining new data from a 2013 national survey of local government executives, this article looks at compensation issues for city, county, and town managers and administrators within the context of the ICMA Guidelines.

9 Police and Fire Personnel, Salaries, and Expenditures for 2013

Continuing the trend identified in 2010 when police and fire departments, like other local government departments, saw their budgets reduced, police and fire expenditures in 2013 are still a concern in some communities. There is hope that, as the housing market continues to strengthen, property tax revenues may slowly increase and that this increase in revenue for municipal budgets may eventually bring a halt to staffing reductions. This article, a longtime staple of *The Municipal Year Book,* is based on the results of an annual survey that is meant to provide a general picture of police and fire personnel and expenditures for each year. It presents the following information for both police and fire departments in tabular form: total personnel, the number of uniformed personnel, minimum crew per fire apparatus, entrance and maximum salaries, information on longevity pay, and a breakdown of departmental expenditures. Data from the 2013 survey are compared with those from 2012.

Directories

Directory 1 comprises eight lists providing the names and websites of U.S. state municipal leagues; provincial and territorial associations and unions in Canada; state agencies for community affairs; provincial and territorial agencies for local affairs in Canada; U.S. municipal management associations; international municipal management associations; state associations of counties; and U.S. councils of governments recognized by ICMA.

Directory 2 presents "Professional, Special Assistance, and Educational Organizations Serving Local and State Governments." The 79 organizations that are included provide educational and research services to members and others, strengthening professionalism in government administration.

Organization of Data

Most of the tabular data for *The Municipal Year Book 2014* were obtained from public officials through questionnaires developed and administered by ICMA. ICMA maintains databases with the results of these surveys. All survey responses are reviewed for errors. Extreme values are identified and investigated; logic checks are applied in the analysis of the results.

Government Definitions

A municipality, by census definition, is a "political subdivision within which a municipal corporation has been established to provide general local government for a specific population concentration in a defined area." This definition includes all active governmental units officially designated as cities, boroughs (except in Alaska), villages, or towns (except in New England, Minnesota, New York, and Wisconsin), and it generally includes all places incorporated under the procedures established by the several states.

Counties are the primary political administrative divisions of the state. In Louisiana these units are called parishes. Alaska has county-type governments called boroughs. There are certain unorganized areas of some states that are not included in the *Year Book* database and that have a county designation from the Census Bureau for strictly administrative purposes. These comprise 11 areas in Alaska, 5 areas in Rhode Island, 8 areas in Connecticut, and 7 areas in Massachusetts.[1]

According to the U.S. Bureau of the Census, in January 2012 there were 90,056 governments in the United States (Table 1).

Municipality Classification

Table 2 details the distribution of all municipalities of 2,500 and over in population by population, geographic region and division, metro status, and form of government.

Table 1 U.S. Local Governments, 2012

Local governments	90,056
County	3,031
Municipal	19,519
Town or township	16,360
School district	12,880
Special district	38,266

Table 2 Cumulative Distribution of U.S. Municipalities with a Population of 2,500 and Over

	Population								
Classification	2,500 and over	5,000 and over	10,000 and over	25,000 and over	50,000 and over	100,000 and over	250,000 and over	500,000 and over	Over 1,000,000
Total, all cities	10,982	6,989	4,229	1,893	863	314	78	34	34
Population group									
Over 1,000,000	9	9	9	9	9	9	9	9	9
500,000–1,000,000	25	25	25	25	25	25	25	25	...[a]
250,000–499,999	44	44	44	44	44	44	44	...	...
100,000–249,999	236	236	236	236	236	236	...	...	...
50,000–99,999	549	549	549	549	549	...	...	...	...
25,000–49,999	1,030	1,030	1,030	1,030	...	...	...	...	...
10,000–24,999	2,336	2,336	2,336	...	...	...	...	...	...
5,000–9,999	2,760	2,760	...	...	...	...	...	...	...
2,500–4,999	3,993	...	...	...	...	...	...	...	...
Geographic region									
Northeast	3,128	1,993	1,101	399	134	35	10	4	2
North-Central	4,313	2,486	1,450	600	247	76	16	5	1
South	2,372	1,550	972	442	216	94	26	14	3
West	1,169	960	706	452	266	109	26	11	3
Geographic division									
New England	810	571	363	143	51	12	1	1	...
Mid-Atlantic	2,319	1,423	738	256	83	23	9	3	2
East North-Central	3,432	1,980	1,160	489	192	57	9	5	1
West North-Central	881	506	291	112	55	19	7	...	...
South Atlantic	1,018	676	442	210	107	43	10	4	...
East South-Central	507	339	195	74	26	13	4	3	...
West South-Central	848	534	334	157	83	38	12	7	3
Mountain	442	331	205	123	63	31	9	5	1
Pacific Coast	725	629	501	329	203	78	17	6	2
Metro status									
Metropolitan Statistical Area	6,667	4,565	2,922	1,530	780	296	76	33	9
Micropolitan Statistical Area	1,790	994	607	107	2	...	...	...	...
New England City and Town Area	524	413	258	67	11	...	...	...	...
Undesignated	2,001	1,017	442	189	70	18	2	1	...
Form of government									
Mayor-council	3,315	2,192	1,328	568	269	104	43	22	6
Council-manager	3,677	2,934	2,040	1,036	484	175	31	11	3
Commission	142	109	70	28	12	5	2	1	...
Town meeting	354	246	116	6	...	...	...	...	...
Representative town meeting	67	57	46	21	5	...	...	...	...
Unknown[b]	3,427	1,451	629	234	93	30	2	...	...

Note: This table comprises *only* city-type local governments with populations of 2,500 and above.

a (...) indicates data not applicable or not reported.

b These local government were brought into ICMA's database from the Census Bureau files, which do not include form of government.

Population   This edition of the *Year Book* generally uses the 2012 Census Bureau figures for placing local governments in the United States into population groups for tabular presentation. The population categories are self-explanatory.

Geographic Classification   Nine geographic divisions and four regions are used by the Bureau of the Census (Figure 1). The nine divisions are *New England*: Connecticut, Maine, Massachusetts, New Hampshire, Rhode Island, and Vermont; *Mid-Atlantic*: New Jersey, New York, and Pennsylvania; *East North-Central*: Illinois, Indiana, Michigan, Ohio, and Wisconsin; *West North-Central*: Iowa, Kansas, Minnesota, Missouri, Nebraska, North Dakota, and South Dakota; *South Atlantic*: Delaware, the District of Columbia, Florida, Georgia, Maryland, North Carolina, South Carolina, Virginia, and West Virginia; *East South-Central*: Alabama, Kentucky, Mississippi, and Tennessee; West South-Central: Arkansas, Louisiana, Oklahoma, and Texas; *Mountain*: Arizona, Colorado, Idaho, Montana, Nevada, New Mexico, Utah, and Wyoming; and *Pacific Coast*: Alaska, California, Hawaii, Oregon, and Washington.

The geographic regions are consolidations of states in divisions: *Northeast*: Connecticut, Maine, Massachusetts, New Hampshire, New Jersey, New York, Pennsylvania, Rhode Island, and Vermont; *North Central*: Illinois, Indiana, Iowa, Kansas, Michigan, Minnesota, Missouri, Nebraska, North Dakota, Ohio, South Dakota, and Wisconsin; *South*: Alabama, Arkansas, Delaware, the District of Columbia, Florida, Georgia, Kentucky, Louisiana, Maryland, Mississippi, North Carolina, Oklahoma, South Carolina, Tennessee, Texas, Virginia, and West Virginia; and *West*: Alaska, Arizona, California, Colorado, Hawaii, Idaho, Montana, Nevada, New Mexico, Oregon, Utah, Washington, and Wyoming.

Metro Status   Metro status refers to the status of a municipality within the context of the U.S. Office of Management and Budget (OMB) definition of a statistical area. In February 2013 the OMB announced new delineations for metropolitan statistical areas, micropolitan statistical areas, nonmetropolitan areas, and non-core-based statistical areas. According to those delineations, "a metropolitan area contains a core urban area of 50,000 or more population, and a micropolitan area contains an urban core of at least

Figure 1   U.S. Bureau of the Census Geographic Regions and Divisions

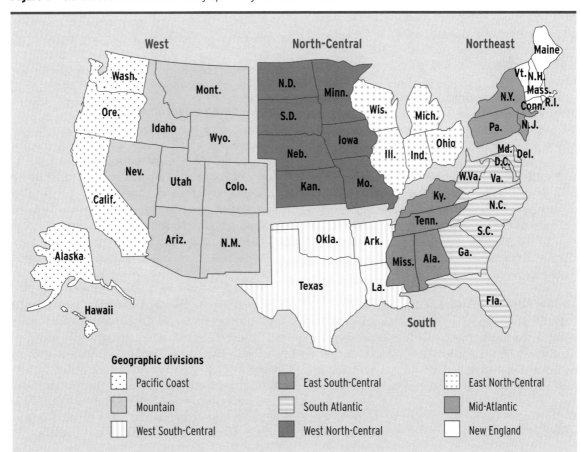

Geographic divisions

- Pacific Coast
- Mountain
- West South-Central
- East South-Central
- South Atlantic
- West North-Central
- East North-Central
- Mid-Atlantic
- New England

10,000 (but less than 50,000) population. Each metro or micro area consists of one or more counties and includes the counties containing the core urban area, as well as any adjacent counties that have a high degree of social and economic integration (as measured by commuting to work) with the urban core." Nonmetropolitan areas include both micropolitan and non-core-based statistical areas (non-CBSA).[2]

Form of Government Form of government relates primarily to the organization of the legislative and executive branches of municipalities and townships.

In the *mayor-council* form, an elected council or board serves as the legislative body. The head of government is the chief elected official, who is generally elected separately from the council and has significant administrative authority.

Many cities with a mayor-council form of government have a city administrator who is appointed by the elected representatives (council) and/or the chief elected official and is responsible to the elected officials. Appointed city administrators in mayor-council governments have limited administrative authority: they often do not directly appoint department heads or other key city personnel, and their responsibility for budget preparation and administration, although significant, is subordinate to that of the elected officials.

Under the *council-manager* form, the elected council or board and chief elected official (e.g., the mayor) are responsible for making policy. A professional administrator appointed by the council or board has full responsibility for the day-to-day operations of the government.

The *commission* form of government operates with an elected commission performing both legislative and executive functions, generally with departmental administration divided among the commissioners.

The *town meeting* form of government is a system in which all qualified voters of a municipality meet to make basic policy and elect officials to carry out the policies.

Under the *representative town meeting* form of government, the voters select a large number of citizens to represent them at the town meeting(s). All citizens can participate in the meeting(s), but only the representatives may vote.

County Classification

Counties are the primary political administrative divisions of the states. The county-type governments in Alaska are called boroughs. Table 3 details the distribution of counties throughout the nation, using the same geographic and population categories as Table 2.

Metro Status Metro status refers to the status of a municipality within the context of the OMB definition

of a statistical area. The OMB has redefined metropolitan statistical areas, metropolitan divisions, micropolitan statistical areas, combined statistical areas, and New England city and town areas in the United States. ICMA has updated its local government records to correspond to these new definitions.

Form of Government For counties, form of government relates to the structural organization of the legislative and executive branches of counties; counties are classified as being with or without an administrator. There are three basic forms of county government: commission, council-administrator, and council–elected executive.

The *commission* form of government is characterized by a governing board that shares the administrative and, to an extent, legislative responsibilities with several independently elected functional officials.

In counties with the *council-administrator* form, an administrator is appointed by, and responsible to, the elected council to carry out directives.

The *council–elected executive* form features two branches of government: the executive and the legislative. The independently elected executive is considered the formal head of the county.

The use of varying types of local government is an institutional response to the needs, requirements, and articulated demands of citizens at the local level. Within each type of local government, structures are developed to provide adequate services. These structural adaptations are a partial result of the geographic location, population, metropolitan status, and form of government of the jurisdiction involved.

Consolidated Governments

The Bureau of the Census defines a consolidated government as a unit of local government in which the functions of a primary incorporated place and its county or minor civil division have merged.[3] There are several categories of consolidations: city-county consolidations operating primarily as cities (Table 4), metropolitan governments operating primarily as cities (Table 5), and areas that maintain certain types of county offices but as part of another city or township government (Table 6). In addition, the District of Columbia is counted by the Census Bureau as a city, a separate county area, and a separate state area. To avoid double counting in survey results, ICMA counts the District of Columbia only as a city.

The Census Bureau defines independent cities as those operating outside of a county area and administering functions commonly performed by counties (Table 7). The bureau counts independent cities as counties. For survey research purposes, ICMA counts independent cities as municipal, not county governments.

Table 3 Cumulative Distribution of U.S. Counties

Classification	All counties	Population 2,500 and over	5,000 and over	10,000 and over	25,000 and over	50,000 and over	100,000 and over	250,000 and over	500,000 and over	Over 1,000,000
Total, all counties	3,031	2,901	2,737	2,358	1,530	916	526	230	106	33
Population group										
Over 1,000,000	33	33	33	33	33	33	33	33	33	33
500,000-1,000,000	73	73	73	73	73	73	73	73	73	...[1]
250,000-499,999	124	124	124	124	124	124	124	124	...	...
100,000-249,999	296	296	296	296	296	296	296	...	...	...
50,000-99,999	390	390	390	390	390	390	...	...	...	...
25,000-49,999	614	614	614	614	614	...	...	...	...	...
10,000-24,999	828	828	828	828	...	...	...	...	...	...
5,000-9,999	379	379	379	...	...	...	...	...	...	...
2,500-4,999	164	164	...	...	...	...	...	...	...	...
Under 2,500	130	...	...	...	...	...	...	...	...	...
Geographic region										
Northeast	189	189	188	183	175	132	86	45	21	3
North-Central	1,051	991	902	730	447	238	133	47	21	6
South	1,366	1,337	1,295	1,152	707	402	212	83	35	11
West	425	384	352	293	201	144	95	55	29	13
Geographic division										
New England	45	45	45	43	40	24	14	6	2	...
Mid-Atlantic	144	144	143	140	135	108	72	39	19	3
East North-Central	436	435	430	403	293	169	98	34	15	5
West North-Central	615	556	472	327	154	69	35	13	6	1
South Atlantic	541	539	533	484	331	209	120	50	21	6
East South-Central	359	357	354	321	179	83	32	7	2	...
West South-Central	466	441	408	347	197	110	60	26	12	5
Mountain	276	244	217	167	97	59	38	18	9	3
Pacific Coast	149	140	135	126	104	85	57	37	20	10
Metro status										
Metropolitan Statistical Area	975	973	970	932	789	653	475	225	104	33
Micropolitan Statistical Area	646	637	631	595	483	206	31	...	...	...
Undesignated	1,410	1,291	1,136	831	258	57	20	5	2	...
Form of government										
County commission	1,724	1,621	1,493	1,210	685	329	151	54	20	6
Council-manager/ administrator	819	804	785	737	559	382	237	103	49	18
Council-elected executive	488	476	459	411	286	205	138	73	37	9

1 (...) indicates data not applicable or not reported.

Table 4 Legally Designated Consolidated City-County Governments Operating Primarily as Cities, 2012

State	Consolidated government
Alaska	City and Borough of Anchorage City and Borough of Juneau City and Borough of Sitka City and Borough of Wrangell
California	City and County of San Francisco
Colorado	City and County of Broomfield City and County of Denver
Hawaii	City and County of Honolulu
Kansas	Kansas City and Wyandotte County City of Tribune and Greeley County
Montana	Anaconda-Deer Lodge Butte-Silver Bow

Table 5 Metropolitan Governments, 2012

State	Consolidated city
Tennessee	Hartsville and Trousdale County Lynchburg and Moore County Nashville and Davidson County

Note: The Census Bureau treats these as consolidated cities.

Uses of Statistical Data

The *Municipal Year Book* uses primary and secondary data sources. ICMA collects and publishes the primary source data. Secondary source data are data collected by another organization. Most of the primary source data are collected through survey research. ICMA develops questionnaires on a variety of subjects during a given year and then pretests and refines them to increase the validity of each survey instrument. Once completed, the surveys are sent to officials in all cities above a given population level (e.g., 2,500 and above, 10,000 and above, etc.). For example, the city managers or chief administrative officers receive the *ICMA Economic Development Survey,* and finance officers receive the *Police and Fire Personnel, Salaries, and Expenditures* survey.

ICMA conducts the *Police and Fire Personnel, Salaries, and Expenditures* survey every year. Other research projects are conducted every five years, and some are one-time efforts to provide information on subjects of current interest.

Limitations of the Data

Regardless of the subject or type of data presented, data should be read cautiously. All policy, political, and

Table 6 Areas That Maintain Certain Types of County Offices but as Part of Another Government, 2012

State	County	Other government
Florida	Duval	City of Jacksonville
Georgia	Chattahoochee	Cusseta-Chattahoochee County unified
	Clarke	Athens-Clarke County unified
	Georgetown-Quitman County	Georgetown-Quitman County unified
	Muscogee	City of Columbus
	Richmond	City of Augusta
	Webster and cities of Preston and Weston	Webster County unified
Hawaii	Kalawao	State of Hawaii
Indiana	Marion	City of Indianapolis
Kentucky	Lexington-Fayette Urban County	Lexington-Fayette
	Louisville-Jefferson County Metro	Louisville-Jefferson
Louisiana	Parish of East Baton Rouge	City of Baton Rouge
	Parish of Lafayette	City of Lafayette
	Parish of Orleans	City of New Orleans
	Terrebonne Parish	Terrebonne Parish consolidated
Massachusetts	County of Nantucket	Town of Nantucket
	County of Suffolk	City of Boston
New York	County of Bronx	New York City
	County of Kings	New York City
	County of New York	New York City
	County of Queens	New York City
	County of Richmond	New York City
Pennsylvania	County of Philadelphia	City of Philadelphia

Table 7 Independent Cities

State	Independent city
Maryland	Baltimore City
Missouri	St. Louis
Nevada	Carson City
Virginia	Alexandria
Virginia	Bedford
Virginia	Bristol
Virginia	Buena Vista
Virginia	Charlottesville
Virginia	Chesapeake
Virginia	Colonial Heights
Virginia	Covington
Virginia	Danville
Virginia	Emporia
Virginia	Fairfax
Virginia	Falls Church
Virginia	Franklin
Virginia	Fredericksburg
Virginia	Galax
Virginia	Hampton
Virginia	Harrisonburg
Virginia	Hopewell
Virginia	Lexington
Virginia	Lynchburg
Virginia	Manassas
Virginia	Manassas Park
Virginia	Martinsville
Virginia	Newport News
Virginia	Norfolk
Virginia	Norton
Virginia	Petersburg
Virginia	Poquoson
Virginia	Portsmouth
Virginia	Radford
Virginia	Richmond
Virginia	Roanoke
Virginia	Salem
Virginia	Staunton
Virginia	Suffolk
Virginia	Virginia Beach
Virginia	Waynesboro
Virginia	Williamsburg
Virginia	Winchester

social data have strengths and limitations. These factors should be considered in any analysis and application. Statistics are no magic guide to perfect understanding and decision making, but they can shed light on particular subjects and questions in lieu of haphazard and subjective information. They can clarify trends in policy expenditures, processes, and impacts and thus assist in evaluating the equity and efficiency of alternative courses of action. Statistical data are most valuable when one remembers their imperfections, both actual and potential, while drawing conclusions.

For example, readers should examine the response bias for each survey. Surveys may be sent to all municipalities above a certain population threshold, but not all of those surveys are necessarily returned. Jurisdictions that do not respond are rarely mirror images of those that do. ICMA reduces the severity of this problem by maximizing the opportunities to respond through second and (sometimes) third requests. But although this practice mitigates the problem, response bias invariably appears. Consequently, ICMA always includes a "Survey Response" table in each article that analyzes the results of a particular survey. This allows the reader to examine the patterns and degrees of response bias through a variety of demographic and structural variables.

Other possible problems can occur with survey data. Local governments have a variety of record-keeping systems. Therefore, some of the data (particularly those on expenditures) may lack uniformity. In addition, no matter how carefully a questionnaire is refined, problems such as divergent interpretations of directions, definitions, and specific questions invariably arise. However, when inconsistencies or apparently extreme data are reported, every attempt is made to verify these responses through follow-up telephone calls.

Types of Statistics

There are basically two types of statistics: descriptive and inferential.

Descriptive

Most of the data presented in this volume are purely descriptive. Descriptive statistics summarize some characteristics of a group of numbers. A few numbers represent many. If someone wants to find out something about the age of a city's workforce, for example, it would be quite cumbersome to read a list of several hundred numbers (each representing the age of individual employees). It would be much easier to have a few summary descriptive statistics, such as the mean (average) or the range (the highest value minus the lowest value). These two "pieces" of information would not convey all the details of the entire data set, but they can help and are much more useful and understandable than complete numerical lists.

There are essentially two types of descriptive statistics: measures of central tendency and measures of dispersion.

Measures of Central Tendency These types of statistics indicate the most common or typical value of a data set. The most popular examples are the mean and median. The mean is simply the arithmetic average. It is calculated by summing the items in a data set and dividing by the total number of items. For example, given the salaries of $15,000, $20,000, $25,000, $30,000, and $35,000, the mean is $25,000 ($125,000 divided by 5).

The mean is the most widely used and intuitively obvious measure of central tendency. However, it is sensitive to extreme values. A few large or small numbers in a data set can produce a mean that is not representative of the "typical" value. Consider the example of the five salaries above. Suppose the highest value was not $35,000 but $135,000. The mean of the data set would now be $45,000 ($225,000 divided by 5). This figure, however, is not representative of this group of numbers because it is substantially greater than four of the five values and is $90,000 below the high score. A data set such as this is "positively skewed" (i.e., it has one or more extremely high scores). Under these circumstances (or when the data set is "negatively skewed" with extremely low scores), it is more appropriate to use the median as a measure of central tendency.

The median is the middle score of a data set that is arranged in order of increasing magnitude. Theoretically, it represents the point that is equivalent to the 50th percentile. For a data set with an odd number of items, the median has the same number of observations above and below it (e.g., the third value in a data set of 5 or the eighth value in a data set of 15). With an even number of cases, the median is the average of the middle two scores (e.g., the seventh and eighth values in a data set of 14). In the example of the five salaries used above, the median is $25,000 regardless of whether the largest score is $35,000 or $135,000. When the mean exceeds the median, the data set is positively skewed. If the median exceeds the mean, it is negatively skewed.

Measures of Dispersion This form of descriptive statistics indicates how widely scattered or spread out the numbers are in a data set. Some common measures of dispersion are the range and the interquartile range. The range is simply the highest value minus the lowest value. For the numbers 3, 7, 50, 80, and 100, the range is 97 (100 − 3 = 97). For the numbers 3, 7, 50, 80, and 1,000, it is 997 (1,000 − 3 = 997). Quartiles divide a data set into four equal parts similar to the way percentiles divide a data set into 100 equal parts. Consequently, the third quartile is equivalent to the 75th percentile, and the first quartile is equivalent to the 25th percentile. The interquartile range is the value of the third quartile minus the value of the first quartile.

Inferential

Inferential statistics permit the social and policy researcher to make inferences about whether a correlation exists between two (or more) variables in a population based on data from a sample. Specifically, inferential statistics provide the probability that the sample results could have occurred by chance if there were really no relationship between the variables in the population as a whole. If the probability of random occurrence is sufficiently low (below the researcher's preestablished significance level), then the null hypothesis—that there is no association between the variables—is rejected. This lends indirect support to the research hypothesis that a correlation does exist. If they can rule out chance factors (the null hypothesis), researchers conclude that they have found a "statistically significant" relationship between the two variables under examination.

Significance tests are those statistics that permit inferences about whether variables are correlated but provide nothing directly about the strength of such correlations. Measures of association, on the other hand, indicate how strong relationships are between variables. These statistics range from a high of + 1.0 (for a perfect positive correlation), to zero (indicating no correlation), to a low of −1.0 (for a perfect negative correlation).

Some common significance tests are the chi square and difference-of-means tests. Some common measures of association are Yule's Q, Sommer's Gamma, Lambda, Cramer's V, Pearson's C, and the correlation coefficient. Anyone seeking further information on these tests and measures should consult any major statistics textbook.

Inferential statistics are used less frequently in this volume than descriptive statistics. However, whenever possible, the data have been presented so that the user can calculate inferential statistics whenever appropriate.

Summary

All social, political, and economic data are collected with imperfect techniques in an imperfect world. Therefore, users of such data should be continuously cognizant of the strengths and weaknesses of the information from which they are attempting to draw conclusions. Readers should note the limitations of the data published in this volume. Particular attention should be paid to the process of data collection and potential problems such as response bias.

Notes

1. The terms *city* and *cities*, as used in this volume, refer to cities, villages, towns, townships, and boroughs.

2. U.S. Department of Commerce, Census Bureau, "Metropolitan and Micropolitan Statistical Areas Main," census.gov/population/metro/; Executive Office of the President, Office of Management and Budget, "Revised Delineations of Metropolitan Statistical Areas, Micropolitan Statistical Areas, and Combined Statistical Areas, and Guidance on Uses of the Delineations of These Areas," whitehouse.gov/sites/default/files/omb/bulletins/2013/b13-01.pdf.

3. See U.S. Census Bureau, *Consolidated Federal Funds Report for Fiscal Year 2009: State and County Areas* (August 2010), Appendix A, census.gov/prod/2010pubs/cffr-09.pdf.

Management Trends and Survey Research

1

Upholding and Expanding the Roles of Local Government Managers: State of the Profession 2012

Kimberly L. Nelson
University of North Carolina at Chapel Hill

James H. Svara
University of North Carolina at Chapel Hill and Arizona State University

Much has changed since the founding of ICMA in 1914. Cities and counties are larger and offer a broader array of services; there are a greater number of local governments; and social and demographic shifts have been considerable. Despite these changes, the basic advisory role of local government managers, as well as their administrative responsibilities, has essentially remained the same. However, the manager's relationship with citizens in the community has evolved and expanded. To understand the nature of local government management in the present and how the profession will meet future challenges, it is important to recall the early experience and aspirations of the founders of the profession. Are managers today acting within the heritage of the founders and their successors, or have they departed from it?

In 1917, Ossian Carr, city manager of Niagara Falls, New York, and third president of ICMA, recognized that managers were pioneers in a new profession with "no precedents."[1] There was guidance, however, in the reports and shared experiences of the early members of ICMA. From those reflections, as well as from the commentary accompanying the Second Model City Charter, which endorsed the council-manager form of government in 1915, it was evident that the reformers did not intend to simply add an administrative technician to oversee the

SELECTED FINDINGS

More than 45% of the responding managers are over 55 years old. Their retirements over the next decade will cause a turnover in the ranks of top administrators, similar to that which occurred during the 1970s. Local governments will have to find—and ICMA will need to help develop—large numbers of persons without prior experience as top administrators to fill the anticipated vacancies.

As they have always done, top administrators are active in offering policy advice to elected officials. Over the past two decades, the commitment to citizen engagement has increased, especially in council-manager municipalities, where nearly 60% of managers reported that they frequently or always engage directly with the public on policy issues.

The effectiveness of the governing board is influenced by the efforts of top administrators to encourage interaction among board members and promote team building. When top administrators always work to promote interaction among council members, 7 of 10 governing boards are highly effective at decision making, compared to 4 in 10 when interaction is never or only occasionally supported.

implementation of policies. Rather, the manager was also expected to "show himself a leader, formulating policies and urging their adoption by the council."[2] In essence, then, managers were expected to have a "double function[:] the conduct of current administration, and persuading the representatives of the public so far as he can that his plans are wise."[3]

And from the beginning, managers filled their dual roles. Reflecting on the experience of managers in the first four years of the association, Carr cautions that the manager should not be concerned when some of his recommendations are rejected by elected officials; perhaps a different approach is best for the community, and ultimately it is the council members who are responsible to the public. Still, the manager's recommendations are on record, and "the commission may come to realize in time that his advice is not lightly given, [and] in fact that his action and advice is exactly what they are paying for."[4]

Statements during the 1930s and in the 1938 Code of Ethics appeared to call for managers to separate themselves from the policy role.[5] However, the code recognized that the manager offers advice and information, and ICMA's first training manual in 1940 makes it clear that these contributions were expected. *The Technique of Municipal Administration* states that "the most difficult and the most important task" of the city manager is "to enlighten the democratic determination of policy by giving adequate information and disinterested expert advice to the governing body."[6] The manager's recommendations are subject to the review and approval of elected officials and must take into account public opinion in the community, but the city manager has "an opportunity to exercise the broadest and most far-reaching influence on the conduct of city government."[7]

Given these examples and the empirical research on city managers during their first 25 years, it is not surprising that a commentator in the *Municipal Year Book 1953* would conclude that "the debate over whether a city manager should be a leader in policy formation seems to have died down, with the weight of evidence indicating that a successful manager inevitably normally performs such a function in one way or another."[8] It is puzzling, however, that the commentator indicated that this role definition "modified appreciably the original theory behind the council-manager plan." As ICMA approached its 40th anniversary, an active policy role for the city manager was accepted, but the historical origins of this role were ignored.

With regard to citizens, the manager promoted democracy by being accountable to the elected representatives of the public. Little attention was given

to interacting directly with the community except for providing information, or what the municipal reformers called a "demand for publicity."[9] The 1924 Code of Ethics obligated managers to "strive to keep the community informed of the plans and purposes of the administrations, remembering that healthy publicity and criticism are an aid to the success of any democracy" [tenet 9]. *The Technique of Municipal Administration* suggests "some modifications of the practice of complete segregation" of citizens and officials, including citizen advisory committees and participation by city employees in organizations and the civic life of the community.[10]

Thus, from the early days of the profession and the council-manager form of government, city managers—as well as top administrators who would come later from counties and from municipalities with other forms of government—have always advised elected officials and supported their work. And from the early days, they have always been involved with citizens although, as noted above, their relationship with citizens has expanded over time.

Whereas there were eight city managers from the 31 cities using the council-manager form who met in Springfield, Ohio, in 1914 to establish the City Managers' Association, there are over 8,800 top administrators in municipalities and counties today, almost 40% of whom are members of ICMA. With tremendous growth in numbers, expansion in the governmental setting in which they work, and 100 years of collective experience, local government administrators may have changed in the way they look at local government and their responsibilities. How do current top administrators view their roles, how do they assess the leadership of elected officials, and what is their level of satisfaction with their position?

The answers are drawn from the *State of the Profession 2012* survey, and comparisons are made (when possible) with the survey findings from the same ICMA survey conducted in 2000 and 2006.[11] The survey does not examine the administrative and managerial responsibilities of top administrators; rather, it focuses on the interaction of those administrators with elected officials in their local governments and on their key relationships outside the governmental sphere. Thus, after a brief review of our methodology and overall response rates, we turn to a description of the managers and administrators who responded to the *State of the Profession 2012* survey; a review of their roles with respect to their governing boards, citizens, and elected officials; and a look at what the changing conditions in local government management today will mean for professional managers in the future.

Survey Methodology and Response Rates

In the summer and fall of 2012, ICMA mailed a *State of the Profession* survey to appointed local government managers and administrators in 7,550 municipalities with populations of 2,500 or more, and to all county governments with an elected executive or manager (n = 1,306). For simplicity in describing governmental structure and officials in cities and counties, we will refer to all municipal governments with an appointed executive as *council-manager* and to all municipal governments with an elected executive as *mayor-council*. Similarly, we will refer to all county governments with an appointed executive as *county manager* and to all county governments with an elected executive as *county executive*. Actual titles vary greatly. *Council* refers to the elected governing body, which may be called a commission, a board of aldermen, or something else. The term *manager* is used to refer to an appointed executive in a city or county, and *administrator* is used to refer to the highest appointed administrative officer in a city or county with an elected executive. The term *top administrator* includes both types.

Respondents were given the option of returning the survey by mail or completing it online. Responses were received from 2,079 municipalities and counties, for an overall response rate of 24%; of those responses, 254 were from counties and 1,825 were from municipalities (not shown). There were also 84 respondents from cities with the commission or town meeting forms of government; these cities are not included in the comparisons by form of government although the respondents are included in analyses of managers and administrators. Finally, a portion of the returned surveys were completed by officials who are not top administrators; because many questions pertain directly to the characteristics, actions, or attitudes of the top administrators themselves, these responses were removed from all the analyses. This brought the total number of respondents who are top administrators to 1,835, for a response rate of 21% (Table 1–1).

There is variation in response from different population groups. The response rates from the smaller (under 50,000) and larger (500,000 and over) jurisdictions are lower than those from the middle-sized jurisdictions. Regionally, the sample is diverse as well, with northeastern communities responding at the lowest rate (14%) and western communities responding at the highest rate (30%).

Response rates vary significantly according to form of government (see Table 1–1). In the case of municipalities, the numbers of council-manager and

Table 1-1 Survey Response

Classification	No. of municipalities[a] surveyed (A)	Respondents No.	Respondents % of (A)
Total	8,856	1,835	21
Municipalities	7,550	1,619	21
Counties	1,306	216	17
Population group			
Over 1,000,000	36	8	22
500,000-1,000,000	84	19	23
250,000-499,999	132	35	27
100,000-249,999	407	112	28
50,000-99,999	698	174	25
25,000-49,999	1,143	251	22
10,000-24,999	2,239	476	21
Under 10,000	4,117	760	19
Geographic region			
Northeast	2,132	304	14
North-Central	2,560	544	21
South	2,824	587	21
West	1,340	400	30
Form of government			
Municipalities			
Mayor-council	3,319	393	12
Council-manager	3,667	1,142	31
Commission	144	19	13
Town meeting	352	55	16
Representative town meeting	68	10	15
Counties			
County executive	489	51	10
County manager	817	165	20

a For a definition of terms, please see "Inside the *Year Book*," xxi-xxiv.

mayor-council communities surveyed are nearly even (3,667 and 3,319, respectively), but the responses are skewed toward those using the council-manager form (31% vs. 12%, respectively). For other forms of municipal government, the response rates are in the teens. Given that this survey was generated by ICMA and that council-manager communities are more likely to be run by ICMA-member managers, this response rate bias is not surprising.

When response rates by form of government are sorted by total municipalities and total counties, however, nearly three-quarters (71%) of the 1,619 responding municipalities and over three-quarters (76%) of the 216 responding counties use the council-manager form, whereas only 24% of both municipalities and counties use the mayor-council/county-executive forms (Table 1–2).

When size of jurisdiction and form of government are considered together, over three in five of the mayor-council respondents are from municipalities under 10,000 in population compared to two in five of the council-manager respondents (not shown). Similarly, 55% of the county executives are from counties under 50,000 in population compared to 35% of the county managers. Thus, the top administrators from jurisdictions with elected executives are more likely to be representing smaller jurisdictions.

One feature of mayor-council governments not included in the survey is the extent of council involvement in appointing the administrator. In only 15% of responding mayor-council municipalities does the mayor alone appoint the administrator (not shown); in 53%, however, the council approves the appointment, and in the remaining 32%, all elected officials choose the administrator.[12] Comparative data on variations within the mayor-council form for 2012 are available only for municipalities over 10,000 in population, but in 25% of those municipalities, the mayor appoints the administrator without council review; in 32%, the mayor and council jointly appoint the

Table 1-2 Breakdown of Responses by Type and Form of Government

	No.	% of total
Total respondents	1,835	100
Municipalities	1,619	88
Counties	216	12
Total responding municipalities by form of government	1,619	100
Mayor-council	393	24
Council-manager	1,142	71
Commission	19	1
Town meeting	55	3
Representative town meeting	10	1
Total responding counties by form of government	216	100
County executive	51	24
County manager	165	76

administrator, and in 45%, the mayor nominates the administrator and the council approves the appointment (not shown).[13] Thus, among the mayor-council administrators in these data, those appointed by the mayor alone are underrepresented while those whose appointment includes participation by the council are overrepresented.

General Characteristics of Responding Top Administrators

A profile of the respondents provides important indicators about how the characteristics/demographics of professional local government top administrators are changing.

Age

For a number of years, researchers have been suggesting that the retirements of baby boomers from top local government management positions could lead to a host of unfilled positions.[14] The results of the *State of the Profession 2012* survey provide evidence for this potentiality. More than 60% of the responding top administrators are over 50 years old (see Figure 1–1). When this survey was administered in 2000, the results were more evenly distributed by age; only 43% of respondents were aged 51 or older and the largest number fell into the middle categories. By 2023, the majority of local government management positions could be turning over.

The question that cannot be answered through this survey is whether there are sufficient numbers of junior-level managers and administrators who are interested in filling the anticipated vacancies. No communities of 100,000 or more employ managers or administrators under age 36. Younger respondents to this survey work exclusively in smaller jurisdictions. Most likely, these top administrators will move into larger jurisdictions as they advance in age and experience, and as they do, more persons who lack prior experience as top administrators may be hired to replace them. In addition, it is possible that an increased number of top administrators will be recruited from organizations outside local government, although these individuals may have worked in local government at some point in their careers.

Sex and Race

Diversity in the local government management profession remains elusive. Although women and minorities have some representation at the top levels of the field, the overwhelming majority of these positions are held by white men. Only 16% of responding top administrators were women (Figure 1–1), compared to 12%

Figure 1-1   Demographic Profile of Top Administrators

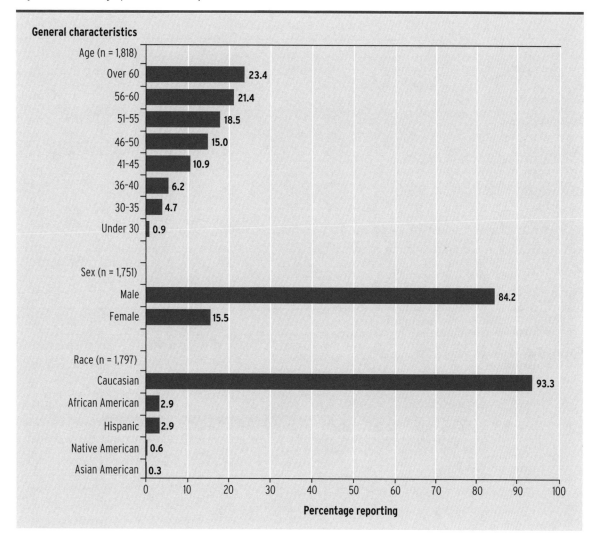

in 2000 and 13% in 2006 (not shown). Women represent about 13% of ICMA's current top administrator membership.

Women serve as managers in some of the largest jurisdictions in the United States, as shown in Table 1–3. The data do not indicate a trend toward higher proportions of women managing in the largest jurisdictions (500,000 and over), but there are increases in all the population categories under 500,000 since 2006. Because of the large number of jurisdictions under 10,000 in population, findings from both 2006 and 2012 show that half of the female top administrators are in these governments, compared to about two-fifths of the male top administrators.

Racial diversity is minimal; only 6.7% of respondents—121 out of the 1,797 top administrators who answered the questions on race and Hispanic background—reported being nonwhite or Hispanic (Figure 1–1). African Americans and Hispanics make up the largest minority among respondents. There was little change in racial and ethnic composition since the survey that was conducted in 2006. Whereas the combined percentage of African Americans and Hispanics was then 3.7%, it was 5.8% in 2012.

Educational Level

Higher education is a prerequisite for nearly every top administrative position. Reflecting this requirement, 93% of the respondents possess a bachelor's degree or higher (see Figure 1–2), and a substantial majority have a postgraduate education; the greatest proportion of those with education beyond college have an MPA degree (43%). Factoring in the other postgraduate degrees brings the proportion of top administrators with postgraduate degrees up to 70%.

Table 1-3   Sex of Top Administrators by Population Category

| | 2006 | | | | | 2012 | | | | |
| | | Men | | Women | | | Men | | Women | |
Population category	Total	No.	%	No.	%	Total	No.	%	No.	%
Total	2,146	1,882	88	264	12	1,751	1,474	84	277	16
500,000 and above	22	18	82	4	18	25	22	88	3	12
250,000-499,999	23	22	96	1	4	33	26	79	7	21
100,000-249,999	95	87	92	8	8	107	88	82	19	18
50,000-99,999	169	157	93	12	7	164	148	90	16	10
25,000-49,999	309	285	92	24	8	239	212	89	27	11
10,000-24,999	580	503	87	77	13	457	391	86	66	14
Under 10,000	948	810	85	138	15	726	587	81	139	19

Source: Data from 2006 are from the ICMA *State of the Profession 2006.* For both years, the data were screened for top administrators.

Figure 1-2   Educational Level of Top Administrators

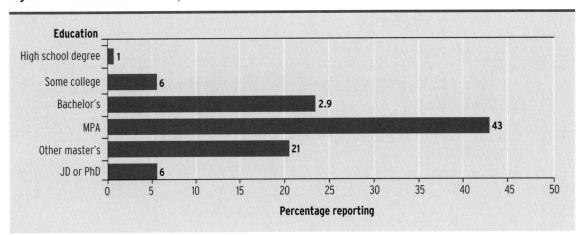

When educational level is broken out by form of government, differences become apparent. In council-manager municipalities, 26% of the respondents have a college degree or less education, compared to 40% in mayor-council municipalities (not shown). Similarly, 31% of managers are without education beyond the bachelor's degree versus 42% of administrators in counties with elected executives. Almost half (47%) of the managers in municipalities and 40% of those in counties have an MPA degree, compared to 34% and 24%, respectively, among administrators in governments with elected mayors or county executives.

Historical trends can be identified only for city managers for whom long-term data are available. As late as 1964 when ICMA turned 50, more than three-quarters of city managers lacked education beyond the bachelor's level, and only 17% had an MPA degree.[15]

Thus, advanced and specialized education in public administration has been a relatively recent development in the local government management profession, and it is still far from universal.

Financial Conditions

The first question on the 2012 survey asked respondents about the financial health of their communities. The majority (62%) described their communities as improving while 4% described them as declining. The remainder reported their communities to be stagnant (34%) (Table 1–4). Managers in council-manager municipalities are most positive about their communities' economies: 65% reported improvement compared to 58% of administrators in mayor-council communities. Respondents from the two types of counties provided similar responses about their financial conditions.

Table 1-4   Economic Status and Form of Government

Form of government	No. reporting (A)	Improving		Stagnant		Declining	
		No.	% of (A)	No.	% of (A)	No.	% of (A)
Total responding	1,794	1,108	62	610	34	76	4
Municipalities							
Mayor-council	385	224	58	137	36	24	6
Council-manager	1,113	720	65	358	32	35	3
Commission	19	12	63	7	37	0	0
Town meeting	55	31	56	22	40	2	4
Representative town meeting	10	6	60	3	30	1	10
Counties							
County executive	49	26	53	21	43	2	4
County manager	163	89	55	62	38	12	7

Advisory Roles of Top Administrators

To learn about the current activities of local government managers, the survey asked respondents to indicate the extent to which they perform a range of major roles in their interactions with their governing boards. Virtually all top administrators reported that they provide information. Beyond that, almost all city managers and a great majority of county managers reported that they identify needs in the community and initiate policy proposals to address those needs, and that they also play a significant role in policy initiation (Table 1–5). Administrators in cities and counties also usually these roles as well, but at lower rates.

These are not new or recent activities for top administrators; such functions have always been integral to the position. Given the emphasis that professional and academic literature has placed on administration, however, it is surprising that nearly 10% of city managers and nearly 20% of county managers rarely provide formal reports on the implementation of policies and programs. Furthermore, one in five city administrators and over a quarter of county administrators rarely provide reports to the governing body. Yet such reports are important to support the governing board in carrying out its oversight function.

It is also striking that nearly 3 in 10 managers reported that they do not exercise significant latitude and discretion in interpreting and implementing governing board policies. The percentage is lower in council-manager municipalities (19%) and counties (31%) than in jurisdictions where the administrator

works with an elected mayor (35%) or county executive (45%) (Table 1–5). The differences may indicate that administrators are more likely to defer to the elected executive in making these judgments. Still, the overall results suggest that local government administrators often seek guidance from elected officials who are close at hand, rather than make their own judgments, as the public administration literature asserts. The results may also suggest that administrators do not recognize the amount of discretion they are exercising. Regardless of which services and programs are adopted, however, almost all administrators strive to ensure that service delivery is equitable and responsive to all citizens.

In addition to providing information and recommendations to assist the local governing board in making decisions, a top administrator may give attention to how the governing board functions as a group. Early commentators of the council-manager form expected that the council and the manager would interact extensively as "two parts of the same mechanism, or . . . two elements in one chemical compound whose combined qualities give the character to the substance,"[16] but there was no discussion of efforts to help the council function. Many top administrators have come to recognize, however, that the governing board does not necessarily work together as a cohesive body without assistance, and a large majority in both municipalities and counties often seek to promote interaction among the board members (Table 1–5). The administrators in county-executive counties are most likely to also seek to promote team building.

Table 1-5 Roles of Administrators with Their Governing Boards

Roles	Municipalities						Counties					
	Mayor-council			Council-manager			County executive			County manager		
	Total (A)	Never/ occasionally % of (A)	Frequently/ always % of (A)	Total (B)	Never/ occasionally % of (B)	Frequently/ always % of (B)	Total (C)	Never/ occasionally % of (C)	Frequently/ always % of (C)	Total (D)	Never/ occasionally % of (D)	Frequently/ always % of (D)
In policy formation and implementation												
Provide information to the governing body	389	1	99	1,133	0	100	51	10	90	163	0	100
Identify community needs and initiate policy proposals	389	13	87	1,133	0	100	51	28	73	163	20	81
Play a significant role in policy initiation	390	14	86	1,138	8	92	51	16	84	163	9	91
Provide the governing body with formal reports documenting policy implementation	389	20	80	1,139	9	91	51	28	73	161	17	83
Exercise significant latitude and discretion in the interpretation and implementation of governing board policy	390	35	65	1,126	19	81	51	45	55	163	31	69
Strive to ensure service delivery is equitable and responsive to citizens	388	3	97	1,130	27	73	51	6	94	163	4	96
In improving council performance												
Promote interaction among the governing body to ensure that there is adequate opportunity for policy discussion and definition	390	16	84	1,132	12	88	51	16	84	161	14	86
Promote team building within the governing body	286	47	54	1,129	42	58	50	36	64	158	42	58
In relating to citizens												
Go out into the community and engage directly with the public on policy issues	389	50	50	1,140	40	60	50	52	48	164	57	43

Note: Percentages may exceed 100% because of rounding.

The Role of Top Administrators in Relating to Citizens

During the early and middle periods of the development of the local government management profession, there were limited expectations for managers to interact with citizens beyond providing information. The role of managers in promoting citizen participation grew with requirements in federal programs in the 1960s,[17] and managers identified the contribution they should make to community building through greater interactions with residents.[18] The 2012 survey indicates how extensive these activities have become and the broadened commitment to citizen engagement that has emerged over the past two decades. These activities appear to be most prevalent in council-manager municipalities. Nearly 60% of these managers reported that they frequently or always go out into the community to engage directly with the public on policy issues, compared to two in five county managers and about half of the administrators in mayor-council municipalities and elected-executive counties (see Table 1–5).

Respondents were asked to indicate their level of agreement with a set of goals that promote citizen participation. Responses by form of government are shown on Table 1–6. To highlight the extent of managers' commitment to active citizen involvement, percentages indicating that managers somewhat agree or do not agree are in bold for the first two goals (minimal mandated activities), and those indicating that managers agree or strongly agree are in bold for the last four (broad approaches).

City managers and administrators responded similarly to this set of statements, although city managers are more likely to disagree that simply meeting minimum requirements for public engagement is sufficient (57% vs. 47%). They are also somewhat more likely than administrators to reject the idea that there should be few public engagement practices beyond minimum requirements and that these should vary by department (61% vs. 52%); and they are more likely to expect that more extensive and deliberative public engagement beyond minimum requirements will be used for local decision making (65% vs. 59%). City managers and administrators also have similar views regarding establishing partnerships and adopting principles for citizen participation, but city administrators are more likely to agree with establishing a body or process related to citizen participation (50% vs. 43%).

In counties, managers are more likely than administrators to disagree that meeting minimum requirements for public engagement is sufficient (57% vs. 45%) and that there should be few public engagement practices beyond minimum requirements (61% vs. 47%) (Table 1–6). County managers and administrators have similar views on the other standards.

Overall, the support for citizen engagement is lower in counties than in municipalities, and counties are less likely to develop partnerships with community organizations to engage the public (40% vs. 63%) (not shown). Despite high levels of support from one or more groups of respondents for certain practices, there is mostly minority agreement across all governments that provisions have been made for community residents to have input into how practices for citizen engagement are established (32%–50%) and that there is an adopted set of principles that define and encourage the use of citizen engagement (35%–47%).

When the goals for public participation are examined, almost all respondents (85% of 1,835) consider the key goal in public engagement to be providing the public with information to assist citizens in understanding an issue (not shown). Other important goals identified by a majority of respondents are working directly with the public to ensure that citizens' concerns are understood (75%), hearing input from a broader cross-section of residents (73%), obtaining feedback from citizens (70%), and partnering with the public in identifying and choosing preferred solutions (57%). However, only 19% overall believe that placing decisions directly in the hands of citizens is an important public participation goal.

Regarding their citizens' level of participation, 55% of administrators from mayor-council municipalities and elected-executive counties reported that a low number of citizens regularly attend activities intended to increase their participation (not shown). Although fewer managers from all council-manager communities reported a low level of participation, the percentage was still very high (45%).[19]

A few local officials have expressed the view that greater participation will lead to more conflict among citizens. They fear that they will experience higher "enragement" rather than "engagement." Furthermore, after a year in which the federal government was shut down for 16 days because both parties in Congress were unable to agree to a continuing budget resolution, there is concern about the increased levels of political conflict. Many states are experiencing a higher level of partisan division in their legislatures as well. As indicated in Table 1–7, however, relatively few local governments are experiencing a high degree of polarization. On the other hand, about a third of municipalities and higher proportions of towns and counties reported some degree of polarized discourse. There is no relationship between the level of participation and the degree of polarization (not shown).

Table 1-6 Acceptance of Standards for Involving Citizens

Goals	Municipalities						Counties					
	Mayor-council			Council-manager			County executive			County manager		
	Total (A)	Strongly agree/agree % of (A)	Somewhat agree/do not agree % of (A)	Total (B)	Strongly agree/agree % of (B)	Somewhat agree/do not agree % of (B)	Total (C)	Strongly agree/agree % of (C)	Somewhat agree/do not agree % of (C)	Total (D)	Strongly agree/agree % of (D)	Somewhat agree/do not agree % of (D)
Attention is primarily to the minimum legal requirements for public engagement, including public comment periods and hearing.	387	40	47	1,129	31	57	51	41	45	159	31	57
There are few public engagement practices beyond minimum requirements, and they vary by department.	394	36	52	1,119	26	61	51	43	47	159	32	61
There are expectations that more extensive and deliberative public engagement beyond minimum requirements will be used for local decision making.	385	59	22	1,126	65	38	51	51	37	162	42	38
There is an adopted set of principles that generally define and encourage the use of effective and inclusive public engagement when/as appropriate.	383	47	28	1,095	45	38	51	47	35	160	42	38
Partnerships are developed with neighborhood and community organizations to involve the public in appropriate public engagement activities over time.	388	63	21	1,134	63	42	50	48	32	162	47	42
There is an established and ongoing body, process, or protocol that provides community representatives with input into the direction, operation, and adaptation of a public engagement plan or set of practices.	388	50	33	1,137	43	40	51	41	43	162	36	40

Note: Percentages do not equal 100% because respondents answering "neutral" are not included on the table.

Table 1-7   Nature of Political Discourse in Local Community in Past Year

Form of government	No. reporting (A)	Very polarized and strident, often rude		Somewhat polarized and strident, occasionally rude		Generally polite and tolerant of different opinions		Very polite and tolerant of different opinions	
		No.	% of (A)	No.	% of (A)	No.	% of (A)	No.	% of (A)
Total	1,814	108	6	604	33	934	52	168	9
Municipalities									
Mayor-council	387	23	6	126	33	205	53	33	8
Council-manager	1,135	59	5	358	32	597	53	121	11
Commission	18	1	6	4	22	11	61	2	11
Town meeting	53	5	9	19	36	27	51	2	4
Representative town meeting	10	0	0	4	40	6	60	0	0
Counties									
County executive	49	7	14	21	43	18	37	3	6
County manager	162	13	8	72	44	70	43	7	4

Note: Percentages may not add to 100% because of rounding.

Top Administrators and the Performance of Elected Officials

Local government is a joint venture between elected and appointed officials. Respondents were asked to assess the effectiveness of their elected councils as decision-making bodies (see Table 1–8). Among the top administrators who responded, only 2% believe that their councils are not effective at all, while 26% rated those bodies as highly effective. Generally, the positive performance ratings (highly to moderately effective) are similar across jurisdiction sizes (with the exception of those jurisdictions in the 500,000–1,000,000 range and those under 2,500).

Comparing council-manager municipalities and counties to mayor-council municipalities and elected-executive counties in this regard reveals only small differences (Figure 1–3). The top "effective" ratings (options 1 and 2) are higher in council-manager municipalities than in mayor-council municipalities and higher in municipalities overall than in counties. Over half of the county managers (53%) rated their councils as effective, compared to 42% of the administrators in elected-executive counties.

A related question asked top administrators to rate the effectiveness of the council's appraisal of their own performance. Respondents provided moderate to high ratings on this question, with fewer than 16% rating their councils as being less than moderately effective (not shown). Results by form of government show slightly higher ratings in municipalities than

in counties and in appointed-executive governments than in elected-executive governments. In municipalities, 48% of top administrators rated the council's appraisal as effective to highly effective regardless of form of government. On the other hand, 49% of county managers provided those ratings compared to only 30% of county administrators.

It appears that the top administrator can have a direct impact on the council's effectiveness by promoting interaction and team building. For governments in which the top administrator never or only occasionally promotes interaction, just over 4 in 10 councils are rated highly effective, compared to over 7 in 10 councils when the top administrator always promotes interaction (Figure 1–4). When the top administrator never or only occasionally promotes team building, just 53% of councils are rated highly effective, compared with 74% of councils when the top administrator always promotes team building. The top administrator's promotion of interaction and team building produces similar differences in the effectiveness of the council when it is appraising the administrator's performance: only 33% of councils are deemed highly effective at appraising the top administrator when they receive little support with team building (not shown).

Another set of questions asked top administrators to evaluate their mayors or board chairs as visionary and facilitative leaders using a five-point scale.[20] First, respondents rated the effectiveness of the elected official at creating a vision and helping to develop goals and policy proposals. Managers in council-manager

Table 1-8 Effectiveness of Council as a Decision-Making Body

Classification	No. reporting (A)	Highly effective (1) No.	Highly effective (1) % of (A)	(2) No.	(2) % of (A)	Moderately effective (3) No.	Moderately effective (3) % of (A)	(4) No.	(4) % of (A)	Not effective (5) No.	Not effective (5) % of (A)
Total	1,793	460	26	620	35	503	28	172	10	38	2
Population group											
Over 1,000,000	6	2	33	2	33	1	17	1	17	0	0
500,000-1,000,000	19	2	11	3	16	10	53	3	16	1	5
250,000-499,999	34	10	29	14	41	7	21	3	9	0	0
100,000-249,999	108	21	19	46	43	28	26	9	8	4	4
50,000-99,999	173	48	28	64	37	38	22	22	13	1	1
25,000-49,999	245	57	23	90	37	75	31	21	9	2	1
10,000-24,999	462	125	27	159	34	124	27	42	9	12	3
5,000-9,999	391	104	27	123	32	120	31	33	8	11	3
2,500-4,999	338	89	26	114	34	92	27	36	11	7	2
Under 2,500	17	2	12	5	29	8	47	2	12	0	0
Form of government											
Municipalities											
Mayor-council	384	95	25	125	33	118	31	43	11	3	1
Council-manager	1,117	315	28	391	35	290	26	97	9	24	1
Commission	17	4	24	7	41	3	18	2	12	1	6
Town meeting	53	8	15	23	43	17	32	4	8	1	2
Representative town meeting	10	0	0	4	40	4	40	2	20	0	0
Counties											
County executive	50	10	20	11	22	22	44	5	10	2	4
County manager	162	28	17	59	36	49	30	19	12	7	4

Note: Percentages may not add to 100% because of rounding.

Figure 1-3 Effectiveness of Council by Form of Government

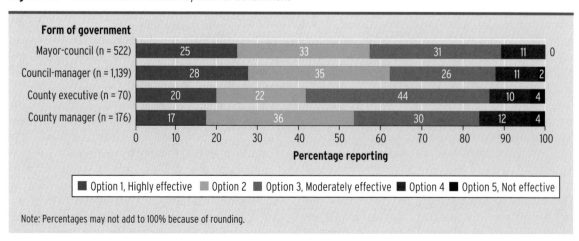

Note: Percentages may not add to 100% because of rounding.

Figure 1-4   Impact of Top Administrator's Promotion of Interaction and Team Building on Council's Effectiveness

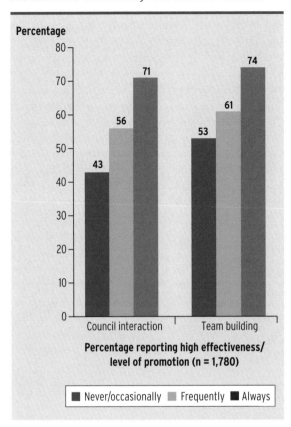

Percentage reporting high effectiveness/
level of promotion (n = 1,780)

municipalities are slightly less likely to consider their mayors to be highly effective visionary leaders (54%) than are administrators in mayor-council municipalities (57%), but a majority of each group viewed effectiveness as high (Figure 1–5), whereas less than 40% of respondents from counties rated their elected executives as highly visionary. There was little difference by form of government in the proportion rating their elected leaders as highly visionary, but one-quarter of the county managers considered those executives to be ineffective as visionaries.

Using the same scale, administrators were asked to evaluate their elected leaders on their effectiveness at facilitative leadership—sharing information, promoting cohesion within the council, and helping to develop goals and proposals. The results are similar to those for the visionary leadership question. Municipal top administrators rated their mayors' facilitative leadership abilities higher than county top administrators did. Despite the argument that the council-manager form provides a more natural setting for facilitative leadership by mayors,[21] there is little difference in the way that managers and administrators in council-manager and mayor-council municipalities, respectively, rated their mayors. Once again, a greater proportion of county managers than of other top administrators rated their commission chairs "not effective" at facilitative leadership.

Figure 1-5   Top Administrator Ratings of Chief Elected Officials' Leadership

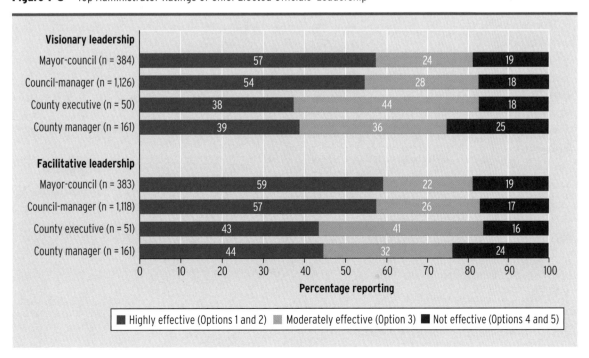

Relationships

A good relationship between the top administrator and the elected officials is critical for effective governance. About 90% of respondents reported that their relationship with their elected officials is either highly collaborative or generally collaborative (Table 1–9), with little difference according to form of government in municipalities. In counties, however, highly collaborative relationships between the top administrator and the elected officials are more common in the county-executive form than in the council-manager form.

As for the level of collaboration among council members, responding top administrators rated that considerably lower, although only 6% rated their boards as not at all collaborative. Whereas 23%

of top administrators rated the relationship among elected officials as highly collaborative (not shown), 49% reported high collaboration between themselves and their elected officials (Table 1–9). The top administrator has an obligation and a practical need to maintain a positive working relationship with each member of the council if possible, but council members can choose whether or not to work with their colleagues. Tellingly, the effectiveness of the council is related to the degree of collaboration among its members. Whereas more than 90% of the boards that are rated as highly collaborative are also rated as highly effective at decision making, less than one-quarter of the boards that are rated as only somewhat collaborative are considered to be effective at decision making (Table 1–10).

Table 1-9   Assessment of Relationship between Top Administrator and Elected Officials

Classification	No. reporting (A)	Highly collaborative		Generally collaborative		Somewhat collaborative		Not collaborative	
		No.	% of (A)	No.	% of (A)	No.	% of (A)	No.	% of (A)
Total	1,823	898	49	737	40	163	9	25	1
Population group									
Over 1,000,000	8	5	63	3	38	0	0	0	0
500,000–1,000,000	19	8	42	9	47	2	11	0	0
250,000–499,999	34	17	50	15	44	2	6	0	0
100,000–249,999	108	48	44	51	47	9	8	0	0
50,000–99,999	172	89	52	72	42	11	6	0	0
25,000–49,999	250	126	50	100	40	23	9	1	*
10,000–24,999	474	238	50	185	39	43	9	8	2
5,000–9,999	399	189	47	165	41	40	10	5	1
2,500–4,999	341	172	50	128	38	31	9	10	3
Under 2,500	18	6	33	9	50	2	11	1	6
Form of government									
Municipalities									
Mayor-council	388	188	49	151	39	44	11	5	1
Council-manager	1,139	572	50	454	40	97	9	16	1
Commission	18	11	61	5	28	2	11	0	0
Town meeting	55	22	40	27	49	5	9	1	2
Representative town meeting	10	3	30	7	70	0	0	0	0
Counties									
County executive	50	27	54	19	38	3	6	1	2
County manager	163	75	46	74	45	12	7	2	1

Note: Percentages may not total 100% because of rounding.

* = Less than 0.5%.

In the follow-up question about the relationship among council members over the past year, responses reveal substantial continuity, with 58% of respondents saying that the relationship has remained the same, one-quarter reporting that it has improved, and 17% indicating that it has worsened (not shown). And when asked to describe how their own relationship with the elected officials has changed over the past year, respondents gave virtually identical assessments (not shown).

The Current Position of Top Administrators

The average tenure of responding top administrators in their current positions is seven years, matching that of respondents in the 2000 and 2006 *State of the Profession* surveys. As for tenure in the local government management profession, the average in 2012 was 21.4 years compared to 20.5 years in 2006.

In the plurality of cases, top administrators served as assistant managers, assistant administrators, or equivalent positions before being appointed to their current positions (36%); 6% were top administrators in another jurisdiction; and about one in five had been department directors in local government (not shown). Ten percent of respondents reported that their previous job was in the private sector (with no distinction between business and nonprofits); this career path is more common in small jurisdictions. In 2006, the top three previous positions were assistant manager, city manager or administrator, and a job in the private sector.

There is some uncertainty about comparing the results from 2012 with those of previous surveys, because the wording of the question has changed slightly.[22] Still, there is a shift evident in the previous positions identified in the last three surveys:

- In 2006, 27% were assistant managers/administrators and 26% were managers/administrators in other governments.

- In 2009, 28% were assistants and 19% were managers/administrators.
- In 2012, 36% were assistants and 6% were managers/administrators (not shown).

It is possible that the increasing proportion of older managers decreases the likelihood that top administrative positions will be filled by managers or administrators who are recruited from other governments. The movement of top administrators across municipalities and counties has previously been a common component of managerial careers, and many local governments have been able to select a manager or administrator with previous experience as a top administrator. As a feature of generational change that is under way, however, it is more likely that governments will select persons who have been assistant managers and administrators. It is also possible that more persons will be recruited from positions outside local government.

Job satisfaction among respondents from the 2012 survey is high, with 71% reporting that they are more than moderately satisfied (Table 1–11). The recession appears to have affected job satisfaction, however, as there was a decline of eight percentage points in satisfaction among respondents who were top administrators between 2006 and 2009. By the same token, over three-quarters of the respondents in jurisdictions with improving economies reported being more than moderately satisfied, compared to 65% in stagnant communities and 54% in declining communities (not shown).

The satisfaction level of managers is related to a number of other factors as well as economic conditions. For example, managers reported lower levels of job satisfaction when the community is polarized, council members are not collaborative, their relationship with the council is weak, and the board is ineffective at making decisions, although personal relationships and performance within the government have a greater negative effect than the state of discourse in the community. But even with the most negative conditions, between 29% and 45% of the managers maintain a fairly

Table 1-10   Internal Collaboration and Effectiveness of Council

Collaboration rating	No. reporting (A)	Rating of governing board decision-making effectiveness					
		Highly effective		Moderately effective		Ineffective	
		No.	% of (A)	No.	% of (A)	No.	% of (A)
Highly collaborative	411	382	93	28	7	1	*
Generally collaborative	830	594	72	218	26	18	2
Somewhat collaborative	431	95	22	225	52	111	26

* = Less than 0.5%.

Table 1-11 Job Satisfaction of Top Administrators by Year

Year	No. reporting	Highly satisfied (%)	Moderately satisfied (%)	Not satisfied (%)
2006	2,050	77	19	4
2009	1,985	69	24	7
2012	1,988	71	22	6

Sources: Data from 2006 and 2009 are based on original analyses of ICMA *State of the Profession* surveys in those years. In both cases, respondents who were not top administrators were removed from the analyses.

Note: Percentages may not total 100% because of rounding.

high level of satisfaction (Table 1–12). And when conditions are most positive, 89%–97% of the managers get substantial satisfaction from their positions. There is no systematic difference in satisfaction level based on form of government, type of jurisdiction, or age.[23]

There was not a substantial difference from 2006 to 2012 in the percentage of respondents who faced pressure to resign. In 2006, only 4.9% of top administrators were fired, forced to resign, or under pressure to resign, while in 2012, the proportion was 6.6%. In both survey years, respondents reported the same top three reasons for being pressured to resign: changes in the elected body following an election (59% in both years); personality conflicts with an elected official (43% in both years); and political pressures (34% in 2006, 39% in 2012) (not shown).

Changing Conditions and Future Challenges

It is possible to infer that support for professional local government administrators has increased dramatically over the past hundred years. The commentary on the Second Model City Charter noted the risk that councils might select political allies for the position of city manager. "Above all, we cannot have expert administration until a large part of the intelligent citizens appreciate the need for it."[24] This prediction appears to have reached fruition. From the early years, when few cities used the council-manager form and it was uncertain what criteria the council would use in filling the manager's position, the use of managers and administrators in cities and counties is now the norm, and it is customary for elected officials to choose well-trained professionals committed to promoting the public interest.

Generally, elected officials have a positive working relationship with top administrators, who have proven to be the active leaders they were expected to be. These professionals bring in information, investigate policy issues, and provide recommendations to elected offi-

cials. This is the "double function" envisioned by the municipal reformers. Most top administrators also help their councils perform better by promoting communication and team building. They have developed a wide range of direct interactions with citizens, and most are committed to expanding citizen engagement far beyond what the founders of ICMA could have imagined. And they generally get substantial satisfaction out of the work they do.

At the same time, they nevertheless face changes and challenges in carrying out their roles. This has always been true, of course, but the challenges have been different. Today's top administrators, for example, are no longer necessarily the primary source of information for elected officials. Increasingly, elected officials find information on the Internet that is inaccurate but that they find credible. They also receive recommendations from advocacy organizations. These other voices may mute the top administrator's policy recommendations. Top administrators must recognize that they are competing with other sources for the attention of elected officials and thus must strive to be effective communicators.

Moreover, the local government management professional is beginning a period of generational turnover on a scale not seen since the early 1970s. There is a challenge in attracting young professionals to local government; those it attracts will come from a wider range of backgrounds and career paths as more managers move between local government and business and nonprofit organizations. The distinct values and skills of young professionals will contribute to the continuing transformation in the way local governments operate and communicate both inside and outside the organization. And to be sure, the profession must diversify its membership if it is to better relate to the population it serves.

Communities are changing as well, and the climate of opinion can challenge sound governance. Only about 6% of jurisdictions are highly polarized and strident, but one-third are at least somewhat

Table 1-12 Percentage of Top Administrators with Above-Moderate Satisfaction in Different Community Conditions

Community condition	Top administrators with above-moderate satisfaction (%)
State of civic discourse in the community (n = 1,771)	
Very polarized and strident	45
Somewhat polarized and strident	60
Generally polite and tolerant	79
Very polite and tolerant	90
Relationship among governing board members (n = 1,776)	
Not collaborative	34
Somewhat collaborative	55
Generally collaborative	77
Highly collaborative	89
Administrator's relationship with elected officials (n = 1,779)	
Not collaborative	29
Somewhat collaborative	31
Generally collaborative	63
Highly collaborative	97
Board performance as a decision-making body (n = 1,751)	
Very low to low	32
Moderately effective	61
Effective	81
Highly effective	89

polarized. Moving forward, the question is whether the tone and tactics of partisan and ideological conflict at the state and federal levels will increasingly come to characterize politics in the local arena.

The professional manager who provides balanced and complete information to elected officials and the public can help to counteract the politicization of issues. As ICMA president Simon Farbrother asserted in 2013 in his closing address at ICMA's 99th Annual Conference, "Now we spend most of our days jointly working with our councils, jointly working with our organizations, jointly working with our community."[25] Trust in local government is higher than it is in other levels of government, where public trust has fluctuated greatly or declined steadily since the early 1970s. Consistently, around 7 in 10 people report that they have a great deal or a fair amount of trust and confidence in the way local governments are handling local problems.[26] The contributions of professional administrators reinforce this trust. Local governments can also build support by continuing to develop new partnerships with citizens in building viable communities.

Overall, a changing environment is producing a different approach to filling professional roles. Local government administrators will need to find new ways to fill both their traditional and their expanding roles in this new environment. However, the local government management profession has continuing strengths as it moves into the future. ICMA should recognize and honor the precedents that its members have established over its history as comprehensive leaders.

Notes

1 Ossian Carr, "The City Managers' Association," *National Municipal Review* (January 1918), 45. This was his presidential address in 1917.

2 Clinton Rogers Woodruff, ed., *A New Municipal Program* (New York: D. Appleton and Company, 1919), 130.

3 Ibid., 38.

4 Carr, "City Managers' Association," 46–47.

5 For example, Clarence C. Ridley and Orin Nolting, *The City Manager Profession* (Chicago: University of Chicago Press, 1934), stated that the manager should not "let himself be driven or led into taking the leadership or responsibility in matters of policy" (30). The 1938 ICMA Code of Ethics stated that "the city manager is in no sense a political leader."

6 Institute for Training in Municipal Administration (ITMA), *The Technique of Municipal Administration* (Chicago: International City Managers' Association, 1940), 24.

7 Ibid., 25.

8 "Municipal Highlights of 1952," *The Municipal Year Book 1953* (Chicago: International City Managers' Association, 1953), 3.

9 Woodruff, *New Municipal Program*, 266. There was amazement that the city manager in Dayton was providing "whole pages of *advertisements*" reporting what the city government was doing (267). The author concluded, "surely we are making progress!" (267).

10 ITMA, *Technique of Municipal Administration*, 468–469.

11 For the 2000 data, see Tari Renner, "The Local Government Management Profession at Century's End," in *The Municipal Year Book 2001* (Washington, D.C.: International City/County Management Association, 2001), 35–46. Data from 2006 (and 2009 data included later) are based on original analyses of ICMA *State of the Profession* surveys in those years. In both cases, respondents who were not top administrators were removed from the analyses.

12 This enhanced dataset for all municipalities over 10,000 in population includes coding for three council-manager variations (mayor selected by council, mayor directly elected, and mayor with additional powers) and four mayor-council variations (the three that differ in how the administrator is selected and the one with no top administrator). This dataset is maintained by

Dr. Kimberly Nelson with the support of the School of Government, University of North Carolina at Chapel Hill.

13 Kimberly L. Nelson and James H. Svara, "Adaptation of Models versus Variations in Form: Classifying Structures of City Government," *Urban Affairs Review* 45, no. 4 (2010): 544–562.

14 For articles discussing the potential for a gap in city manager ranks, see Ralph Blumenthal, "Unfilled City Manager Posts Hint at Future Gap," *New York Times*, January 11, 2007, nytimes.com/2007/01/11/us/11managers.html?hp&ex = 1168578000&en = a5f8 bcfecfcc850f&ei = 5094&partner = homepage&_r = 0; Gerald Gabris, Trenton Davis, and Kimberly Nelson, "Demand versus Supply: Can MPA Programs Satisfy the Need for Professional Management in Local Government?" *Journal of Public Affairs Education* 16, no. 3 (2010): 379–399.

15 "City Manager Profession and Directory," *The Municipal Year Book 1964* (Chicago: International City Managers' Association, 1964), 500.

16 Woodruff, *New Municipal Program*, 37.

17 A precedent was set in intergovernmental programs in the 1930s. When recommending citizen advisory committees in 1940, the authors of *The Technique of Municipal Administration* offered the example of committees established for welfare and juvenile delinquency programs (468).

18 John Nalbandian, "Facilitating Community, Enabling Democracy: New Roles for Local Government Managers," *Public Administration Review* 59 (May/June 1999): 187–197.

19 Only 10% of respondents from representative town meeting municipalities reported low levels of citizen participation.

20 For a discussion of mayoral leadership roles, see James H. Svara, ed., *The Facilitative Leader in City Hall: Reexamining the Scope and Contributions* (Boca Raton, Fla.: CRC Press, 2009), chapter 1.

21 Ibid. As noted previously, there are fewer "strong mayor" cities where the mayor appoints the administrator without council participation than in the overall population of cities.

22 In 2006 and 2009 the question was, "what was your previous position"; in the 2012 survey it was, "what was your most recent position before being appointed as chief administrative officer/city or county manager?"

23 It is interesting to note that 88% of the top administrators over age 70 have higher-than-moderate satisfaction levels.

24 Woodruff, *New Municipal Program*, 36.

25 Simon Farbrother, "Closing Address," ICMA's 99th Annual Conference, Boston, Mass., September 22–25, 2013.

26 Gallup, Annual Governance Survey Results (2012), gallup .com/poll/157700/trust-state-local-governments.aspx.

2

100 Years of Tackling Societal Challenges

Elizabeth K. Kellar
Center for State and Local Government Excellence

Were early local government managers focused only on directing staff, establishing professional practices, and improving basic services for the communities they served? Or were they visionary, creative, and innovative in tacking societal problems? A review of ICMA publications reveals that many managers were not only good administrators but also keen observers of societal problems—and committed to addressing them. As one might expect from a profession rooted in the progressive reforms of the early 20th century, evidence-based management was one of the hallmarks of the profession. And from the beginning, local government managers were eager to share best practices for every conceivable aspect of local government administration, from revenue generation to planning, protecting public safety, and choosing staff.

In the early years of the 20th century, pressure to improve services was driven by rapid urbanization and growing populations that were straining local governments' management capacity. Corruption was a major problem, creating an opening for trained, professional public servants who would treat all citizens equally. While Congress addressed child labor and antitrust issues, state and local governments focused on home rule, the short ballot, and new forms of government that were designed to combat "boss politics." At the time of ICMA's founding, professional organizations

SELECTED FOCAL POINTS

Early local government managers marshaled every resource they could find to tackle public health and other community problems.

Whether facing the struggles of the Great Depression or the social turmoil of the 1960s, local government managers recognized the importance of making every man and woman feel like they were part of the government.

Idealism, foresight, innovation, and evidence-based solutions have been hallmarks of the local government management profession for the last 100 years.

for chiefs of police, fire chiefs, municipal engineers, and finance officers already existed. Council-manager government, however, created the position of chief appointed executive to oversee service provision in a professional, nonpartisan way.

With support from the National Municipal League, the League of Women Voters, and the Chamber of Commerce, the commission plan and the council-manager form of government became popular alternatives to big-city machine politics. By 1908, Staunton,

Virginia, had appointed Charles E. Ashburner as its first city manager; in 1913, Dayton, Ohio, became the first large city to adopt council-manager government; and in 1914, 8 of the 31 city managers in the United States met in Springfield, Ohio, for their first annual conference.

The Early Years: Public Health, Citizen Engagement, and Revenue

Like their modern counterparts, early local government managers faced daunting challenges and insufficient financial resources. In addition to building and maintaining infrastructure, providing basic services, and establishing professional public safety departments, they tackled pressing issues such as public health. And as they looked for ways to address broad community needs, managers quickly realized that progress depended on reaching out to residents and community organizations to engage them in developing solutions.

Public Health

In 1921, speaking at the eighth annual conference of the City Managers' Association, Louis Brownlow, city manager of Petersburg, Virginia, challenged attendees to think broadly about their mission, reminding them that they should not be "content with improving the quality and efficiency of the ordinary functions of municipal government—a great achievement, truly, but not enough."[1] Reflecting on his accomplishments in Petersburg, Brownlow noted that the best thing he had done was to marshal community resources to improve public health:

> The city has its health officer and its registrar of vital statistics and its bacteriological laboratory. It has its tuberculosis clinic and nurse, its contagious disease service and its venereal disease clinic. It has its food inspectors and its sanitary inspectors. All are housed under one roof. Under that same roof is the Red Cross Child Welfare station. . . . The bacteriological laboratory [at the Health Center] . . . is at the service of every practicing physician in the city. The school nurses, although under independent control of the school board, voluntarily report there every day. Boards of directors and executive committees of social workers' organizations meet there as a matter of course.[2]

A year later, Brownlow reported the results of this public health initiative, comparing outcomes for 1922 to those of two years earlier:

The general death rate has decreased from 19.12 to 16.64 [per 1,000 population]. . . . After two years it is impossible to discover . . . what part of the health work is done by the city, what by the Red Cross, the King's Daughters, the Tuberculosis Society, the Milk fund. . . . The decrease in the white death rate has been from 14.07 to 13.35 and in the negro death rate from 25.60 to 20.90. . . . The infant mortality rate has decreased from 189 to 106. . . .

Perhaps it would be more conventional to put the sewer and water mains laid under the heading of public works, but as a matter of fact, the council undertook the expenditure of about $300,000 . . . as a health measure.[3]

Brownlow was not alone in his concern for public health: in 1921, George J. Roark, city manager of Beaumont, Texas, reported that he had hired "the best sanitary engineer available" and given him oversight over all public health matters. The results were impressive:

> Malaria, for which this section has been famous, has been reduced 50 percent. An excellent record has been established in stamping out bubonic plague. The water supply is under daily chemical control. Tuberculosis among cattle furnishing city milk has been eliminated. We have not needed the smallpox pest house for a year.[4]

In addition to tracking data on public health goals, I. B. Ellison, city manager of Muskegon, Michigan, used graphs, charts, and stories to communicate progress to citizens. Ellison's annual report to residents explained government functions by focusing on results: "from infant mortality through the health department, and engineers and works department (amount of sewers and sidewalks laid monthly etc.) to the amount of snow shoveled in July."[5]

Some early local government managers were so confident of having made progress in public health that they began to focus on wellness and other health issues. F. H. Locke, city manager of Grand Rapids, Michigan, lamented that science had not yet found a way to treat "the diseased mind," but he believed that would change. He also predicted that

> the health work of the future, based on control of communicable disease as a fact accomplished, will be a work of health promotion and not of disease prevention. It will be positive, not negative, creative and not preventive. [It] . . . will begin with the unborn babe and

will secure to the expectant mother the sort of life which will promote the development of a sound, healthy, and vigorous fetus.[6]

Tapping Every Resource in the Community

Along with evidence-based management, the notion of enlisting every resource in the community was a common theme among early local government managers. Brownlow put it this way at the 1921 annual meeting:

This new thing I suggest to you, that you strive earnestly every day, so that in time to come every civic secretary, every social worker, every church worker, every worker for the public good of any kind, will turn naturally to our successor as his natural leader— the City Manager of Tomorrow.[7]

Charles E. Ashburner, city manager of Norfolk, Virginia, emphasized the importance of connecting government to citizens:

Make them feel that no matter what the distress, whether it be in family troubles or financial troubles or need of employment, that the city is the ultimate place to come if they can't get their want somewhere else. Have a human soul in your city administration and have every one feel that no man has a drag with the administration any more than the other. I say, get your Republican, your Democrat, your Jew, your Gentile, your Protestant and your Catholic believing that there is a soul in the administration. Then, my friends, they will follow you for anything you want to do.[8]

Two years later, Clarence E. Ridley, city manager of Bluefield, West Virginia, presented a paper at the 1923 annual meeting titled "The Relation of the City Manager with the Public," in which he noted that

a Manager's success will depend upon a proper relationship with the public. Why is this true? Because, in the first place, no council will long retain a Manager who cannot and does not command the respect and confidence of the public, even tho he may clearly demonstrate that he is a man of high integrity and efficiency. . . . If a Manager cannot sell a certain policy to his council, then something is wrong, and the chances are ten to one that it is in the policy. . . .

We should strive to give the people of a city the best possible government they will accept, and then constantly raise the standard

until they in turn not only desire a better government, but demand it.

The great secret of good government is to make every man and woman feel that they are a part of the government, and that you are personally interested in their troubles and problems, even tho you may not be able to comply with their requests.[9]

Revenue Sources: Paying for Services and Public Ownership of Utilities

Municipal revenues, bond measures, and state limitations on taxation have been on the policy agendas of local government managers from the earliest days. At the 1922 convention, C. A. Bingham, city manager of Lima, Ohio, presented a paper titled "Miscellaneous Municipal Revenue," in which he noted that property taxes made up approximately 65% of local revenue in the United States; other sources—such as gifts, the earnings of public service departments, and revenue from business taxes—made up the rest. Bingham also commented on differences between local governments: "Where the business tax average throughout the country is 3.2 percent, we find our brother managers throughout Virginia receiving five or six times the average, as example Norfolk 15 percent, Roanoke 17.1 percent and Lynchburg 18.9 percent."[10] After Bingham's talk, attendees discussed a variety of other taxes, including an automobile tax, a gasoline tax, and licenses for soft drink parlors.

Another hot topic at the 1922 convention was municipal ownership of utilities. During a debate with Paul Haynes, former chairman of the Indiana State Utilities Commission, Delos F. Wilcox, a public utility consultant for New York City, argued that municipalities should own public utilities, noting "the necessity for reasonable conservatism in the financing and development of public utilities, . . . because private ownership . . . is characterized by such reckless and fraudulent financing as ought never to be tolerated in an age in any country in connection with services that are public in their nature."[11] He further argued that public regulation had been tried and had failed, that public functions should be performed by public agencies, and that private utilities hired former judges and elected officials to "fight the public with the public's money."

For his part, Haynes argued that "no city, the policies of which are determined by popular vote, can long continue to apply sound economic principles and business methods to its ownership and operation of utility properties—and the simple reason is that cities are essentially political agencies—not necessarily partisan, but broadly speaking, political."[12]

Clyde Seavey, city manager of Sacramento, California, stands as an example of leadership in addressing his community's long-term water and power needs. Advocating for a $500 million bond issue that would conserve water, generate hydroelectricity, and permit the development of millions of acres of land (through irrigation and reclamation), Seavey made two arguments: first, that the proposed measure would "relieve the present danger of water shortage in different parts of the State"; and second, that the state had "already proved that public enterprises can be underwritten and be made self-sustaining without adding to the tax burden."[13]

Holding that the measure would ensure sufficient water for irrigation and hydroelectricity "at cost," Seavey also noted that it would allow "the people of California [to] wrest the control of the water and power resources of the State from the grasp of the private interests."[14] Finally, citing examples from several cities in Ohio and Canada, Seavey observed that municipally owned service enterprises had led to lower water and power rates.

"A Letter from New Zealand," written by Charles Dash, borough manager of Rangiora, New Zealand, and published in 1924 in the *Tenth Yearbook,* was prompted by lengthy discussions in ICMA literature of tax challenges and variations in taxing authority across the United States. Having been "struck by the apparent want of uniformity in the statutory rights of your cities," Dash suggested that "with all your experience and powers of boosting, you could still learn from your friend, little New Zealand"—where the municipal powers of 117 boroughs and cities are "practically uniform throughout the dominion" and "the rights and privileges conferred by incorporation are the same for the smallest borough as for the largest city."[15]

Women and Minorities

Even in the early years, the local government management profession often viewed women and members of minorities as untapped resources that could play key roles in addressing local concerns, including crime and public health. For example, Louis Brownlow, speaking at the 1921 annual meeting, advocated appointing women to the police force, noting that only the addition of two women to the Petersburg Police Department had made it possible to know "what was going on in town."[16] Brownlow cited three advantages to the appointment of women police officers:

First, they are the only means of reaching the cases of feminine juvenile delinquency.

Second, the presence of women on the police force changes the attitude of the policemen toward sex cases.

Third, they are the only means by which the police department can learn all that is going on in the city.[17]

Brownlow noted not only that the Petersburg force included two women but also that one woman was white and one was "colored": "Putting a colored person on the police force . . . without having one word of adverse criticism from any source whatever, is something that I count an achievement. It was done because we had women of the town behind it."[18]

Brownlow's era also saw social tensions and divisions, however, including a 1922 incident in Columbus, Georgia, that was covered in three consecutive issues of the monthly *City Manager Bulletin*. As reported in the May issue,

about 8:30 p.m. on April 21st, as . . . City Manager [Hinkle] was walking along one of the central business streets, three men sprang from an automobile and attacked him from the rear, striking him a glancing blow on the head with a "billy" and inflicting a deep cut. Letters threatening the Mayor and the City Manager had been sent to each ever since Commission-Manager government was inaugurated in January. . . . The day following the assault on the City Manager, the Mayor and the Manager each received letters threatening death unless the Manager resigned within 48 hours. On May 21st, the Mayor's residence was damaged by a bomb placed or thrown onto the front porch. . . . It has been both accused and denied that the K.K.K. had anything to do with these actions.[19]

The following month, ICMA Executive Secretary Paul Wilcox noted in the *City Manager Bulletin* that although the attacks and threats had indeed occurred, local viewpoints varied. One local newspaper said that Hinkle's "inability to hit it off with our folks made him an unwise choice for City Manager."[20] Wilcox observed that the account from this newspaper would "allow us to see the Columbus situation as some others see it."[21]

In July, Wilcox published a perspective from another Columbus newspaper, which observed that "City Manager Hinkle knew his business, proceeding in a business-like way, without any regard whatsoever for politics—and that is where some of the trouble came in."[22] In a response published in the following issue of the *City Manager Bulletin,* one manager suggested that the *Bulletin* "not take sides on the K.K.K. controversy."[23]

In the early decades of the 20th century, local government managers sometimes accepted community traditions without much reflection. In an article published in the *Ninth Yearbook*, for example, V. J. Hultquist, city manager of Alcoa, Tennessee, described his city's "well laid out plan" and mentioned in passing that "the white and colored population of the city is divided by extensive industrial areas."[24] In fact, services were often organized along segregated lines. In an article about Dayton, Ohio's substantial commitment to parks and recreation, Ethel Armes, of the Playground and Recreation Association, noted that Dayton, the "first city of consequence to try the City Management plan," boasted "25 recreation centers" that were used by "ten thousand people a day."[25] She further observed that the "Federation for Social Service" was "responsible for work with colored people," and that

> the colored center, . . . located on the grounds of the city welfare department, with which it closely cooperates, has tennis courts and the space of a city block for horseshoe pitching. The activities include day nursery, old folks' home, dramatic club, athletics for young men and women, children's drama group, a junior orchestra, and a community choral society. The center is financed from the Federated Community Chest.[26]

When it came to parks and public spaces, the profession embraced the broad goals of community well-being and providing for the next generation. Like others writing in this era, Armes focused on results, noting that

> through an organized recreation system, crime and juvenile delinquency have been reduced; an improvement in health and hygienic conditions has been marked, to say nothing of a new outward aspect, the grace and beauty coming to a town with many parks, little green squares and circles, tree and flower planting, and all the gifts of the outdoors which the recreation movement lays at the feet of the people.[27]

Writing in July 1922, Paul Wilcox exhorted managers to think ahead 25 to 50 years:

> Do you realize the rapidity with which our urban population is increasing? And do you realize that above all city chief executives, the City Managers of the country whose profession is founded and built on the "rock of foresight" rather than on the "shifting sands of political issues"—do you realize that you,

above all, have a moral obligation to our unborn posterity of the second and third generation?[28]

The Big Squeeze of the Depression Years

By 1932, local government managers were hearing from taxpayer groups who were worried about the cost of government and about debt service in particular. To cut costs, many managers focused on what they called "scientific budget procedures."[29] But managers also faced shrinking revenues—partly because of tax delinquencies and partly because bank failures had depleted municipal assets. Unemployment relief was yet another strain on local revenues. Although the federal Reconstruction Finance Corporation had lent over $60 million to state and local governments, many smaller local governments had nonetheless defaulted on principal or interest payments, giving rise to worries that some of the nation's largest cities might default as well.[30]

Writing in 1933, C. E. Richtor, controller of Detroit, Michigan, estimated that reductions in local government expenses came primarily from "salary and wage reductions of . . . 10–25 percent or even more."[31] Richtor also observed that

> one of the lessons learned as a result of the current pressure upon cities for retrenchment is that a long-term financial program is needed in every city, and that the capital outlays for any one year should be included with the current operating budget and co-ordinated with revenues in order that the total tax levy may be kept on an even keel.[32]

During the Great Depression, citizens and public officials became more aware of local governments' dependence on the state for a balanced revenue system. As it became increasingly clear that the property tax was not sufficient to meet communities' most basic needs, local governments pressed for a greater share of state revenues. Meanwhile, the federal government had recognized the plight of local governments and, for the first time, was considering direct grants-in-aid to cities.[33]

Throughout the depression years, local government managers continued to apply innovative strategies. In Michigan, for example, cooperative purchasing helped small cities save money. In New York State, sharing information about prices they had been charged for various items enabled municipal managers to negotiate for more favorable prices.

And in Cincinnati, Ohio, the university joined with city and county government to centralize purchasing, saving money and improving operations. The State of Maine established centralized purchasing in 1932 and recorded substantial savings in the first nine months of operation.[34]

The popularity of council-manager government continued throughout the 1930s. In 1932, Arlington County, Virginia, became—in the words of Paul W. Wager, assistant professor of rural social economics at University of North Carolina—the first county in the United States "to have a manager in the fullest and best sense."[35] Wager also singled out Virginia and California for having made the greatest gains in county management, awarding Virginia first place because of its enactment of supportive state legislation.[36]

Nevertheless, the era's harsh economic realities led to substantial retrenchment. As physician W. F. Walker noted in 1933,

> The continued mental strain of our present economic condition, and in many cases actual privation, is having its effect upon people and will ultimately be reflected in a lowered resistance. Health departments are facing difficulties in two directions. Increased demands are being made upon their services because of lowered economic status and a direct reduction is being made in their budgets. . . . Services for child welfare and public health nursing, because they have loomed larger in the budget, have generally borne the brunt of reduction.[37]

And in an article for the *City Manager Yearbook 1933,* Donald C. Stone, research director for the International City Managers' Association, observed that robbery and larceny rates had increased from 1930 to 1932.[38]

Local managers dealt with difficult economic conditions through vision and resolve. In an article titled "The Real Cost of Municipal Retrenchment," C. A. Dykstra, city manager of Cincinnati, Ohio, cited a Cincinnati newspaper editorial on "spendthrift cities," in which a French president was quoted as having said that "to govern is to foresee." The editorial went on to say that "the peculiar task of government is to see farther than individuals or profit-making corporations can afford to see."[39]

Dykstra observed that of all public officials, local government managers were the most free to think in nonpolitical terms. He expressed concern, however, that managers could

> fall into the error in such a time as this of
> cutting public service costs so low that the

health and welfare of city populations for years to come will suffer out of all proportion to the savings we are making. Our municipal community is a great family. The interests of all must be our paramount concern. It is the business of the public official to foresee what is ahead. Only as we do this do we merit the confidence of our citizens and deserve to be in places of authority.[40]

Economic struggles continued—but by 1934, there were signs of improvement, particularly in the public's understanding of local government problems. In that year, Louis Brownlow wrote that

> the principal municipal task was making buckle and tongue meet; the immediate fiscal problem overshadowed all others. During the year the financial position of municipal and other local governments improved. Budgets were balanced, credits were improved, interest rates were reduced, payroll arrears were caught up, forced pay cuts were restored, tax collections improved and tax delinquencies decreased as the tax strikes faded from the picture. In the process of achieving this improvement, which of course was not universal, the cities as governments, to an extent never before known, co-operated with each other; and sought, as never before, the co-operation of state and federal governments.[41]

Looking back on those years, L. P. Cookingham focused on the people:

> We all learned that there were people problems that had never confronted city officials before, at least in our generation. . . . I happened to be serving the Detroit area which was probably hit harder than any other area in the U.S. At one time, about a third of Wayne County's population depended on relief to stay alive.[42]

The War Years

With so many men deployed in the war effort, local governments had difficulty finding staff for essential jobs. Many cities expanded their labor pool by hiring women, along with others who had previously been excluded from the workforce. In 1943, *Public Management (PM)* magazine reported that Asheville, North Carolina, had recently employed eight married women as traffic officers: "The city furnishes flaming red capes and red overseas caps, raincoats and rain helmets. Other clothing is supplied by the women themselves and most have purchased olive-drab ski suits."[43] Meanwhile, Los Angeles County hired "500 housewives as personal property appraisers. The jobs, of a temporary nature, usually are filled by men. All were put through an intensive training course . . . and are ready to carry out the assessment task as efficiently and as accurately as it had been done in previous years."[44]

Regular federal bulletins affected personnel practices, resource use, and security efforts. In 1943, for example, when President Franklin Delano Roosevelt issued an executive order creating the 48-hour workweek, municipalities were quick to respond—even though there was no mandate for local governments to comply. Detroit was the first city in an area suffering from labor shortages to voluntarily implement the policy. The Detroit city council also voted to increase municipal wages by 4.54% to bring them more in line with private sector wages.[45]

As early as 1943, local government managers had begun to plan for the postwar period. An editorial published in the April 1943 issue of *Public Management* noted that cities around the world—from Europe to Asia and South America—were getting ready for an unprecedented rebuilding effort, while in the United States,

> the cooperative efforts of all levels of government and all types of private enterprise have created a new wartime pattern of industry, commerce, and transportation. By the same kind of cooperative effort, all of these institutions may achieve for the American people in peacetime a national income and a national standard of living higher than we have heretofore thought possible, and a place of responsible leadership in the community of nations.[46]

The challenges facing North American cities, however, paled in comparison with those facing cities elsewhere. Speaking at the ICMA conference in Chicago in September 1943, Arthur Collins, who had served as chief financial officer for several public authorities in Great Britain, observed that

> over the whole of Great Britain, one home in every five has been destroyed or damaged. . . . In Clydeback, Scotland, out of 12,000 houses with 60,000 population, only 10 were left intact after two nights' consecutive bombing. . . . All over the country there are cities and towns awaiting a new creation. Here is an opportunity to rebuild for new life.[47]

Although labor shortages were a major concern, planning for the postwar period energized managers. Don Price, assistant director of the Public Admin-

istration Clearing House, observed that ICMA's 1943 annual conference "was devoted to business to a degree unusual even for city managers, who are perhaps the world's most avid shop-talkers."[48] Price was struck by the difficulties local governments faced in their efforts to keep "functioning during the dislocations of wartime," but also by the way managers looked

> beyond the end of the war with imagination, with purpose, and even with elation . . . toward the building of a better world in which city governments would come closer to making their greatest possible contribution to human welfare, and city managers would take their part in leading communities throughout the world toward the great human freedoms.[49]

The war years also saw federal, state, and local governments working together toward common goals, setting the stage for an era of united purpose, as cities around the world built (or rebuilt) schools, houses, highways, water and sewer systems, and other essential infrastructure.

Social Unrest and Urban Challenges: The 1960s and 1970s

The 1960s were a period of social upheaval and of soul searching within the local government management profession. In 1964, ICMA celebrated its 50th anniversary at the annual conference in Chicago; in his presidential address, Bert Johnson, county manager of Arlington County, Virginia, speculated about ICMA's centennial celebration in 2014:

> Change is the only constant on the urban scene. We would find that automation had continued to be the most important single development affecting municipal administration. We would also see that the social revolution had persisted and that managers had moved forward in their capacity with the "people problem" to help citizens work toward a well-adjusted society. . . . Citizenship training would become more important as citizens demand answers to regional problems that ignore city boundaries.[50]

At the annual conference three years later, ICMA president David D. Rowlands, city manager of Tacoma, Washington, introduced the executive board's plan to engage the membership in an extensive review of the association's goals:

> We are in the midst of an urban revolution in the United States—an economic, social, moral, and cultural ferment that pervades

all elements of our lives. Millions of Americans—formerly apathetic onlookers on the urban scene—are now involved activists who are demanding a greater share of the benefits of our way of life. We may call these people the disadvantaged minorities, the economically depressed, the rural remnants, or the militant unionists, but these are the people and the groups who are challenging our values and the institutions that preserve those values.[51]

One year later, in a *Public Management* article titled "City Hall Can't Go It Alone," John Gardner, chairman of the Urban Coalition, warned, "This is not a time for business as usual. This is a time to think and act imaginatively and responsibly to hold the nation together and move it toward a constructive future." Gardner also identified constructive solutions:

We have the technology and the means of advancing that technology. We have the intellectual talent and the institutions to develop it and liberate it. We have it in our power to build the systems and organizations, public and private, through which our common goals can be pursued.[52]

In 1968, the ICMA Executive Board published *ICMA Goals: A Proposal,* which had been prompted by deep reflection about the challenges of the previous decade. The document noted that "urban affairs, the dimensions of urban problems, the urgency of success in urban management all have acquired new importance. . . . Over the life of our profession, city managers have been in the vanguard of leadership and initiative toward coping with the challenges of urban change." Among the proposed goals was "to contribute to the understanding and resolution of urban government issues."[53] The board felt that "the Association can—and should—respond affirmatively to problems that are common to all cities, whether at the state, regional, or national levels."[54]

As has been the tradition when ICMA shifts its values or priorities, the board also proposed rewriting the ICMA Code of Ethics to include all urban managers eligible for membership, not just those working in council-manager governments. The board noted that "the city manager no longer is the only professional urban manager. In the maze of jurisdictions sharing responsibility over our urban society, there are many units of government, following many different forms."[55]

To broaden the membership, the executive board also proposed changing ICMA's name from the International City Managers' Association to the International City Management Association, or ICMA.[56] The membership approved the change, and the new name went into effect on July 1, 1969.

Later that year, at ICMA's annual conference in New York, members approved a statement urging local government to take the lead in managing for social and economic opportunity. The statement, developed with guidance from a 100-member task force appointed in 1968, read, in part:

The ICMA members hereby rededicate their professional careers to the compassion for individual citizens which is basic to the City Management Code of Ethics. . . .

Cities, counties, and other local governments are the agencies through which citizens establish community standards and provide for their common welfare and security. Local government is also the delivery system for many of the most essential of state and federal services. . . .

Local governments' efforts to assure justice and provide service equally to all citizens have failed too often to serve adequately those whose needs are greatest. The poor, the old, the handicapped, the subjects of ethnic and racial discrimination have often been overlooked by local government. . . .

Local government has a unique opportunity to provide the focus of leadership necessary to eliminate discrimination in all its forms.

This cannot be done with good intentions alone. Positive programs are necessary. Each professional must devote his position of responsibility in the local government structure to the fundamental objective of achieving social and economic justice.[57]

Examples of efforts to promote social justice included reaching out to disparate community groups; ensuring equitable distribution of services; examining recruitment, job requirements, and hiring practices to ensure public employment opportunities for all; and encouraging the development of low-income housing.[58]

Beyond Piecemeal Approaches

As it became clear, over the course of the 1960s, that local governments, however well intentioned, could not address urban problems alone, ICMA joined forces with state, county, and municipal associations to develop a more focused, national approach to pressing social issues. In his presidential address at the 1970 annual conference, David A. Burkhalter, city manager of Springfield, Missouri, spoke of the sharp contrast between those whose economic circumstances were secure, and those who struggled for shelter and food; he then noted that

> social unrest, campus disorders, and civil disturbances are headlines familiar to every manager. It is in this sphere that state and local responsibilities become more complex and consequently more painful to explore. State and national decisions on public welfare, housing, national defense, education, and other social areas usually trigger the upheaval at the local level. . . . Our task . . . is to allocate the responsibilities for action and get on with the job.[59]

At the 1970 annual business meeting, ICMA members approved a statement on revenue sharing that read, in part,

> Responsive local government is an absolutely essential element of the federal system. Members of ICMA are deeply concerned about inadequate local resources. The costs of rendering local services, at even the same level in an ascending economy, are rising at a more rapid rate than revenues from traditional municipal sources. The maintenance of the most essential services is threatened.
>
> The local property tax is rapidly reaching its practical limits. This tax and the other sources of local revenues are not responsive to inflation and are inadequate to meet the growing service needs of an urban population. These limitations on local revenue sources seriously limit the ability of local government to respond effectively to local needs as well as to national problems.[60]

Speaking at the 1970 ICMA annual conference, John DeBolske, executive director of the League of Arizona Cities and Towns, observed that in the early 1960s, local governments had turned to the federal government for help

> more as an act of last resort rather than choice. . . . We learned to our surprise that federal officials often had a better grasp of city problems than did their counterparts in state government. Most significantly, our new-found friends brought with them tangible evidence of their support—a broad range of grant-in-aid programs.[61]

DeBolske also observed that by the late 1960s, the special rapport between the federal government and urban centers was threatening the traditional relationship between the states and their local governments. "Together the states and local government can do much to shape the future of urban America; divided, our effectiveness and credibility will be lessened.[62]

Taxes, Deficits, and Local Authority

Since the advent of the local government management profession, managers have been mindful of the limitations of the property tax to finance basic services. Writing in *Public Management* in 1970, John Shannon, assistant director of the Advisory Commission on Intergovernmental Relations, observed that "the property tax should be freed up for local government use";[63] he noted that in 1942, about one-third of all property tax revenue was being funneled to schools, but that by 1968, schools consumed over half of property taxes. Shannon argued that public education was a state and national priority, and that state revenue sources were better equipped to "assure equalization of educational opportunities."[64] He also advocated the sharing of federal income tax revenues with states and localities.

Even with revenue sharing, however, citizens launched property tax revolts: in June 1978, when California voters passed Proposition 13 by a 2-to-1 margin, the referendum was viewed as a vote against "big government." The proposition—which, among other things, cut the property tax rate from an average of 2.6% to 1% in every county, and capped the annual increase in assessed values at 2% unless the property was sold—ushered in an era of fiscal constraint, during which supermajorities were often required to raise local taxes. In the view of Mark E. Keane, executive director of ICMA, Proposition 13 represented "the crumbling consensus": it meant that "California voters did not trust public officials . . . who said passage . . . would hurt badly."[65]

Back to the Future

Shortly after the shock wave of Proposition 13, ICMA's Committee on Future Horizons issued its 1979 report, *New Worlds of Service*, which predicted what local government would be like in the year 2000. The report identified key issues, from energy and water resources to poverty and infrastructure:

> Politics will be characterized by a continuation of relative powerlessness among elected and appointed officials. . . .
>
> The maintenance of the infrastructure will be a major agenda item for the future. It will be very tempting, in the next two decades of modest resources, to ignore the problems that citizens do not see. The continual, and expensive, maintenance of water and sewer lines, bridges, power plants, [and] utility connections must continue. Deferred costs of

maintenance, repair, and replacement are simply additions to the mortgages of the future.[66]

Other key issues addressed in the report include demographic change, atomized and aging populations, the environment, the state role in national policy making, developments in telecommunications, and intergovernmental relations. The trends identified in that report have persisted well into the 21st century.

In 1981, ICMA issued a follow-up report that considered the implementation of recommendations made in the report of the Committee on Future Horizons. Regarding telecommunications, the report was prescient, noting that "we still will rely heavily on print media and face-to-face communication, but we also will work with teleconferencing, telephone adaptations, satellite communications, national cable hookups, and other demands and benefits of the telecommunications age."[67]

21st-Century Challenges: Thinking Globally, Preparing Locally

The 1990s saw an economic boom and technological advances that dramatically changed the way government works. The first decade of the 21st century was sobering: in the wake of the attacks of September 11, 2001, local governments faced new responsibilities to help detect potential acts of terrorism. Since 2001, federal, state, and local governments—along with their counterparts around the world—have worked intensively to harden targets and better coordinate intelligence.

Just four years after the events of 9/11, local governments were stunned to find the nation ill prepared to respond to a more predictable threat: Hurricane Katrina. One reason for the lack of preparedness was that a key intergovernmental partner, the Federal Emergency Management Agency (FEMA), had lost capacity when it was brought under the umbrella of the Department of Homeland Security. Local government managers nationwide did what they could to help hard-hit communities in Alabama, Louisiana, and Mississippi—often working around FEMA, which could not keep up with the requests for assistance. The new, state-coordinated Emergency Management Assistance Compact (EMAC) provided an alternative legal authority capable of granting local governments permission to cross state lines in order to send response and recovery teams into flood-damaged communities. Although the EMAC system also became overwhelmed, it expanded the number of local government teams that were able to provide help.

In Katrina's aftermath, managers argued for a networked approach to emergency management. In a white paper developed for ICMA's Governmental Affairs and Policy Committee and published in August 2006, Robert J. O'Neill, executive director of ICMA, wrote that the country needed to improve the entire intergovernmental system by creating "a network of partnerships among cities and counties . . . supported by state governments and a sophisticated database."[68] Such an approach would give the nation "the flexibility to move resources and assets where they need to be, when they need to be there."[69] Although there have been some improvements in the coordination of local, state, and federal resources, the networked system O'Neill envisioned is not yet functioning. Nevertheless, local governments have acted independently to expand mutual aid agreements, sometimes throughout a state and sometimes across state lines.

The worldwide economic meltdown of 2008 led to a bailout of major banks and unprecedented federal intervention to avoid even greater economic hardships. The economic recovery has been slow, and the federal government has taken on more debt. As Congress and the White House look for ways to address long-term fiscal issues, highly valued programs, such as Community Development Block Grants, have been cut back. From the local government perspective, among the most important programs under threat is tax-exempt financing—which was also threatened in the 1980s, when federal budget cutters were similarly looking for ways to address federal debt.

In the local government realm, demographics are destiny—which makes immigration a pressing issue for municipal and county managers. The number of undocumented immigrants in the United States is estimated at 11.7 million, 6 million of whom were born in Mexico.[70] A 2008 ICMA white paper on immigration reform recommended a comprehensive national immigration policy that (1) "provide[s] fair and lawful ways for businesses . . . to hire much-needed immigrant workers" and (2) focuses enforcement efforts on the "coyotes, human smugglers, employers, and others who take advantage of and profit from vulnerable immigrants."[71]

Particularly in the areas of public health, public safety, and education, local government managers see the importance of integrating immigrants into their communities. For example, crimes sometimes go unreported because residents do not speak English or are fearful of deportation. Another issue is that local governments incur costs for providing immigrants with services, such as education and health care, but do not receive federal revenues to offset those costs. As the ICMA white paper noted,

> Whether immigrants are generally perceived as making a positive contribution to a community or considered a threat, local officials

agree on one thing: insufficient resources are provided by the federal government to help local governments respond to immigration. . . . Roughly two-thirds of taxes generated by immigrants go to the federal government, whereas two-thirds of the costs are borne at local and state level.[72]

Sustainability in the face of climate change is another major issue facing local government managers. More severe and more frequent weather events have caused widespread destruction, and rising sea levels are prompting careful analysis of development decisions. As municipal and county managers give more attention to creating livable, sustainable, and resilient communities, ICMA has stepped up research, training, and education in these areas.

Many of the concerns confronting local government managers today evoke ICMA's "Declaration of Ideals," prepared by the Assistants Steering Committee and released in 1981.[73] The declaration, in turn, inspired portions of a 1988 speech given by ICMA president Curtis Branscome, as he looked ahead to ICMA's 75th anniversary in 1989:

The unending tension that we live with is that we must be good leaders and, at the same time, we must be good followers. . . . Stated another way, we must seek to improve our communities without becoming celebrities ourselves.

As we move into the future, we must focus on our responsibility to the stakeholders—all the stakeholders who are affected by the actions of our communities, the rich and the poor, the enfranchised and the disenfranchised, the citizens and the noncitizens, the born and the unborn.[74]

Branscome then read all 11 principles of the declaration, closing with this one: "Take actions to create diverse opportunities in housing, employment, and cultural activity in every community for all people." "In *every* community for *all* people," he repeated. "That, ladies and gentlemen, is the stuff of heroes! That is where the future of our profession lies."

Idealism, foresight, innovation, and evidence-based solutions have been hallmarks of the local government management profession for the last 100 years. And they will remain its hallmarks throughout the 21st century.

Notes

1 Louis Brownlow, "Some Suggestions for Improved Service to Citizens," in *Eighth Yearbook* (East Cleveland, Ohio: City Managers' Association, 1922), 93–96.

2 Ibid.

3 Louis Brownlow, "New Government in an Old City," in *Ninth Yearbook* (Lawrence, Kans.: City Managers' Association, 1923), 11.

4 George J. Roark, "City Management in Beaumont," in *Ninth Yearbook,* 27.

5 "An Innovation," *City Manager Bulletin,* July 1922, 6.

6 F. H. Locke, "Public Welfare," in *Eighth Yearbook,* 141.

7 Brownlow, "Some Suggestions," 97.

8 Charles E. Ashburner, remarks in response to Brownlow, "Some Suggestions," 101.

9 Clarence E. Ridley, "The Relation of the City Manager with the Public," in *Tenth Yearbook* (Lawrence, Kans.: City Managers' Association, 1924), 75–76.

10 C. A. Bingham, "Miscellaneous Municipal Revenue," in *Ninth Yearbook,* 100.

11 "Debate: 'Resolved: That Municipal Ownership of Public Utilities in City Manager Cities Is Desirable,'" in *Ninth Yearbook,* 161–167.

12 Ibid., 170.

13 Paul Wilcox, "Public Ownership," *City Manager Bulletin,* April 1922, 15.

14 Ibid., 16.

15 Charles Dash, "A Letter from New Zealand," in *Tenth Yearbook,* 24.

16 Harvey Walker, "The Kansas City Conference," *City Manager Bulletin,* December 1922, 4.

17 Louis Brownlow, "Public Safety," in *Eighth Yearbook,* 179.

18 Ibid., 180.

19 Paul B. Wilcox, "Things Have Been Happening in Columbus," *City Manager Bulletin,* May 1922, 7.

20 Paul B. Wilcox, "One Side," *City Manager Bulletin,* June 1922, 6.

21 Ibid.

22 Paul B. Wilcox, "The Other Side," *City Manager Bulletin,* July 1922, 9.

23 Quoted in Paul B. Wilcox, "Read This," *City Manager Bulletin,* August 1922, 5.

24 V. J. Hultquist, "City Management in Alcoa," in *Ninth Yearbook,* 48–49.

25 Ethel Armes, "Results of the Recreation Movement in City Manager Cities," *City Manager Bulletin,* June 1922, 11.

26 Ibid. Groups such as the Federated Community Chest were precursors of the United Way.

27 Ibid.

28 Paul B. Wilcox, "An Opportunity," *City Manager Bulletin,* July 1922, 4.

29 C. E. Richtor, "Financial Planning," in *City Manager Yearbook 1933* (Chicago: International City Managers' Association, 1933), 2.

30 Ibid. Established in 1932 during the administration of President Herbert Hoover, the Reconstruction Finance Corporation (RFC) was an independent agency of the U.S. government that provided aid to state and local governments as well as loans to banks, railroads, mortgage associations, and other businesses. The RFC's relief programs were taken over by the New Deal in 1933.

31 Ibid.

32 Ibid.

33 Simeon E. Leland, "Municipal Revenues," in *City Manager Yearbook 1933*, 8.

34 Russell Forbes, "Public Purchasing," in *City Manager Yearbook 1933*, 12.

35 Paul W. Wager, "County Government," in *City Manager Yearbook 1933*, 40.

36 Ibid., 41.

37 W. F. Walker, "Public Health," in *City Manager Yearbook 1933*, 28–29.

38 Donald C. Stone, "Police Administration," in *City Manager Yearbook 1933*, 30–31.

39 C. A. Dykstra, "The Real Cost of Municipal Retrenchment," in *City Manager Yearbook 1933*, 53.

40 Ibid., 67.

41 Louis Brownlow, "Municipal Administration in 1934," in *The Municipal Year Book 1935* (Chicago: International City Managers' Association, 1935), 4.

42 Quoted in Al Bohling, "The Dean Looks Back—and Ahead," *Public Management (PM)*, May 1970, 8. Cookingham, often referred to as "the Dean of City Management," served for 19 years as the city manager of Kansas City, Missouri, starting in 1940. He also served as city manager of three Michigan cities: Clawson, Plymouth, and Saginaw. He ended his city management career in Fort Worth, Texas.

43 "What American Cities Are Doing," *Public Management*, January 1943, 87.

44 Ibid.

45 "Effect of the 48–Hour Week on Municipal Employment," *Public Management*, January 1943, 80.

46 "Editorial Comment: The Role of Cities in Postwar Democracies," *Public Management*, April 1943.

47 Arthur Collins, "Some Observations on American City Management," *Public Management*, September 1943, 258–259.

48 Don K. Price, "Listening in at the Managers' Conference," *Public Management*, October 1943, 286.

49 Ibid.

50 Bert Johnson, "Prepare for the Future," in *1964 Conference Proceedings: Summary of the 50th Annual Conference of the International City Managers' Association, Chicago, Illinois* (Chicago: International City Managers' Association, 1964), 10–11.

51 David D. Rowlands, "Creative Urbanism," in *Proceedings, 53rd Annual Conference, International City Managers' Association, October 8–11, 1967, New Orleans* (Washington, D.C.: International City Managers' Association, 1967), 8–9.

52 John Gardner, "City Hall Can't Go It Alone," *Public Management*, November 1968, 266–267.

53 International City Managers' Association Executive Board, sidebar adjacent to "Goals in Brief," in *ICMA Goals: A Proposal* (Washington, D.C.: International City Managers' Association, 1968).

54 International City Managers' Association Executive Board, "Goals in Brief," in *ICMA Goals: A Proposal*.

55 "Prologue," in *ICMA Goals: A Proposal*.

56 Some advocated changing the name to the International Urban Management Association, but that view did not prevail.

57 "Highlights of the Conference," in *1969 Conference Proceedings of the International City Management Association, New York Hilton Hotel, New York, NY* (Washington, D.C.: ICMA, 1969), 3.

58 Ibid., 2–3.

59 David A. Burkhalter, "Presidential Address," in *Proceedings, 56th Annual Conference, International City Management Association, September 20–24, 1970, San Diego* (Washington, D.C.: ICMA, 1970), 8–10.

60 "Highlights of the Conference," in *Proceedings, 56th Annual Conference*, 4–5.

61 John J. DeBolske, "Luncheon Address," in *Proceedings, 56th Annual Conference*, 21.

62 Ibid., 22.

63 John Shannon, "Fiscal Mismatch," *Public Management*, August 1970, 12.

64 Ibid.

65 Mark E. Keane, "The Crumbling Consensus," *Public Management*, August 1978.

66 ICMA Committee on Future Horizons, *New Worlds of Service* (Washington, D.C.: ICMA, 1979), 6, 10.

67 *ICMA and New Worlds of Service: Report of the Committee to Implement the Report of the Future Horizons Committee and City Management Declaration of Ideals* (Washington, D.C.: ICMA, August 1981), 7–8.

68 Robert J. O'Neill, *A Networked Approach to Improvements in Emergency Management* (Washington, D.C.: ICMA, August 2006), 2, icma.org/en/icma/knowledge_network/documents/kn/Document/2535/A_Networked_Approach_to_Improvements_in_Emergency_Management.

69 Ibid., 3.

70 Julia Preston, "Number of Illegal Immigrants in the U.S. May Be on Rise Again, Estimates Say," *New York Times*, September 23, 2013, nytimes.com/2013/09/24/us/immigrant-population-shows-signs-of-growth-estimates-show.html (accessed January 12, 2014).

71 Nadia Rubaii–Barrett, *Immigration Reform—An Intergovernmental Imperative* (Washington, D.C.: ICMA, October 2008), 5–6, icma.org/en/icma/knowledge_network/documents/kn/Document/6275/Immigration_ReformAn_Intergovernmental_Imperative.

72 Ibid., 31–32.

73 ICMA, "Declaration of Ideals," icma.org/en/icma/about/organization_overview/who_we_are/ideals.

74 Curtis Branscome, unpublished speech given after he was installed as ICMA's president at the closing celebration for the 1988 ICMA Annual Conference, Charlotte, North Carolina.

3

100 Years...and We Are Still Reinventing Government!

Ted A. Gaebler
Rancho Cordova, California

Cheryl Hilvert
ICMA

Troy Holt
Rancho Cordova, California

As ICMA celebrates its 100th anniversary in 2014, we are reminded of the significance that professional local government management has had in communities around the world. Since December 1914, when 8 of the 31 existing city managers in the United States met in Springfield, Ohio, and formed the City Managers' Association, ICMA's goal has been to "promote the efficiency of city managers and municipal work in general."[1] And since that time, as the role of the local government manager has grown, particularly in small to mid-sized cities, counties, and other quasi-public organizations, the enduring goal of managers has remained the same: to improve the quality of communities and local government services. ICMA supports this goal through its mission to "create excellence in local governance by developing and fostering professional local government management worldwide."[2]

Throughout the history of our profession, managers have also been called upon to constantly improve and "reinvent" themselves and the ways in which local governments conduct their business. For the current generation of managers, perhaps the most significant call to action was the book *Reinventing Government: How the Entrepreneurial Spirit Is Transforming the Public Sector,* by David Osborne and Ted Gaebler.[3] Published in 1992, this best seller has been printed in 22 languages, and its authors have become

SELECTED FOCAL POINTS

Since *Reinventing Government* was published in 1992, local governments have been supporting initiatives focused on improving customer service, contracting and partnering for service delivery, using enterprise funds, and imposing fees to generate revenue, and they have made increasing use of technology in their operations.

Reinventing Government remains relevant today, more than 20 years after its publication, and managers have suggested that its initiatives will continue to provide a way forward for local governments in the future.

internationally recognized experts in government reform. The recommendations in the book formed the basis of the "New Public Administration" movement, which encouraged local governments to be more "entrepreneurial" in their work.[4] The book continues to be used today in many master of public administration programs, and it has inspired countless progressive managers who believe that governments need to be more mission driven, customer focused, and results oriented.

Robert J. O'Neill, executive director of ICMA, says of *Reinventing Government:* "It would be hard to over-estimate the impact the book has had on government at all levels—an impact not unlike that of the reform-ers who transformed our cities, towns, and coun-ties more than a century ago when they introduced the concept of professional management."[5] Thus, as we celebrate the 100th anniversary of ICMA and of professional local government management, we also celebrate the continuing relevance of *Reinventing Gov-ernment* for the profession today, more than 20 years after its first publication.

Reinventing Government

A central premise of *Reinventing Government* is that the system of American governmental bureaucracy was fitting during the industrial era and times of eco-nomic and military crisis, but that it is not the best system of governance for the postindustrial infor-mation age. The American public wants quality and choice of goods and services, and efficiency of pro-ducers; however, quality and choice are not what bureaucratic systems are designed to provide, and efficiency is nearly impossible in a system of complex rules and lengthy decision making.

Different sectors of the economy (public, private, and nonprofit) should provide the goods and services that each sector produces best—separately or as a collective effort. Government is broad in scope and capacity and is run democratically; thus, it is best at providing policy, social equity, and direction to the economy as well as at preventing discrimination. The private sector, with the flexibility of the market and the forces of competition, is best at providing choices and quality goods and services to consum-ers. The nonprofit, "voluntary," or "third" sector is best at providing human services and goods that do not yield a profit because of the generally small scale and local focus of nonprofit organizations.

In *Reinventing Government,* Osborne and Gaebler emphasize two points: (1) government cannot simply be "run like a business" because business and govern-ment each serve valuable and necessary, but differ-ent, purposes; and (2) the question is not *how much* government we have, but *what kind.* The authors introduce the concept of entrepreneurial government, which focuses on results, decentralizes authority, reduces bureaucracy, and promotes competition both inside and outside government. Using numerous case studies of governments in the United States as well as abroad,[6] Osborne and Gaebler propose 10 principles for transformation:

1. *Catalytic Government: Steering Rather Than Row-ing.* Catalytic governments steer—they set policy, offer guidance, provide funds to operational

bodies, and evaluate performance—and they allow the private and nonprofit sectors to row—to pro-duce the goods and services that those sectors pro-vide best. As examples of steering organizations, *Reinventing Government* cites private industry councils made up of local public and private lead-ers whom the federal Job Training Partnership Act (JTPA) has brought together to manage job training activities within their regions, and transportation management districts that work with employers to reduce commuter traffic (*RG* 40–41). The JTPA was most recently reauthorized by Congress as the Workforce Investment Act of 2013 (H.R. 798), and transportation management districts are active in both Houston, Texas, and Southern California.[7]

In local government, the Cordova Community Council in Rancho Cordova, California, backed by a relatively small financial investment by the city, provides volunteers to perform community service and manage large events (e.g., the annual Fourth of July Celebration, Kids' Day)—activi-ties that would otherwise require a great deal of city staff time. The council leverages the city's money to raise additional funds through commu-nity donations, while the city maintains a seat on the council's board of directors to ensure that the investment is well spent.[8]

2. *Community-Owned Government: Empowering Rather Than Serving.* Bringing communities into the picture empowers people who are the intended recipients of services and also results in better per-formance. The success of this approach is evident in community-oriented policing and in the efforts of parents, community leaders, churches, and vol-unteers to improve service in areas ranging from recycling to public schools. In 2009, Brooklyn Park, Minnesota, embarked upon a Community Engagement Initiative in which a community-wide strategic planning process was designed to engage residents in achieving social control, developing shared expectations of action, and establishing a working trust among the diverse community.[9] Decatur, Georgia, is also a leader in the field of community engagement and building through its efforts in strategic planning, collaborative budget-ing, and community festivals and celebrations.[10]

3. *Competitive Government: Injecting Competition into Service Delivery.* More effective than regu-lation, competition—whether between public agencies and private firms, among private firms, or among public agencies—is possibly the most important element for improving both the qual-ity and the cost-effectiveness of government ser-vices. It can be instrumental in providing not only services to the public but also internal services,

such as printing, accounting, purchasing, and repair. Examples cited in *Reinventing Government* include Phoenix, Arizona's public works department, which competes with the private sector to provide lower-cost trash collection services (*RG* 76–78), and merit pay for high-performing schools (not individual teachers), which boosts competition between teams to build morale and encourage creativity (*RG* 80). Today, the city of Carrollton, Texas, is a leader in injecting competition into many of its public services, including utility operations and billing, parks maintenance, building inspection and planning, payroll/accounting, and library services, saving an estimated $30 million in its first decade as a managed competition "practitioner."[11]

4. *Mission-Driven Government: Transforming Rule-Driven Organizations.* Public organizations should be driven by their missions, not by their rules and budgets. Rules on operations, personnel, procurement, and accounting are embedded in rule-driven systems, resulting in wasted time and inefficiency. By contrast, mission-driven systems free their employees to pursue the organization's mission, resulting in more efficiency, effectiveness, innovation, and flexibility. As examples, Osborne and Gaebler cite the federal China Lake Experiment authorized in 1978, which classified jobs by functions and in wide bands to help managers manage rather than waste time dealing with arcane personnel classification issues (*RG* 128–129); and teachers in East Harlem, who were able to run efficient schools because they were given permission to break the rules (*RG* 100). Today, Fort Collins, Colorado, exemplifies mission-driven government through its core philosophy of sustainability, which underpins every city effort, from the smallest daily tasks to the largest multiyear initiatives.[12]

5. *Results-Oriented Government: Funding Outcomes, Not Inputs.* Governments should focus on outcomes—accountability, performance, and results—rather than inputs. Instead of rewarding managers for protecting their jobs and pursuing larger budgets, larger staffs, and more authority, governments should implement a results- or performance-oriented environment, one that calls for new ways of measuring and rewarding outcomes. This can be applied in various fields, such as job training, vocational education, housing, highway construction, and even the courts system. An example given in *Reinventing Government* is Sunnyvale, California, where managers measure the quantity, quality, and cost of every service they deliver in terms of four categories: goals, community condition indicators, objectives, and performance indicators.

The switch to this system led to the elimination of many rules and budget line items, and brought high productivity, smaller staff levels (by 35%–45%), higher salaries, and lower costs (*RG* 145).

Today, Kansas City, Missouri, has a centralized office of performance management that works closely with its 3-1-1 call center to identify departments and services that can benefit from a performance management approach. For example, with an enormous backload of code enforcement and nuisance abatement requests for service (and unacceptable time frames for addressing those requests), the Neighborhood Preservation Division (NPD) and housing department quickly emerged as a public-facing service area in need of improvement. Eager to use the data-driven process, NPD managers and department leaders quickly took action. Through a combination of key indicator data analysis, updated technology, and strong leadership willing to make large-scale management decisions, the NPD's efficiency and effectiveness have improved dramatically.[13]

More recently, starting in 2010, Bellevue, Washington, began using a "budgeting for outcomes" methodology and logic model approach to connect the budgeting process to the strategic outcome areas determined by the city council. Its neighborhood traffic safety program, for example, uses educational and engineering efforts to address traffic concerns in a project related specifically to the citywide goal of improved mobility. The program details the inputs to be used—such as staff time, capital funding, materials, and equipment—to develop and produce traffic action plans, conduct neighborhood-wide surveys, and produce educational materials. From these actions and strategies the city can anticipate increased knowledge of traffic laws and best practices among residents of Bellevue, a more engaged community on traffic issues, heightened pedestrian and bicycle safety, and an enhanced neighborhood identity, all of which contribute to the council's desired outcome of improved mobility.[14]

6. *Customer-Driven Government: Meeting the Needs of the Customer, Not the Bureaucracy.* Whereas businesses have a nexus between customer revenues and service delivery, government does not; this is because most funding comes from legislative bodies and not directly from customers. As a result, even though society has become more complex and diverse so that the needs and preferences of customers are no longer homogeneous, governments still provide standardized services. They must instead make a greater effort to identify their customers' needs and preferences and provide a

choice of producers. This can be accomplished by providing resources such as vouchers and cash grants. With the GI Bill program, for example, Congress made funding available for military personnel returning from World War II to get a college education, and by allowing GIs to attend the accredited university, college, or technical school of their choice, Congress forced service providers (educational institutions) to be accountable to their customers. As Osborne and Gaebler point out, "Congress turned millions of battle-scarred young men into the educated backbone of a 30-year economic boom" (*RG* 181). Today, Mountain View, California, operates a waste collection program for large item and excess trash that offers customers a variety of options for pickup and collection to suit their individual needs.[15]

7. *Enterprising Government: Earning Rather Than Spending.* Government is under constant pressure to keep taxes down. Some enterprising state and local governments have learned to recognize their assets and use innovative methods to generate revenues that would otherwise come from tax increases. Examples include (1) charging user fees for services provided as private goods, such as municipal golf courses and tennis courts; (2) introducing a loan pool against which entrepreneurial managers can automatically borrow funds to use for explorational purposes; and (3) spending money to protect land under intense development pressure that would otherwise require massive government investment in the future (e.g., spend now to save later). Boulder County and the City of Ft. Collins, Colorado, for example, use "pay as you throw" programs for trash collection, in which the local government imposes a fee based on the volume of trash generated by the household or business. These programs can have ancillary benefits in that they tend to increase recycling rates and eliminate greenhouse gas emissions in a fair and equitable manner through user fees.[16]

8. *Anticipatory Government: Prevention Rather Than Cure.* Many city, state, and federal governments have incorporated mechanisms into their decision-making processes to plan for the future. The central idea driving this trend is the realization that prevention—think fire or crime—costs less and is much easier to effect than suppression. This approach allows them to integrate rising costs with the short-term decisions that politicians make to maintain the approval of special-interest groups. The State of New Jersey, for example, seeks to prevent homelessness by intervening *before* people lose their homes, providing one-time

loans, security deposits, or rent payments.[17] Organizations such as BUILD Baltimore (buildiaf.org/) and the Greater Indianapolis Progress Committee (indygipc.org/) have become, in essence, stakeholders of the future as they assess government policy for its long-term practicality and lobby decision makers. And many local governments use strategic planning and visioning processes to plan for the future. Flagstaff, Arizona, for example, created a Municipal Resiliency and Preparedness Study to address the significant public service challenge of reducing vulnerability and building local resilience to climate variability and climate-related disasters.[18]

9. *Decentralized Government: From Hierarchy to Participation and Teamwork.* Centralized decision making can cripple the ability of organizations to respond to various challenges. In centralized systems, knowledge accumulates at the top of an organization, where decision makers are far removed from frontline staff. Decentralized organizations seek to empower those individuals who are in the best position to develop effective and innovative solutions to problems. Osborne and Gaebler recount, for example, how when given the authority to study a problem that was causing a driver backup at the Energy Recovery Plant, solid-waste employees in Madison, Wisconsin, came up with a schedule-based solution that obviated the need for the city to spend $1 million on facility-based improvements (*RG* 260–261). Additionally, the Madison police department created an experimental unit in which employees elected their own captain and lieutenants, developed their own staffing and work schedules, and designed and built their own district building—all resulting in a high job satisfaction rating among employees and in lower rates of absenteeism and workers' compensation claims (*RG* 260). Today, the cities of Olathe, Kansas,[19] and Montgomery, Ohio,[20] make extensive use of employee teams and, in so doing, successfully drive leadership and decision making down into the organization to create stewardship for the organization among all employees.

10. *Market-Oriented Government: Leveraging Change through the Market.* "Cities are . . . like markets— vast, complex aggregations of people and institutions, each constantly making decisions and each adjusting to the other's behavior based on the incentives and information available to them" (*RG* 282). The most effective way for government to meet the public needs of this local marketplace is not by attempting to control it directly through administrative programs, but by using policy to steer the decisions and activities of its players. One example is the creation of a market-based regulatory policy

to create incentives rather than demands, such as building into the cost of a polluting product (e.g., gasoline and pesticides) the cost imposed on society by the polluter (*RG* 302). Consumers need no sophistication about which product is more environmentally damaging than another; they simply have to look at the price. Another example, seen in many cities such as San Francisco, is the creation of regulations to encourage the use of customer-owned grocery/shopping bags while charging a fee for store-provided bags in order to address adverse environmental impacts created by these products.[21]

What Has Changed since 1992?

To repeat, *Reinventing Government* encouraged managers at all levels of government to abandon more industrial-era approaches and become more entrepreneurial—mission driven, results oriented, and customer focused, with decentralized authority and less reliance on rules and regulations. At a special session commemorating its 20th anniversary, Ted Gaebler stated that the book "paved the way for us to be mavericks in local government."[22] But the question is, *have* managers been mavericks who have succeeded in transforming government, or do we need a reminder to continue the government reinvention that Osborne and Gaebler called for in 1992? The answer is, probably both.

In 2003, ICMA surveyed all chief executive officers in municipalities of 10,000 or greater to assess the reinventing government paradigm in municipal government.[23] City managers who responded indicated a high level of support for the primary reinventing government principles and for the actions needed to implement them. Survey respondents reported significant implementation of those principles in the following budget-related areas:

- Use of enterprise funds in budgeting, 88%
- Funds for customer service training for municipal employees, 72%
- Funds for citizen surveys, 71%
- Funds to train employees in decision-making skills for response to customer complaints, 71%
- Funds to train neighborhood organizations in decision making, 69%
- Funds for e-government initiatives, 69%
- Fee increases instead of tax increases, 69%
- Partnering to provide a program or service, 68%
- Contracting out a municipal service, 68%
- Entrepreneurial program funding, 59%[24]

In the years since the 2003 ICMA survey, local governments have continued to support initiatives focused on improved customer service, contracting and

partnering for service delivery, the use of enterprise funds, and the imposition of fees for revenue. Additionally, they have made increasing use of technology in their operations, taking advantage of the efficiency and enhanced service delivery that this advancement has facilitated. Performance budgeting has become increasingly more common among local governments since *Reinventing Government* was published.

Survey results from 2003 show that in their budget recommendations, managers most commonly cited fee increases instead of tax hikes (86%). A majority of managers also recommended funding for customer service training (71%), partnering with private and nonprofit organizations to provide services (71%), using enterprise funds (67%), funding e-government initiatives (68%), contracting out services (66%), training employees in decision making for citizen complaints (64%), and funding citizen satisfaction surveys (56%).[25] These items indicate strong acceptance of the customer service principle so deeply embedded in the reinventing government concept. As Richard Kearney states, "The reinventing government movement does appear to be firmly established as the local government management paradigm."[26]

In 2013, during a special session celebrating the 20th anniversary of *Reinventing Government* at ICMA's annual conference, a panel of local government managers identified the following areas where continuing work is needed:[27]

- *Making the mission the focus of the entire organization.* While local governments today are indeed more mission driven in their approach, this focus needs to extend beyond the manager and elected officials to individuals throughout the organization. Employees need a "clear line of sight" between the work they do each day and fulfillment of the organization's mission. They need to focus on the things that matter most in achieving that mission, which can mean abandoning the way work "has always been done." This can be achieved, for example, by pursuing high-performance organization (HPO) strategies,[28] which seek to align all departments and employees with the mission of the organization to improve performance and achieve excellence in work products.

- *Empowering the organization to solve problems and identify opportunities.* Once all parts of the organization are aligned with its mission, managers must empower staff to solve problems and create opportunities that make a difference for the organization and its stakeholders, the community, and themselves. In the 1960s, Rensis Likert developed his "organizational systems theory," which supports the concept that employee empowerment creates better "outputs" for an organization.[29] To achieve this goal, managers must not only ensure alignment with the organization's mission but also address antiquated job descriptions that focus employee attention solely on technical task work. They must develop the competencies of leadership and management in all their staff members, train employees with the basic skills necessary for teamwork and problem solving, provide general direction and support to allow employees to develop those skills, and then *listen* to the employees' ideas. This approach can improve both the organization's capacity for problem solving and its ability to recognize opportunities for new strategies and innovative ideas that can reinvent local government and its work.

- *Understanding the critical difference between leadership and management.* Leadership and management entail very different approaches, and it is critical that managers understand the difference. It has been said that "a leader is someone you follow because you want to" while "a manager is someone you follow because you have to." Osborne and Gaebler define *leadership* as "steering" the organization toward the future and *management* as "rowing" the organization along a predetermined path. Leadership has also been defined as making a difference "more than a year from the now" while management is more "in the minute." HPO strategies suggest that the work of leadership is understanding the customers/stakeholders and what they value; creating both a vision and a culture for the organization; cultivating "stewardship" for the whole organization; learning, thinking, changing, and renewing; and enabling, energizing, and empowering the organization. Management, on the other hand, is more centered on the organization's business functions, including finance and budget, human resources and supervision, project oversight, process improvement, and technology.

  It is also critical that managers understand that leadership is not "positional." It can be demonstrated by individuals at all levels of the organization, not just by the city/county/town manager or chief elected official. Thus, managers must seek to develop the leadership skills within all employees in the organization, a characteristic that is critical to reinventing government.

- *Putting more emphasis on achieving results and on using those results in making decisions.* Many local governments today are using performance measurement and benchmarking; ultimately, however, the local government business is not about "crunching" more numbers than anyone else but about using those numbers to be a change

agent for the community. Specifically, data should be used to enable managers to think differently about what and how their organizations deliver services, to ensure that projects and services are linked to the organization's mission and goals, to identify community outcomes derived from those projects and services, and to make continuous improvements in that work.

Resources such as the National Citizen's Survey™[30] and ICMA's Performance Measurement programs, as well as innovative approaches such as Priority-Based Budgeting,[31] all provide ways in which managers can effectively use data to manage their organizations and the services they provide. At the same time, "big data" will continue to make more and more information available to managers. It is important that local governments recognize the importance of data and be prepared to use the massive amounts of information available in its decision-making and service delivery processes.

- *Sharpening the customer/stakeholder focus in service delivery while recognizing the importance of the citizen/co-owner. Reinventing Government* discusses the importance of a customer-driven focus, and many local governments use methods, including surveys, to determine the types of services that their customers (i.e., citizens) value. However, some argue that calling citizens "customers" minimizes the role of citizens as stakeholders in the community and creates a "vending machine" mentality in which citizens' relationship with local government is "transactional," leaving them with little or no ability to influence the services they receive.[32] Thus, to continue reinventing government, managers need to sharpen their focus on "customer-driven government," give citizens the "power of customers," and be proactive and responsive in service delivery. At the same time, they also need to recognize the value of civic engagement and of developing a strong relationship with their citizens. When managers are willing to admit that they cannot do it all, they will realize how important relationships are in quality local decision making, linking the work of the local government to the goals of the community, and in many cases they will find allies that make their work easier and more fulfilling.

- *Being more anticipatory to better see the needs of the future.* Solving problems and delivering services is no longer enough for local governments. While many managers do strategic planning, they need to look beyond that vehicle to anticipate the work of local government in the future. Having a longer-term vision will enable managers to be more proactive in their approach to service delivery and less reactive to the latest problems, trends, or citizen demands.

- *Letting go of programs and services that can be better supplied by others in order to focus on the things that really matter.* The important message for managers today is that government is not the sole solution provider, even though citizens often want it to be. With limited financial resources, managers must look to alternative methods for service delivery (and possibly shedding services altogether) so that they can direct those resources where they are most needed. While *Reinventing Government* focused much of its attention on public-private contracting, managers should consider all forms of collaborative service delivery, including public-private partnerships, regionalism, and consolidation. The nonprofit community and citizen groups are also possible providers of services and partners for local governments.

However, while contracting/partnering can be a good approach, it is important to remember that it can be done poorly, resulting in bad contracts and contractual relationships. In the December 2013 *State and Local Government Review* article "Collaborative Service Delivery: What Every Local Government Manager Should Know,"[33] managers considering collaboration are urged to

1. examine the reasons behind any proposal to learn if they are legitimate and in the best interests of the parties involved
2. carefully examine the type of collaboration proposed to determine whether it is the best approach to achieving the goal
3. determine the correct number of partners to be included
4. determine—on the basis of financial analysis, ease of service delivery, and the private sector's need to generate profit—whether the service is best kept in-house
5. assess the difficulties involved with contract specification and management, including the management of relationships
6. identify the barriers
7. identify the benefits.

- *Creating a culture of innovation.* Typical bureaucracies can hinder creativity and innovation, as can an organizational culture that does not value and encourage such characteristics. Managers need to avoid the "siloes" of a typical bureaucracy, in which departments and employees focus on the technical aspect of their jobs, rarely collaborate outside their siloes, rely heavily on rules and regulations that impede the organization's ability to reinvent itself,

and spend their time simply "turning the crank." In such an environment, it often takes a crisis, such as the fiscal crisis of 2008, to get workers to approach work differently. Unfortunately, when the crisis passes, so too does the innovation.

Bureaucratic barriers can be broken down by eliminating processes and systems that do not support organizational values, encouraging teamwork across the organization, empowering staff to make decisions, giving meaning to the work they do, and creating managers and leaders from employees at all levels of the organization. Creating a culture of innovation as well as excellence in service delivery requires a deliberate focus on developing and supporting organizational values, aligning systems of government to reflect those values, making a commitment to excellence, creating trust within the organization, and supporting a willingness to take risks. It also requires consistent feedback to personnel—and to the organization as a whole—on progress made toward that goal. Again, managers can use HPO strategies, as well as the work of the Alliance for Innovation and its Enhanced Research Partnership with Arizona State University and ICMA's Center for Management Strategies, to support their efforts to create a culture of innovation in their organizations.

The Enduring Reinvention Imperative

As we enter the second century of professional local government management, the recommendations of Osborne and Gaebler are still as timely as they were 20 years ago. In an October 2013 *ICMA Newsletter* article titled "Local Governments' Enduring Reinvention Imperative," Bob O'Neill states that "during the past two decades, local governments have become increasingly engaged in the process of reinvention."[34] Largely driven by factors both inside and outside their organizations—including the changing landscapes and demographics of communities; challenging economic climates; difficult, multijurisdictional problems; polarizing politics; and technology advancement—managers have increasingly turned to new and different approaches to service delivery and problem solving. Citing the innovative approaches used by seven local governments to reinvent the services and programs they provide, he hails these jurisdictions as exemplifying the kind of entrepreneurial governments that Osborne and Gaebler champion in *Reinventing Government:*[35]

- Hampton, Virginia, made its activities and services more transparent; increased opportunities for citizens to become involved in the work of their local government; and developed new ways for representatives of the public, private, and non-profit sectors to effectively work together in service to their city.

- Decatur, Georgia, engaged more than 2,000 of its 20,000 residents, both online and in person, to create its 2010 strategic plan.
- Fort Collins, Colorado, honored by *Money* magazine as one of its 2006 "Best Places to Live," boasts award-winning schools, a globally focused university, excellent shopping and restaurants, a flourishing arts community, and outstanding outdoor activities enhanced by hundreds of miles of biking and walking trails.
- Olathe, Kansas, one of the fastest-growing communities in the country, has become an economic powerhouse by attracting such highly visible businesses as Honeywell, Garmin, ALDI, and Farmers Insurance Group.
- Durham, North Carolina, was one of 33 cities worldwide to receive an IBM "Smarter Cities Challenge" grant to develop a coordinated strategy for addressing disenfranchised youth and positioning them to become contributing members of the community by age 25.
- Palo Alto, California, has been nationally recognized for its cloud-based open data sites, which foster transparency and trust in government by providing new opportunities for citizen communication and participation.
- Needham, Massachusetts, adopted the town-manager form of government in 2005, which resulted in an approach to infrastructure investment that has radically revitalized the community.

These local governments took standard public services and programs that are used in other locations—such as those promoting strategic planning, youth outreach, economic development, financial management, and quality of life—and raised them to a higher level through an approach that echoes the *Reinventing Government* message of 20 years ago. In other words, being mission driven, customer focused, and results oriented continue to be viable goals for local government managers today.

This "reinventing" approach and the success stories it engenders do not just happen by accident. O'Neill suggests that "reinvention-minded" local governments share a set of principles that imbed a culture of sustained innovation within the organization; abandoning the status quo, these principles instead focus on achieving results, measuring performance, and adhering to the core mission:[36]

Ted Gaebler and Reinventing Government

Since the release of *Reinventing Government,* Ted Gaebler has been both the chief executive officer for a county government and the founding city manager for Rancho Cordova, California. In that city's first decade of cityhood (with Gaebler as its only city manager), Gaebler's methods of reinvention and entrepreneurial government, along with his creation of a great employee culture, resulted in $25 million in federal funding for infrastructure improvements and enhancements in service while $400 million in local dollars were kept in Rancho Cordova. The city has garnered a budget surplus every year since incorporation.

Today the city is financially stable, with $1.4 billion in commercial, retail, residential, and other investments. Neighborhoods have been dramatically improved through aggressive, yet collaborative, code enforcement. Rancho Cordova was named an All America City in 2010 and is the first local government to be named a *Fortune* "Great Place to Work." Four of the founding city council members remain, and none has ever lost a bid for reelection.

- *Consistency and perseverance.* Change is difficult in an organization, and the manager must remain strongly committed to the goal and motivated to see the change through to fruition.
- *Stable leadership.* Consistent and stable leadership in an organization, regardless of political change, is critical. Even with a change in the top management position, the organization's leaders should remain focused on achieving the organization's mission and goals.
- *Earned trust.* Because local government leaders are closer to the people they serve than are other government leaders, citizens often have higher levels of confidence and trust in their local governments than in their state and federal governments. Local officials can use this trust to support efforts to reinvent the local government and, often, the community itself.
- *A focus on issues that matter.* A community that is interested in innovation and reinvention must stay focused not only on its mission but also on the work necessary to achieve that mission. It must be disciplined enough not to get sidetracked by opportunities that offer short-term benefits but overlook or even undermine established priorities and long-term goals.

- *High levels of citizen/resident engagement.* Engaging all sectors of the community in local decision making as it relates to strategic plans and community priorities creates support for reinvention work and new initiatives.

- *Tolerance for risk.* Reinvention requires challenging assumptions and abandoning the status quo, actions for which a certain amount of risk taking is critical. During times of crisis, superior organizations embark on "creative destruction,"[37] deliberately abandoning the traditional ways of thinking and doing in order to achieve innovation.

- *A sustainable culture of excellence.* Creating an organizational culture that supports excellence, innovation, and reinvention requires a commitment to mission and goals, performance management, accountability for results, and engagement of the organization's staff and of the community.

Managers who desire to reinvent themselves and their local governments would be well served to cultivate these principles in their organizations. They would also be well served to learn from the innovative approaches exemplified by the seven communities cited above. In doing so, they can continue to pursue the challenge to reinvent themselves that Osborne and Gaebler issued to government managers everywhere.

Conclusion

In addition to writing about the principles that are necessary to sustain innovation over time, Bob O'Neill has written about "The Coming Decade of Local Government," in which he describes both challenges and opportunities for local government managers. In this June 2012 *Governing* article, he states that

the next decade will be a time in which the fiscal woes of federal and state governments will leave local and regional governments on their own, struggling to balance the need for innovation against the necessity of making tough choices. But . . . it also will be a decade in which local government will lead the way in developing creative solutions to extraordinary problems.

There are a number of reasons to be optimistic about this coming decade of local government.[38]

Similarly, in a *New York Times* op-ed article in January 2014, David Brooks refers to two authors from the Brookings Institution who "argue that Washington paralysis is already leading to a power inversion. As the federal government becomes less energetic, city governments become more so."[39]

As we approach this "coming decade of local government"—and the 100th anniversary of ICMA—managers should be optimistic and energetic about their roles and the roles of local government. These roles will continue to expand along the paths of reinvention, innovation, excellence, risk tolerance, leadership, trust, collaboration, and a focus on what matters.

Effecting substantial change within a government organization is a major challenge. Bob O'Neill reminds us that "reinvention can happen only when the government enterprise has the discipline required to abandon the status quo and focus on achieving momentum toward positive results. That is the enduring lesson of *Reinventing Government*."[40] The book that challenged managers to greater heights of performance in 1992 continues to be a call to action as we enter the next century of ICMA and professional local government management. Are you up to the challenge?

Notes

1   ICMA Constitution adopted at the second annual conference in Dayton, Ohio, November 1915.

2   Mission Statement, ICMA 2008 Strategic Plan, icma.org/en/icma/about/organization_overview/strategic_plan.

3   David Osborne and Ted Gaebler, *Reinventing Government: How the Entrepreneurial Spirit Is Transforming the Public Sector* (New York: Plume Publishing, a division of Penguin Books, 1992). For all future references to this source, page numbers are provided parenthetically in the text, preceded by *RG*.

4   Mildred Warner, "Restructuring Local Government" (Ithaca, New York: Cornell University College of Architecture, Art, and Planning, 2014), mildredwarner.org.

5   Bob O'Neill, "Local Governments' Enduring Reinvention Imperative," *ICMA Newsletter*, October 31, 2013, icma.org/en/icma/newsroom/highlights/Article/103867/Local_Governments_Endur.

6   Case studies from outside the United States were taken from Australia, Belgium, Canada, Denmark, England, Germany, Greece, Iraq, Israel, Italy, Japan, New Zealand, Norway, the Philippines, Poland, Singapore, South Africa, Spain, Sweden, Turkey, Vietnam, and Yugoslavia.

7   See Houston-Galveston Area Council, "Transportation Management Organizations" (n.d.), mysolutionis.com/partners/transportation-management-organizations/default.aspx, and South Coast Air Quality Management District, aqmd.gov/trans/doc/tma_tmo_list.pdf.

8   See National Civil League, "Success Stories: Rancho Cordova's 'Three-Legged Stool,'" July 26, 2010, allamericacity.award.com/2010/07/26/rancho-cordova-city-hall/.

9   James Verbrugge, "Case Study: Community Engagement Initiative in Brooklyn Park, MN," ICMA Knowledge Network (2012), icma.org/en/icma/knowledge_network/documents/kn/Document/304087/Case_Study_Community_Engagement_Initiative_in_Brooklyn_Park_MN.

10 See Decatur, Georgia, "Strategic Planning and Community Engagement: Whose Vision Is It, Anyway?," ICMA Knowledge Network (2013), icma.org/en/icma/knowledge_network/documents/kn/Document/304469/Strategic_Planning_and_Community_Engagement_Whose_Vision_is_it_Anyway; Meredith Roark, "Collaborative Budgeting Process in Decatur, Georgia," ICMA Knowledge Network (2010), icma.org/en/icma/knowledge_network/documents/kn/Document/301578/Collaborative_Budgeting_Process_in_Decatur_Georgia; and "The Magic of Festivals: A Bold Approach to Building Community and Economic Development," ICMA Knowledge Network (2011), icma.org/en/icma/knowledge_network/documents/kn/Documnt/302701/The_Magic_of_Festivals_A_Bold_Approach_to_Building_Community_and_Economic_Development.

11 Carrollton, Texas, *Managed Competition: A Decade of Transformation* (March 20, 2012), cityofcarrollton.com/modules/showdocument.aspx?documentid=10082.

12 Darin Atteberry, "Sustainability Services: How Economic Health, Environmental Services and Social Services Join Together to Build Community" (2013), transformgov.org/en/knowledge_network/documents/kn/document/305112/sustainability_services_how_economic_health_environmental_services_and_social_services_join_together.

13 See City of Kansas City, Mo., "Neighborhood Preservation Division," kcmo.org/CKCMO/Depts/NeighborhoodAndCommunityServices/Preservation/index.htm.

14 Hannah Wolford, Corey Orlosky, and Kira Hasbargen, "Using Performance Measurement for Effective Strategic Planning," *InFocus* 44, no. 6 (2012): 5–12.

15 City of Mountain View, "Clean Up Programs, Bulky Goods & Vouchers" (Mountain View, Calif., 2014), ci.mtnview.ca.us/city_hall/public_works/garbage_and_recycling/clean_up_programs.asp.

16 Lisa Skumatz, "Pay as You Throw," *Colorado Municipalities* (April 2008), transformgov.org/en/knowledge_network/documents/kn/document/2596/pay_as_you_throw.

17 State of New Jersey, Department of Community Affairs, "Homelessness Prevention" (2014), state.nj.us/dca/divisions/dhcr/offices/hpp.html.

18 City of Flagstaff, *Resiliency and Preparedness Study* (Flagstaff, Ariz.: September 2012), flagstaff.az.gov/DocumentCenter/Home/View/38841.

19 Marnie Green, "Tidbits from TLG: Seven Innovative Ideas for Engaging Public Employees," ICMA Knowledge Network (April 21, 2012), icma.org/en/icma/knowledge_network/blogs/blogpost/658/Tidbits_from_TLG_Seven_Innovative_Ideas_for_Engaging_Public_Employees.

20 Matthew Vanderhorst, "Changing the Public Perspective of Local Governments," ICMA Knowledge Network (2011), icma.org/en/icma/knowledge_network/documents/kn/Document/303024/ICMA_Strategic_Leadership__Governance_Awards.

21 SF Environment, "Checkout Bag Ordinance" (n.d.), sfenvironment.org/article/prevent-waste/checkout-bag-ordinance.

22 Quote from Ted Gaebler, *"Reinventing Government:* The Book's Impact after 20 Years and Its Continuing Relevance for the Future," special session held at ICMA's 99th Annual Conference, Boston, Mass., September 15, 2013.

23 Richard C. Kearney, "Reinventing Government and Battling Budget Crises: Manager and Municipal Government Actions in 2003," in *The Municipal Year Book 2005* (Washington, D.C.: ICMA, 2005), 27–32.

24 Ibid., 29.

25 Ibid.

26 Ibid., 32.

27 *"Reinventing Government:* The Book's Impact after 20 Years and Its Continuing Relevance for the Future," special session held at ICMA's 99th Annual Conference, Boston, Mass., September 15, 2013. Session participants were Bill Horne, city manager of Clearwater, Florida; Craig Gerhart, former manager of Prince William County, Virginia; Bob O'Neill, ICMA executive director; Mary Bunting, city manager of Hampton, Virginia; and Nicole Lance, assistant to the town manager, Town of Gilbert, Arizona.

28 See Commonwealth Centers for High Performance Organizations, Charlottesville, Va., highperformanceorg.com/, and ICMA Center for Management Strategies, icma.org/en/results/management_strategies/leading_practices/hpo.

29 Rensis Likert, *The Human Organization: Its Management and Value* (New York: McGraw-Hill, 1967).

30 The National Citizens' Survey™ is a product of the National Research Center in Boulder, Colo., and is offered as a leading practice by the ICMA Center for Management Strategies; see icma.org/strategies.

31 Priority Based Budgeting is a product of the Center for Priority Based Budgeting™ of Denver, Colo., and is offered as a leading practice by the ICMA Center for Management Strategies; see icma.org/strategies.

32 See, for example, Donald Kettl, *The Next Government of the United States: Why Our Institutions Fail Us and How to Fix Them*" (New York: W. W. Norton, 2009), 29–31.

33 Cheryl Hilvert and David Swindell, "Collaborative Service Delivery: What Every Local Government Manager Should Know," *State and Local Government Review* 45, no. 4 (December 2013): 240–254.

34 O'Neill, "Local Government's Enduring Reinvention Imperative."

35 Ibid.

36 Ibid.

37 Robert J. O'Neill Jr., "Local Government in an Era of Creative Destruction," *Governing*, May 1, 2013, governing.com/columns/mgmt-insights/col-local-government-creative-destruction-challenges-leadership.html.

38 Robert J. O'Neill Jr., "The Coming Decade of Local Government," *Governing*, June 27, 2012, governing.com/columns/mgmt-insights/col-coming-decade-local-government-citizen-trust.html?utm_source=related&utm_medium=direct&utm_campaign=col-coming-decade-local-government-citizen-trust.

39 David Brooks, "The Power Inversion," *New York Times*, June 6, 2013, nytimes.com/2013/06/07/opinion/brooks-the-power-inversion.html?_r=4& (accessed January 8, 2014).

40 O'Neill, "Local Government's Enduring Reinvention Imperative."

4

ICMA's Evolution as an International Organization

Barbara H. Moore
ICMA

ICMA's vision of an international presence started as early as 1924—when, just ten years after its founding, the City Managers' Association added "International" to its name. Although the organization had been founded with an eye to professionalizing local government in the United States, its reach soon extended to other countries—such as Canada, Great Britain, and New Zealand. In fact, the 1924 annual conference was in Montreal, so the stage was set for what ultimately became a truly international organization.

The "I" in ICMA was advanced substantially by executive director Orin Nolting. During his tenure, from 1956 to 1967, Nolting traveled abroad extensively, especially in Western Europe, to promote the council-manager plan, attend biennial congresses of the International Union of Local Authorities, and further the exchange of ideas and experiences between

The author thanks the following people for their contributions to this article: David Grossman, director, ICMA International; Elizabeth K. Kellar, deputy executive director, ICMA; Michael Murphy, former director of ICMA's International Municipal Programs; and Rita Ossolinski, director, state and affiliate relations, ICMA. This article is based on interviews with these individuals; staff reports to the ICMA Executive Board; and articles in *Public Management (PM)* magazine and other ICMA publications.

SELECTED FOCAL POINTS

Although ICMA has fostered connections across international borders throughout most of its 100-year history, the "I" in ICMA assumed new meaning with a significant award from the U.S. Agency for International Development in 1989. As municipalities worldwide absorbed new responsibilities–and faced new challenges–in the face of urbanization and decentralization, ICMA's mission, vision, and core values proved to be perfectly in sync with new emphases in U.S. foreign assistance policy goals.

In its international work, ICMA seeks to identify local solutions to local challenges–and then put in place programs ensuring that improvements in governance and service delivery can be sustained into the future.

ICMA's members–professional managers in local government–have eagerly embraced city-to-city partnerships to share knowledge and best practices with their counterparts in developing and decentralizing countries. Partnerships and friendships enrich all participants and frequently endure after project funding ends.

U.S. and Canadian managers and their counterparts in other countries.[1]

Building on Nolting's legacy, ICMA's leadership and members became eager to expand the organization's international activities, and members began to make more connections with officials in European cities. In 1976, with funding from the Charles F. Kettering Foundation and the participation of Antioch College, the European Task Force—which included U.S. and Canadian local government managers, several academics, and the deputy director of ICMA—spent three weeks traveling in England, the Netherlands, and the Federal Republic of Germany, meeting with high-level officials and exploring how ideas generated in European cities might be applied in the United States.

The task force focused on intergovernmental relations, planning (physical, social, and economic), and downtown (core) redevelopment and beautification. Upon their return from Europe, participants formed the ICMA Task Force on International Education to disseminate the lessons learned. The early reports of the task force covered affordable housing, downtown revitalization (including public art and pedestrian- and bike-friendly layouts), and alternative approaches to policy development and service delivery.[2]

ICMA also undertook a few small-scale projects funded by donor organizations—including, in the 1970s, a program in the Philippines and, in the late 1980s, a United Nations–funded technical-assistance training program that was conducted in Jordan and attended by administrators and mayors from Arab nations.

A Funding Opportunity

The late 1980s was a period of rapid urbanization in Africa, Asia, and Latin America. Particularly in developing countries, cities were ill equipped to handle the influx of people from rural areas, which overwhelmed already deficient public services. In response, the federal Agency for International Development (commonly referred to as USAID) began to develop new strategies to strengthen the capacity of local leaders to address urban problems, including service provision.

Meanwhile, it was becoming clear that U.S. foreign assistance policy goals—which provide direction for USAID—were perfectly in sync with the mission, vision, and core values of ICMA. ICMA staff member Elizabeth Kellar began attending USAID conferences and meetings to learn more, recognizing that the agency's new emphasis on urbanization presented a perfect opportunity to bring ICMA's substantial municipal management knowledge and resources to bear on a worldwide scale. As word got out that

USAID was planning to issue a request for proposals (RFP) focusing on municipal networking, longtime international contractors began exploring the possibility of having ICMA participate as a subcontractor. Given the depth of the organization's expertise, however, ICMA staff decided that the association had the necessary strengths to be a credible contractor in its own right.

In 1989, with ICMA executive director William H. Hansell's encouragement and support, ICMA took on the challenge of writing the association's first proposal to USAID. Staff put together a proposal team and met with representatives of other local government organizations—including the American Public Works Association, the Government Finance Officers Association, and several municipal leagues—to solicit letters of support. When USAID's Office of Housing and Urban Programs issued the RFP, it was a perfect fit for ICMA, and ICMA was ready.

The solicitation asked for proposals to provide municipal development, management, finance, and training services in a number of developing areas in Africa, Latin America, and elsewhere. The ICMA proposal highlighted the association's significant qualifications for the work:

- A core membership of local government professionals with hands-on experience, numbering 7,500 at the time
- State-of-the-art training materials that were tested, proven, and easily adaptable
- An unequaled information center with the ability to respond quickly to inquiries
- A network of professionals who could facilitate international study tours, exchanges, and peer-to-peer relationships, including affiliate relationships with organizations in Australia, Canada, England, New Zealand, and the Middle East
- An institutional vision, commitment, and strategy focused on expanding and strengthening professional local government management worldwide.

ICMA's proposal was successful, and in late 1989, the association was awarded the multimillion-dollar Municipal Development and Management Project to assist local government officials in developing countries.

ICMA Hits the Ground Running

To meet the financial, contractual, and logistical demands of international work, ICMA established the International Municipal Programs department and quickly assembled the necessary resources. In addition to building a talent bank and hiring staff with specialized expertise, ICMA needed to invest in technology to facilitate international communications. The new program faced a host of unfamiliar management challenges—health risks; safety issues, particularly in postconflict areas; and even the psychological stress of culture shock, as U.S. and Canadian managers were suddenly transported to unfamiliar physical, cultural, and political environments.

ICMA's members were eager to help. In response to announcements in the association newsletter, ICMA received more than 600 résumés from candidates for international positions—most of them from members. Staff also conducted a language survey of members and received more than 1,000 responses, 850 of which indicated some proficiency in a language other than English.

An additional challenge for ICMA was the need to continuously market the project. The contract was structured in a way that required "buy-ins" from USAID country missions, bureaus, and regional housing and development offices. During the first year, ICMA visited USAID missions and other offices in Ecuador, Honduras, Hungary, Indonesia, the Ivory Coast, Jamaica, Kenya, the Philippines, Poland, Thailand, and Tunisia, and responded to more than 60 requests for services around the world. The following are among the tasks that ICMA undertook in fulfillment of the contract:

- Recruiting trainers and training coordinators for wide-ranging assignments, including the development of an urban environmental strategy and a proposal to establish new toll roads in Jamaica, support for the privatization of solid-waste services in Botswana and Costa Rica, and the design of a computer-based land management system in Morocco

- Arranging for the placement of an engineer from Morocco with public works officials in St. Petersburg, Orlando, and Dade County, Florida, for on-the-job training in the management of sewer treatment facilities

- Conducting studies of local currency and municipal bond guaranty in Indonesia and Kenya

- Arranging study tours, training events, and conferences in venues that included Czechoslovakia, Honduras, Poland, and Senegal.

New Forces at Work: Decentralization and Democratization

Just as the ICMA program was getting up and running, two historic events occurred: the fall of the Berlin Wall in late 1989 and the dissolution of the Soviet Union in 1991. These events precipitated a rapid devolution of responsibility from the national to the subnational level in Central and Eastern Europe and Central Asia. As the attention of the world—and USAID—turned to Central and Eastern Europe, the agency modified the scope of the ICMA program to include that region.

After centuries of centralized control of political and financial power, the former Soviet states had virtually no history of autonomous local government.[3] Nevertheless, many Central and Eastern European countries set about establishing independent local governments with surprising enthusiasm. Michael Murphy, who served for ten years as the first director of ICMA's international program, cites examples:[4]

- In Poland, in order to counter the discredited, top-down communist system and develop a local political base, the Solidarity-backed central government sought to establish democratic municipal elections.

- In Hungary, the first democratically elected government enacted legislation to create local governments and to decentralize responsibility for many public services to the local level.

ICMA's Approach

From the very beginning, ICMA's international projects have been guided by a core set of principles:

- Leverage the experience and expertise of ICMA's members, their professional staff members, and the resources developed by ICMA's U.S.-focused programs, and apply them to the challenges of developing and decentralizing countries.
- Develop partnerships and networks for sharing information and best practices.
- Engage as many stakeholders as possible, including appointed and elected local officials, nongovernmental organizations, national ministries and agencies, the private sector, and civil society.
- Develop locally appropriate solutions to challenges identified collaboratively with local stakeholders.
- Focus on developing local capacity so that programmatic improvements can be sustained after donor funding ends.

To implement its projects, ICMA has assembled a diverse pool of experts in the subspecialties of municipal management (finance, public works, economic development) and a flexible tool kit of approaches (e.g., assessments, training programs) that can be tailored as needed. The resources developed by ICMA's U.S.-based programs have been the impetus for expanding the international program into such areas as public safety and violence prevention, climate adaptation and sustainability, and performance measurement.

Decentralization brought new challenges to municipalities with no history of self-government. In Central and Eastern Europe, local leaders, no matter how educated and astute, lacked the experience that would have allowed them to develop decision-making, citizen engagement, and other public leadership skills. With new responsibility for service delivery, local governments needed access to financial resources—either from the national government, which was often reluctant to share revenues, or from local sources, which required new practices, such as assigning property values to establish a base for local taxes.

Among the significant projects in Central Europe, Eastern Europe, and Central Asia during the early 1990s—all funded by USAID—were the three-year Hungary Public Administration Program and multiyear public administration programs in Armenia,

Kazakhstan, Kyrgyzstan, Romania, and Slovakia. All these programs focused on decentralization, fiscal and administrative management, and capacity building.

Decentralization was occurring at the same time in Latin America, but there the drivers were practical as well as political. In the face of economic pressures and demographic shifts toward urban areas, central governments recognized the advantage of placing responsibility for services at the local level, where they could be delivered more efficiently. Direct local election of mayors became the norm; the new mayors, who were often from the business community, appreciated the value of professional and technical staff in service delivery. Unlike their counterparts in Central and Eastern Europe, Latin American local governments had access to revenue sharing from the central government, which relieved some of the need for locally generated revenue sources.

In South Africa, democratization came about through the fall of apartheid in 1994 and the nation's first multiracial elections, which led to the presidency of Nelson Mandela. ICMA was called on to help in a number of ways. Historically, the city managers' association in South Africa had been all white. ICMA began working with a newly emerging association of black local government professionals who eventually became the core of a new professional association. Leaders of the association visited ICMA and attended ICMA conferences; partnerships were established between a number of South African and U.S. cities; and Bill Hansell, executive director of ICMA, and Jim Knight, director of the Federation of Canadian Municipalities, went to South Africa to meet with a committee of the South African Parliament, which wanted to consult with them on proposed new local government legislation (see photo).

A delegation of ICMA members and staff, including (from left to right) ICMA executive director Bill Hansell, ICMA staff member Russell Hawkins, and former ICMA president Sylvester Murray, with Nelson Mandela in South Africa.

Despite differences in context, the twin trends of decentralization and democratization set the stage for the largest projects of the early years—in Poland and Honduras.

Poland

After decades of Soviet rule, Poland was entering a period of rapid change in the direction of democratization, decentralization, and the introduction of a market economy. The Local Self-Government Act became law in 1990, and municipal elections were held shortly thereafter.[5] As part of decentralization, the national government had drastically decreased subsidies to cities, which now needed to build institutions for public representation and effective service delivery, and to secure sufficient financial resources to carry out their responsibilities. Many local governments in Poland had serious fiscal deficits and housing shortages; they were also taking charge of a large share of public property (land, housing, economic enterprises)—a complex and lengthy process.[6]

ICMA's assistance project in Poland began in 1990 with two cities: Warsaw, the capital, and Slupsk, near the Baltic Sea. Technical assistance teams met with city officials to identify problems and recommend solutions for housing, infrastructure, finance, land valuation, and municipal management. Particular emphasis was placed on the transfer of land and property: ICMA conducted "train the trainer" sessions on land use management, land appraisal, and communal housing.

Honduras

In 1990, the Municipal Reform Law granted Honduran municipalities financial resources, more control over local resources, and increased autonomy from the central government. These changes satisfied a fundamental prerequisite for USAID funding and set the stage (and created a need) for management at the local level. ICMA's Honduran Municipal Development Project provided technical assistance and training in taxation, general management, public works, community participation, and other skills and practices that establish a foundation for professional administration.[7]

The first step for project staff was to gain political support from the mayors of the municipalities that had been selected to participate in the initial phase of the project. Their support—and the support of the central government—were critical to the program's ultimate success. The project made significant contributions:

- Strengthening and promoting the Association of Honduran Municipalities (AMHON) as a national organization representing the interests of member municipalities. AMHON began convening well-attended national mayors' conferences and became a visible force for the Honduran municipal reform movement.

- Introducing the concept of the professional administrator as someone who manages day-to-day service provision.

- Documenting practices and delivering training for mayors, council members, and staff to systematize municipal tax administration and revenue enhancement, budget development and administration, accounting standards and financial controls, and other basic management activities.

- Providing mayors with guidance on how to hold successful open town meetings—something they had been reluctant to do for fear of losing control of the forum.

- Improving the delivery and management of public works projects—which included persuading many municipalities of the need for a trained engineer, rather than just a project manager, to plan and execute projects.

- Developing and leaving in place a cadre of more than 50 local consultants to continue working with municipalities after the end of the funded portion of the project.

The Birth of CityLinks

ICMA's flagship international program, now called CityLinks, was established in 1997 as Resource Cities, funded by USAID. Under this program, U.S. local governments formed partnerships with their counterparts in Africa, Asia, and Latin America to jointly address local challenges in the non-U.S. countries. These partnerships provided new opportunities for ICMA's members to participate directly in international contract activities; for many of them, the experience was inspiring and eye-opening. Because members and their professional staffs donated their labor (see photo), the arrangement was also a plus for the funding agency, whose dollars could go further.

During a CityLinks partnership between Tirana, Albania, and Catawba County, North Carolina, Catawba county manager Tom Lundy (left) participates in a cleanup day in the Albanian city.

CityLinks continued through 2008 and resumed with new funding in 2011. Through close to 100 projects, CityLinks partners have assisted municipalities around the world as they seek to improve public works facilities and services, plan and organize for local economic development, initiate citizen participation mechanisms, develop and enhance local revenue sources, and meet dozens of other challenges in just about every realm that local government touches—from public health to transportation, emergency services, tourism development, and code enforcement.

From the start, ICMA's approach has been to put in place policies and practices that can be sustained locally after funding ends. And CityLinks has achieved some remarkable successes, with lasting results. In the past decade, for example,

- A consortium of cities in Bulgaria, together with a national local-government reform foundation, established a local economic development certification program, launched a website to market local assets to investors, and institutionalized training for economic development professionals. Three years after the program's end, these efforts had yielded 2,500 new jobs, €140 million of investment in new and expanding businesses, and a fully established certification program.
- Through the Post Tsunami Recovery Program, Cuddalore and Nagapattinam, two tsunami-

ravaged cities in India, restored damaged property; designed and built community playgrounds; modified infrastructure to mitigate flooding from typhoons; educated citizens about public services; and increased access to reliable, safe drinking water for residents. The program drew on the experience of three Florida cities—Oldsmar, Palm Bay, and Port Orange—that had learned to live with the constant threat of hurricanes and remain prepared for them.

- In Jordan, CityLinks partners designed and implemented centralized medical waste collection and disposal practices that helped safeguard community health and protect the country's precious water supply from contamination. Partners were the Jordan University of Science and Technology, the Jordan Ministry of Health, and East Carolina University. When the program ended in 2005, 21 hospitals were safely incinerating their waste. By 2012, 109 were doing so, thanks to practices that had been put in place during the project.

In addition to programmatic sustainability, City-Links has fostered lasting partnerships between cities:

- After serving as a key adviser on a program in Dire Dawa, Ethiopia, the fire chief of Oldsmar, Florida, arranged for the donation and shipment of protective equipment for local firefighters, who were at constant risk of injury because they lacked proper gear.
- Three years after the two cities' formal partnership ended, the city of Tigard, Oregon, dedicated an Indonesian-style park pavilion in honor of its partnership with the city of Samarinda.
- Years after their CityLinks partnership ended, the director of utilities and engineering in Catawba County, North Carolina, continued to advise public works and planning staff from Tirana, Albania, on materials, guidelines, and management practices.
- Similar continuing relationships exist between Golden, Colorado, and Veliko Turnovo, Bulgaria; Port Townsend, Washington, and Umag, Croatia; and West Bend, Wisconsin, and Pazardjik, Bulgaria.

Global Reach

As ICMA's global reach grew, the organization began to set up field offices and form partnerships to solidify its worldwide presence. The first field offices were established in Honduras and were organized shortly after the Honduras program started in 1990. In 1994, ICMA opened its first field office in Eastern Europe—in Romania—and continued to establish field offices for large programs in Central Europe, Eastern Europe, and Central Asia, including Armenia, Hungary, Kazakhstan, Kyrgyzstan, Poland, and Slovakia. The overseas offices were staffed by a combination of U.S. local government professionals and support staff from the country being served. ICMA staff in Washington, D.C., supervised overseas operations and kept USAID informed of program results.

In 2004, ICMA built on earlier successes in Mexico by launching an office in Guadalajara—ICMA Latinoamérica, later renamed ICMA México-Latinoamérica —to provide a presence in Latin America and the Caribbean. ICMA-ML provides direct services to Mexican cities and promotes professionalism and transparency. A significant step forward occurred in February 2014, when the governing council (*ayuntamiento*) in Navolato, in the state of Sinaloa, created the position of municipal administrator as a nonpolitical council appointee.

In the late 1990s, ICMA began establishing a presence in South Asia, working with the Urban Management Centre (UMC) in Ahmedabad, India, as its project office. By 2005, UMC had evolved into an independent nongovernmental organization that continues to serve as ICMA's "anchor" in the region.

As China became a greater player in the global political and economic arenas, ICMA sought to develop professional relationships there as well. Starting with small-scale projects to provide study tours, training, and technical assistance—and after considerable due diligence—ICMA eventually identified the China University of Political Science and Law (CUPL) as a viable long-term partner.

In 2011, ICMA and CUPL established the ICMA China Center at the university's campus in Beijing. Shortly thereafter, the center was welcomed into the U.S. Department of State's competitive EcoPartnerships program, in recognition of its commitment to addressing common challenges related to energy and the environment. In 2013, the center facilitated a trip by two ICMA members to address local government officials and university students; and in May 2014, it will host the first ICMA International Regional Summit in Yangzhou.

By 2014, ICMA's international "reach" embraced nearly 70 countries in which full-scale projects had been implemented, and perhaps a dozen more countries whose professionals have participated in training, exchanges, and other programs.

Diversification

USAID was the primary funder for many of ICMA's early projects, but as the international program matured, it attracted awards from other donors and undertook projects in a wider range of technical areas:

- The World Bank, through the Public-Private Infrastructure Advisory Facility, funded the Regional Credit Rating Improvement Program, which guided subnational governments in Argentina, Costa Rica, and Mexico as they established practices that would increase their ability to borrow for infrastructure projects.

- The U.S. Department of State has selected ICMA to manage portions of its Professional Fellows program, which has provided reciprocal exchanges for professionals from Australia, China, Indonesia, New Zealand, Thailand, and Timor-Leste and their counterparts in U.S. cities and counties. The first program managed by ICMA focused on sustainable communities, and two others have focused on the legislative process, governance, and transparency.

- The U.S. Department of Defense Southern Command (SOUTHCOM) tasked ICMA with assessing the disaster readiness of communities on Guatemala's Pacific coast and developing a training and exercise program for them. Following the 2010 earthquake in Haiti, SOUTHCOM also engaged ICMA to support a network of new fire and emergency services stations by making recommendations for organization, staffing, and equipment procurement and designing a program of instruction for personnel.

Conflict and Postconflict Countries

Starting with its projects in Central and Eastern Europe, ICMA often found itself working in conflict and postconflict environments. In such settings, a guiding principle of ICMA's work has been that sound governance and good service delivery are keys to promoting stability.

Following the war in Iraq, for example, ICMA was engaged as a subcontractor to provide support to new local leaders; as part of ICMA's fulfillment of that contract, several ICMA members accepted long-term assignments to provide training in basic management. Later, ICMA assisted newly elected local council members as they learned how to relate to local citizens and to the national government. To help ensure that the success of the project would be sustained, ICMA employed a "train the trainer" approach—teaching local trainers who could, in turn, train current and future council members (see top-left photo on following page).

Conflict in Afghanistan set the stage for ICMA's largest portfolio of international projects, starting in 2004 with a USAID-funded program to strengthen the capacity of the municipality of Kabul, a city whose infrastructure and public services had deteriorated

Participants in a "train the trainers" workshop conducted by ICMA in Karbala, Iraq, record their points on a flip chart.

through years of neglect and war-related damage. Not only were physical facilities in disrepair, but the city lacked the capacity to plan for and manage services. The goal of the project was twofold: to tackle the infrastructure problems and to establish sustainable public services by introducing practices and approaches that could be replicated elsewhere in the country.

Because of the volatile political environment and pockets of anti-American sentiment, project staff generally worked through the mayor's office or municipal departments so that accomplishments were perceived as originating locally. Using a "learning by doing" approach, ICMA placed local workers in project-funded jobs at various skill levels so that they could perform the needed work while gaining new skills.

Working in several neighborhoods, ICMA was able to help local officials and citizens achieve some welcome progress:

- Basic infrastructure improvements: cobblestone-paved streets, roadside drainage ditches cleaned of trash and sewage, restoration of parks and other public spaces, and identification of private sector organizations that would cover the costs of future maintenance. (For example, a cell phone company agreed to partner with the municipality by committing six maintenance workers to the upkeep of a newly improved park for a year.)

- Solid-waste management improvements: creation of a routing system, acquisition of equipment, closure of illegal dump sites, and education of citizens about their role in packaging waste and placing it at curbside for pickup.

- Pleasant recreation areas and green space provided for families and children.

- Street marking and traffic signage to improve vehicular and pedestrian safety.

Because of the success of the Kabul project, USAID awarded ICMA the contract for the Afghanistan Municipal Strengthening Program (AMSP), which extended ICMA's previous work to 12 provincial capitals. Only a detailed list of accomplishments can provide a full picture of what "strengthening" meant in the Afghan context: by the end of its lifespan (May 2007–November 2010), AMSP had

- Implemented 81 small-scale municipal infrastructure projects, and collected and removed 88,100 cubic meters of trash

- Provided 184,000 worker-days of employment and paid $1.1 million in wages to temporary local laborers

- Leveraged $4.3 million in funds from other donors

- Provided 6,700 hours of training and technical assistance to partner municipalities

- Provided opportunities for youth to engage productively in their communities (4,530 boys and 1,234 girls were involved in capacity-building activities, sports, internships, and jobs)

- Prepared digitized, geographic-information-system–based maps for AMSP municipalities

- Facilitated citizen-driven, strategic municipal action plans for six cities

- Achieved improvements in citizens' perceptions of quality of life and municipal services (as assessed by citizen satisfaction surveys).

In 2008, ICMA was awarded another major project in Afghanistan: the Commercialization of Afghanistan Water and Sanitation Activity (CAWSA). Scheduled to continue through May 2014, CAWSA works with local water-supply companies to help them establish the physical and management infrastructure to support

One improvement engineered by ICMA programs in Afghanistan was the conversion of manual records to computerized ones.

eventual privatization. Activities include repairing damaged or neglected wells, pipes, and other infrastructure and introducing basic business practices (e.g., computerization of records, financial management, revenue collection, preventive maintenance, and customer service). Management improvements have produced measurable results:

- Thousands of new connections delivering reliable water service to customers
- Reductions in the unit cost of water production
- Improvements in cost-recovery ratios
- Faster response times to emergency calls
- Improved customer service.

ICMA has rounded out its Afghanistan portfolio by serving as a subcontractor on other projects. All of the resulting activities—among them, change management assistance for a national ministry and gender awareness training—have been designed to develop the capacity of Afghans to ensure their country's future. While the future of U.S. involvement in Afghanistan remained uncertain at the time of this writing, ICMA is hopeful that its projects will have a lasting positive impact.

Looking Ahead

As ICMA marks its 100th anniversary, ICMA International is turning 25. The USAID award in 1989 served to solidify the "I" in ICMA, enabling the organization to carry out its mission worldwide and satisfying members' desire to make contributions beyond their jurisdictions' borders. Since that time, awards from

other donors have given ICMA further opportunities to establish a sound reputation in the international development community. ICMA understands that cities learn best from other cities; thus, the association serves as a convener of local government practitioners, supporting a global local government network and providing a platform for continuous learning and information sharing.

Not surprisingly, the focus and direction of ICMA's international program over the years have been steered by worldwide trends and events—decentralization, democratization, urbanization, conflict and other social upheavals, and climate change. Programs are also driven by national priorities, such as crime and violence prevention, ethics and transparency, environmental protection, citizen involvement, and the empowerment of women.

In 1914, only 15% of the world's 1.6 billion people lived in cities, yet ICMA's founders saw the need for an association that would promote good governance and professionalism in local government. Today, as ICMA enters its next 100 years, more than half of the world's 7 billion inhabitants live in cities; and by the turn of the century, that is expected to be true for a projected 85% of the world's 11 billion people. The urbanization megatrend, if well managed, will have enormous economic, political, demographic, social, public health, and ecological benefits for all humankind. Clearly, ICMA is well positioned to contribute to global efforts to ensure that our cities are places in which citizens can enjoy safe, prosperous, and productive lives. The "I" in ICMA is more relevant than ever.

Notes

1 David S. Arnold, "ICMA—A Chronicle of Service," unpublished history of ICMA, July 1986, icma.org/chronicle.

2 "The European Connection," *Public Management (PM),* July 1976.

3 Michael Murphy, "Progress of Local Government Worldwide," *Public Management,* March 2001, 6–10.

4 Ibid.

5 Renata Frenzen, "ICMA Activities in Poland," *Public Management,* June 1991, 13.

6 Ibid.

7 Ann E. Bueche, *Making Cities Work: The Honduran Municipal Development Project* (Washington, D.C: ICMA, 1994); a summary of the project appears in Ann Bueche and Pablo Salcido, "Did ICMA Meet Its Goal on the Honduran Project?" *Public Management,* July 1994, 19–22.

5

Intermunicipal Cooperation: The Growing Reform

George C. Homsy
Department of Public Administration
Binghamton University

Mildred E. Warner
Department of City and Regional Planning
Cornell University

Local governments have been under increased stress since the Great Recession of 2008. Declining revenues have created intense fiscal pressures while the need for public services has risen. In the face of this challenge, we were especially curious to see if ICMA's 2012 alternative service delivery (ASD) survey would show any increases in outsourcing.

ICMA has measured local government use of ASD mechanisms since 1982. This ongoing survey allows us to track experimentation and innovation at the local level. Service delivery strategies vary widely as managers must respond to citizen preferences, local capacity and needs, and differences in local market conditions. In the last decade, privatization has dropped slightly (from 18% of all service delivery in 2002 to 16% in 2012),[1] while intermunicipal cooperation has grown (from 17% of all service delivery in 2002 to almost 24% in 2012). Intermunicipal contracting is now the most common delivery alternative—more common than for-profit contracting.

This *Year Book* article explores some of the factors explaining this trend. It also discusses motivators and obstacles to ASD, and it presents a disturbing fact about local government evaluation of ASD mechanisms: the data show that monitoring and evaluation of contracted services continue to be low.

SELECTED FINDINGS

Intermunicipal cooperation is the only alternative service delivery strategy that continues to grow among local governments, having increased from 17% in 2002 to almost 24% in 2012.

Contracting out service provision to for-profit companies dropped slightly in 2012, even in the face of fiscal stress caused by the 2008 recession.

Eighty-two percent of jurisdictions participate in a regional organization of some sort. While most of this cooperation (68%) involves roads and highways, nearly two-thirds (62%) of it is focused on economic development.

Evaluation of private contracts is inadequate. More attention needs to be given to the evaluation of private contracts and intermunicipal agreements.

Survey Response and Methodology

ICMA's *Profile of Local Government Service Delivery Choices, 2012* survey was mailed to the chief administrative officers in all municipalities with city-type governments and a population over 2,500 as well as to all functioning counties—a total of 10,552 jurisdictions across the United States. In prior years, only one in four municipalities under 10,000 in population and all counties under 25,000 in population were included in the sample. In 2012, however, the U.S. Department of Agriculture funded the survey, so ICMA made a special effort to reach small and rural municipalities.[2] Although expansion of the sample frame resulted in a drop in the response rate from 26% to 21%, the 2012 survey had responses from 471 more municipalities and 114 more counties than did the 2007 survey (Table 5–1). These extra governments are primarily in the under-10,000 population category.

As in the past, the response rate from municipalities is higher than that from counties. Apart from the smallest jurisdictions, the distribution of survey response by population group is relatively consistent, ranging from 20% to 25%, with the rates being slightly higher in the bigger cities (above 100,000). Geographically, the response rates are highest in the Pacific Coast, South Atlantic, and Mountain geographic divisions and lowest in the East South-Central, Mid-Atlantic, New England, and West South-Central divisions. While in the past ICMA reported responses by metro status using U.S. Census-bureau designations (metro core, suburban, independent), in this survey ICMA reports responses by metro status using U.S. Office of Management and Budget designations.[3] Municipalities are assigned to categories based on the designation of the county in which they sit. Within metropolitan areas, principal cities and counties are designated using Census Bureau definitions. For this survey, the highest response rate (29%) is from principal cities or counties in a metropolitan statistical area; the lowest (17%) is from local governments in non-core-based statistical areas (non-CBSAs), which represent the most rural places in the country.

The 2012 survey lists 76 services and asks local managers to describe which of those services they provide and the manner in which each is delivered (i.e., by public employees entirely, by public employees in part, in partnership with another government or agency, contracted out to a for-profit company, contracted out to a nonprofit organization, by franchise, with subsidies, or by volunteers).[4] This survey presents 13 services that were not listed in 2007 (while merging 7 of the 67 services shown in 2007 into three broader categories). The new services, which are marked with an asterisk in Table 5–2, include additional social services for children and seniors as well as important local government planning functions, such as land use review, economic development, affordable housing, and comprehensive planning.

Table 5-1   Survey Response

Classification	No. of municipalities/ countiesª surveyed (A)	Respondents No.	% of (A)
All	10,552	2,184	21
Municipalities	7,515	1,715	23
Counties	3,037	469	15
Population group			
Over 1,000,000	42	10	24
500,000-1,000,000	99	23	23
250,000-499,999	166	37	22
100,000-249,999	504	125	25
50,000-99,999	875	186	21
25,000-49,999	1,499	305	20
10,000-24,999	2,760	554	20
5,000-9,999	2,300	466	20
2,500-4,999	2,045	447	22
Under 2,500	262	31	12
Geographic division			
New England	797	132	17
Mid-Atlantic	1,415	208	15
East North-Central	1,901	437	23
West North-Central	1,339	298	22
South Atlantic	1,484	377	25
East South-Central	827	112	14
West South-Central	1,246	213	17
Mountain	687	167	24
Pacific Coast	856	240	28
Metro status			
Metropolitan (principal city or county)	641	185	29
Metropolitan (other)	5,955	1,299	22
Micropolitan (rural)	1,707	327	19
Other rural (non-CBSA)	2,249	373	17

a   For a definition of terms, please see "Inside the *Year Book*," xxi-xxiv

The survey also explores different aspects of service delivery, including motivators for and obstacles to implementing private service delivery and intergovernmental contracting. Finally, two new questions are on the 2012 survey: one asks about participation in regional government organizations and the service delivery areas encompassed by those arrangements; the other inquires about methods of raising revenue beyond the property tax.

Table 5-2 Use of Public Service Delivery Strategies, 2012

	No. reporting	Public services provided by				
		Public employees entirely, %	Public employees in part, %	Another government or entity, %	Private for-profit company, %	Private nonprofit organization, %
Average		44.6	16.3	23.6	15.5	9.9
Public works/transportation						
Residential solid-waste collection	1,213	28.3	5.4	5.7	50.9	0.9
Commercial solid-waste collection	947	19.0	8.4	5.8	59.5	0.7
Recycling*	748	32.1	18.2	6.8	40.1	3.2
Solid-waste disposal	652	38.5	11.3	15.2	32.8	1.2
Street repair	1,454	42.0	48.4	6.1	28.9	0.4
Street/parking lot cleaning	1,040	75.4	15.4	2.3	14.3	0.4
Snow plowing/sanding	1,163	75.2	20.0	5.9	10.0	0.3
Traffic sign/signal installation/maintenance	1,240	49.0	32.3	17.6	18.5	0.2
Parking meter maintenance and collection	235	74.0	17.9	3.8	13.2	0.9
Street tree trimming and planting	1,205	43.4	43.7	3.6	30.0	2.1
Maintenance/administration of cemeteries	634	66.9	15.5	4.6	10.1	7.9
Inspection/code enforcement	1,384	75.0	17.0	7.1	9.2	0.4
Operation of parking lots and garages	410	69.8	12.9	8.0	15.1	1.0
Operation/maintenance of bus transit system	390	25.6	9.0	46.9	15.4	9.0
Operation/maintenance of paratransit system	343	23.6	9.9	40.2	16.9	13.1
Operation of airports	395	45.8	19.0	27.8	16.5	0.8
Water distribution	1,082	73.3	9.8	15.2	6.1	0.8
Water treatment	1,027	68.4	8.2	22.0	5.5	0.6
Sewage collection and treatment	1,124	59.9	15.7	27.1	6.0	1.2
Disposal of sludge	908	35.9	13.3	25.0	30.1	2.1
Disposal of hazardous materials	639	19.1	19.7	36.2	32.4	2.8
Public utilities						
Electric/gas utility operation and management	429	32.4	5.8	13.5	42.2	5.6
Utility meter reading and billing	716	81.8	11.2	3.5	7.8	0.8
Public safety						
Crime prevention/patrol	1,296	87.0	6.9	8.6	0.4	0.5
Police/fire communications	1,011	67.1	15.7	23.9	0.6	0.8
Fire prevention/suppression	1,276	58.9	9.3	20.5	1.3	2.8
Emergency medical service	1,170	39.8	15.1	26.4	13.3	8.9
Ambulance service	1,097	29.7	9.0	27.6	23.1	11.3
Traffic control/parking enforcement	1,156	82.9	8.0	9.8	2.2	0.3
Vehicle towing and storage	764	11.6	9.0	7.1	69.0	5.1
Health and human services						
Prisons/jails	975	35.2	9.2	57.5	2.3	0.8
Sanitary inspection	886	37.5	11.1	50.9	4.4	0.8
Insect/rodent control	657	21.3	12.8	44.9	25.6	2.1
Animal control	1,125	55.0	13.6	26.3	5.8	6.7

continued

Table 5-2 Use of Public Service Delivery Strategies, 2012

	No. reporting	Public services provided by				
		Public employees entirely, %	Public employees in part, %	Another government or entity, %	Private for-profit company, %	Private nonprofit organization, %
Operation of animal shelters	735	32.1	9.5	34.6	8.0	20.3
Operation of day care facilities	288	13.2	6.3	22.9	48.6	26.0
Child welfare programs	423	16.5	15.6	58.9	6.4	12.3
Programs for the elderly	744	24.5	31.2	37.9	7.7	23.0
In-home safety improvements for seniors*	397	13.1	18.1	45.3	14.4	24.9
Home health care/visiting nurse*	381	12.6	12.1	40.9	28.1	24.4
Programs to address hunger*	467	4.7	21.6	38.3	5.6	48.4
Elder nutrition programs (e.g., Meals on Wheels)*	625	8.5	18.4	37.0	5.1	41.4
Operation/management of hospitals	488	3.1	1.0	36.7	36.9	36.3
Public health programs	263	39.9	29.7	29.7	5.3	13.7
Drug and alcohol treatment programs	443	8.8	12.2	50.8	18.5	34.1
Operation of mental health/mental retardation programs and facilities	397	7.3	10.6	57.9	16.9	30.0
Operation of homeless shelters	307	3.3	4.6	45.6	7.5	52.1
Workforce development/job training programs	417	8.9	15.3	65.7	8.6	23.3
Youth employment programs*	389	11.8	18.8	55.0	7.2	23.7
Intake/eligibility determination for welfare programs	426	26.5	10.1	58.5	3.8	9.6
Parks and recreation						
Operation/maintenance of recreation facilities	1,357	72.0	20.4	9.3	6.4	5.1
Parks landscaping/maintenance	1,357	67.8	23.7	5.7	14.2	1.5
Operation of convention centers and auditoriums	417	51.1	15.6	19.9	13.2	7.9
Before-/after-school programs or summer camps*	777	47.1	21.8	20.6	8.4	20.3
Youth recreation programs*	1,027	48.8	27.0	14.7	6.2	18.9
Senior recreation programs*	859	44.7	27.4	19.2	5.0	19.3
Cultural and arts programs						
Operation of cultural and arts programs	574	21.8	32.9	16.7	9.2	37.8
Operation of libraries	903	46.6	10.2	35.7	1.3	8.6
Operation of museums	476	18.5	16.4	22.7	4.6	39.7
Land use and economic development						
Comprehensive land use planning*	1,350	67.3	22.3	9.9	11.0	1.6
Land use review and permitting*	1,394	77.8	15.8	6.6	7.6	0.6
Affordable housing*	707	27.4	30.3	41.2	9.9	20.9
Economic development*	1,253	42.1	35.0	23.1	6.4	16.5
Support functions						
Buildings and grounds maintenance	1,464	68.0	27.5	1.2	19.3	1.1
Building security	1,079	72.6	14.9	2.1	18.3	0.4
Fleet management/vehicle maintenance	1,398	57.7	32.6	2.4	25.1	1.0

continued

Table 5-2   Use of Public Service Delivery Strategies, 2012

	No. reporting	Public services provided by				
		Public employees entirely, %	Public employees in part, %	Another government or entity, %	Private for-profit company, %	Private nonprofit organization, %
Payroll	1,492	87.6	7.0	1.1	8.6	0.3
Tax bill processing	1,109	57.4	13.3	30.2	6.3	0.5
Tax assessing	995	44.0	10.6	42.1	8.9	0.4
Data processing	1,279	71.4	18.9	7.8	12.2	0.6
Collection of delinquent taxes	1,080	47.5	16.7	35.2	11.6	1.1
Title records/plat map maintenance	954	45.9	17.3	40.0	8.4	0.4
Legal services	1,158	33.3	18.3	4.8	51.4	2.7
Secretarial services	1,277	93.2	5.2	0.9	2.1	0.0
Personnel services	1,324	89.0	8.9	1.4	5.3	0.5
Public relations/public information	1,127	88.6	10.1	1.3	4.5	1.3

* Denotes new service added to survey in 2012.

As in all ICMA *Year Book* reports, percentages for specific answers throughout the survey are based on the number of respondents to that particular question and not on the entire sample. Comparisons between questions, as well as between years, should therefore be treated carefully because of the different base numbers of respondents in each particular instance.

The Continuing Rise of Intermunicipal Cooperation

Direct public delivery continues to be the dominant form of local government service provision, accounting for 45% of delivery on average across all services (Table 5–2). The majority of services continue to be provided entirely by public employees, a delivery strategy most commonly found in support functions, followed by public safety. For example, the top six services provided directly by local government employees are, in order, secretarial (93%), personnel (89%), public relations (89%), payroll (88%), crime prevention/patrol (87%), and traffic control/parking enforcement (83%). Twenty-nine services have public delivery rates over 50%. Police, fire, roads, parks and buildings maintenance, and land use planning are all core services that the majority of governments do not contract out. The lowest use of public employees is in the social services area, where intermunicipal cooperation and nonprofit delivery are more common.

Along with the prevalence of direct public delivery, the 2012 survey found that intermunicipal cooperation is the only service delivery strategy to increase in usage among local governments since 2007 (from 20% to 24%). Intermunicipal cooperation typically occurs between neighboring cities and towns or between municipalities and the county in which they sit. Municipalities that are not adjacent may form partnerships if they share similar social factors and concerns. Sometimes the collaboration is with a single-purpose governmental organization, such as a transit authority or an economic development agency. Contracting with another government or governmental authority represents an effort on the part of local leaders to find economic efficiencies by working across multiple jurisdictions while keeping service delivery in the public sector. Research has demonstrated that intermunicipal contracting yields similar fiscal gains as privatization but produces better results in terms of equity and citizen responsiveness.[5]

Responses to the 2012 survey show that the most common services provided in collaboration with another government entity are social programs (see Table 5–2), for which economies of scale and regional coordination are important. Respondents reported that workforce development/job training is the most commonly shared service (66%), followed by child welfare programs (59%), welfare administration (59%), operation of mental health facilities (58%), and operation of prisons/jails (58%). Some of these may be collaborations between cities and counties. Other commonly shared services include tax assessing and collection, affordable housing, economic development, and transit services. Forty services have sharing rates over 20%.

By contrast, only 17 services have for-profit delivery rates over 20%, and only 4 of them—vehicle towing, legal services, and commercial and residential solid waste—show private for-profit contracting in the majority of responding jurisdictions (Table 5–2). These are services in which private markets are well established, and as might be expected, most of them have low levels (20% or less) of intermunicipal sharing. For example, only 5% of legal services are shared among municipalities, but more than half (51%) of respondents contract with private law firms. Similarly, solid-waste collection has a low rate of sharing (6% for both residential and commercial collection) but a high rate of privatization (51% for residential and 60% for commercial), and vehicle towing has a 7% rate of sharing compared to a 69% rate of privatization. Critical differences between these services and the ones that rank high in cooperation are that these services tend to be easier to specify in a contract and do not require close regional coordination.

Typically, services with high citizen contact show lower rates of for-profit delivery. Such services are more likely to be provided by intermunicipal cooperative agreements or contracts with nonprofits. Surprisingly, only 9% of respondents reported contracting out payroll, a service that computer technology should make easily scalable. Some large cities have sufficient scale to perform this efficiently in-house, but smaller municipalities might benefit from outsourcing. Growth in privatization might be anticipated in this area.

Nonprofit delivery is the third most common alternative. Seventeen services have nonprofit delivery rates over 20%; these include nutrition and homeless services, culture and art, day care facilities and senior services, affordable housing, and workforce development (Table 5–2). As with intermunicipal contracting, nonprofit delivery is more common for services that involve high human interaction and require some level of community coordination.

Motivators for and Obstacles to Alternative Service Delivery

The most common motivators for intermunicipal cooperation are to save money (81%) and to achieve economies of scale (70%) (Figure 5–1). This drive for fiscal benefit coincides with the number one reason that local government leaders study options for privatization (Figure 5–1). However, the other important motivators for cooperation and privatization indicate that these leaders have very different perspectives on the two approaches. The next most important motivators for intermunicipal cooperation are the desire to strengthen intergovernmental relations (62%), to promote higher-quality/more effective service delivery (60%), and to promote regional service integration (54%). These are more community-oriented goals and are markedly different from those for privatiza-

tion, which remain driven by fiscal gain and, to a lesser extent, antigovernment ideology.

Significantly fewer respondents indicated obstacles to contracting with a private provider than to contracting with another local government (Figure 5–2). Moreover, the most important obstacles to the two service delivery strategies are different. Leaders reported that the biggest barriers to sharing service delivery with other governments are a concern for loss of community (69%), lack of a common vision/mission with potential partners (46%), and lack of trust (43%). By contrast, the most common obstacles encountered by governments studying privatization are related to labor: opposition from employees (56%), opposition from elected officials (43%), and restrictive labor contracts (36%). Intermunicipal cooperation may be seen as less threatening to jobs than privatization.

Another component of intergovernmental cooperation is local government participation in a regional organization. In many cases, such an entity can organize public service delivery across numerous municipalities and offer greater economies of scale and expertise than can individual local governments. In a new question on the 2012 survey, local leaders were asked if they participate in a regional council of governments, metropolitan planning organization, or regional planning agency. A large majority of municipalities and counties (82%) indicated that they do participate in such a regional entity (Figure 5–3). As expected, most of this cooperation involves roads and highways (68%). Nearly two-thirds (62%) of the regional agencies focus on economic development, an endeavor that research indicates is more successful when it is coordinated across a region.[6] Public transit is the focus for 54% of respondents, while nearly half of all local governments (46%) collaborate with regional organizations for disaster planning.

The Maturation of Privatization

Contracting with private for-profit companies for public service delivery dipped slightly from 2007 (from 18% to 16%) after having basically been flat since 2002. Outsourcing to private nonprofit organizations has remained steady. While privatization has increased in some service areas (e.g., a majority of respondents now report for-profit delivery in waste collection), most local leaders have enough experience to understand which services are best privatized in their communities and which are not. Even the fiscal stress of the 2008 recession did not lead to more privatization.

Despite the stable usage of private contracting, the motivations for engaging a for-profit company to provide public services have changed since 2007

Figure 5-1   Drivers of Alternative Service Delivery Strategies, 2007 and 2012

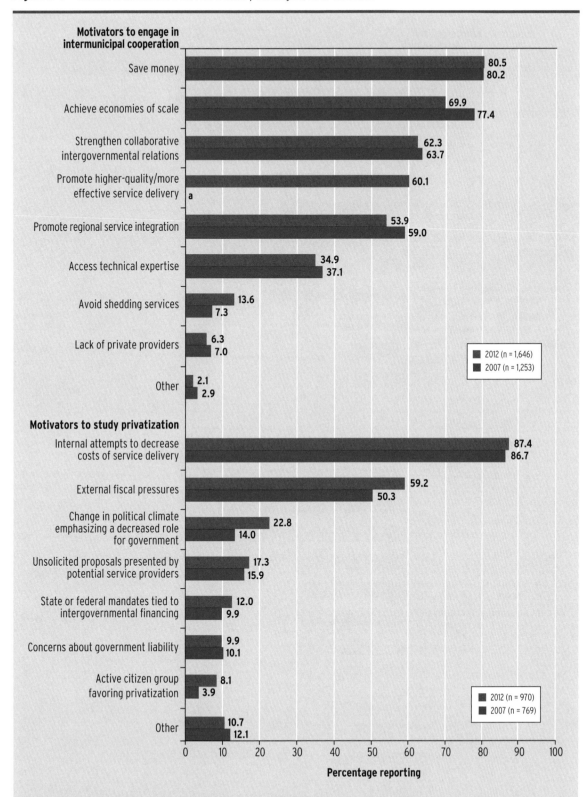

Source for 2007 figures: Mildred E. Warner and Amir Hefetz, "Cooperative Competition: Alternative Service Delivery, 2002-2007," in *The Municipal Year Book 2009* (Washington, D.C.: ICMA Press, 2009), 11-20, Figure 2-1 and Table 2-6.

a Not included in the 2007 survey.

Figure 5-2   Obstacles to Alternative Service Delivery Strategies, 2012

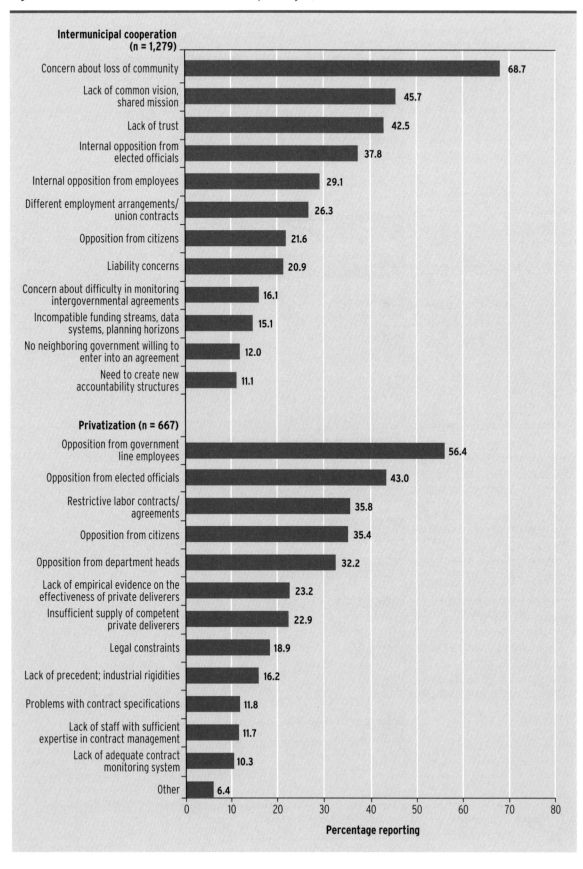

Figure 5-3   Participation in Regional Organizations, 2012

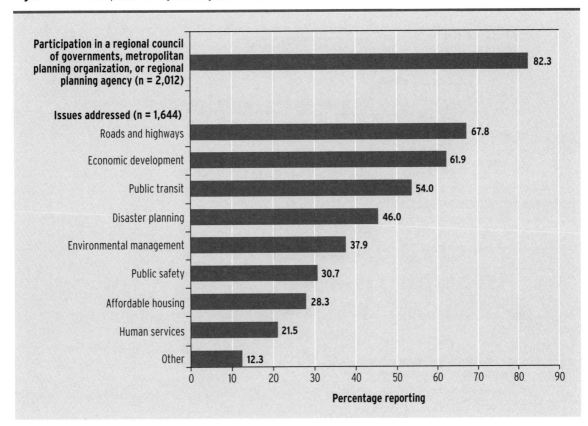

(Figure 5–1). While the number one motivation to privatize—the drive to decrease the cost of service delivery (87%)—remains unchanged, shifts in the other drivers are worth noting. The percentage of jurisdictions reporting external fiscal pressures (e.g., restrictions on raising taxes) as a driver jumped from 50% in 2007 to 59% in 2012, likely as a result of the recession. Similarly, the number of places indicating ideology as a motivator (i.e., "change in political climate emphasizing a decreased role for government") grew from 14% in 2007 to 23% in 2012.

In 2012, only 31% of jurisdictions reported engaging in any activities to ensure the success of privatization (Figure 5–4); that rate is down from 38% in 2007 and from 44% in 2002 (not shown). This may be another sign of maturity, with local leaders better able to grasp which services are appropriate for contracting to private firms and which are not. In those jurisdictions that do engage in activities to ensure the success of privatization, the number one activity is identifying successful efforts in other jurisdictions (71%). Such learning can take place informally among neighbors; through associations of local government officials, which present case studies at

conferences; and through professional publications. Activities used much less frequently include hiring consultants to do feasibility studies (26%), proposing privatization on a trial basis (26%), and allowing government departments to compete in the bidding process (23%).

Monitoring of Service Agreements

Once private sector agreements are in place, the 2012 survey reveals that only about one-third of local governments (37%) monitor their service delivery contracts (Figure 5–5). This is down from just under half (45%) in 2007 (not shown). Among those municipalities that do conduct evaluations, cost is the most frequently monitored factor, considered by 87% of municipalities. Contract compliance is next (79%), followed by measurement of citizen satisfaction (58%). The low evaluation levels raise concerns about the maintenance of service quality.

In those places that evaluate private sector contracts, most (71%) monitor citizen complaints as part of the process (Figure 5–5). Data and records analysis and observations in the field are each used by 69% of local governments; only one-quarter use citizen

Figure 5-4   Ensuring the Success of Privatization, 2012

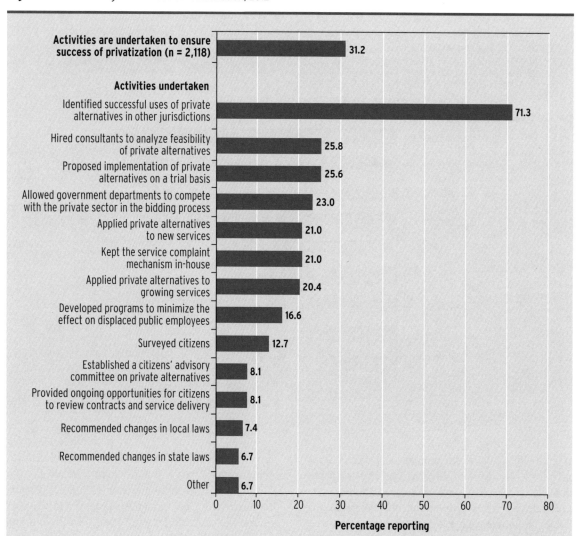

Activities are undertaken to ensure success of privatization (n = 2,118): 31.2

Activities undertaken

Identified successful uses of private alternatives in other jurisdictions: 71.3

Hired consultants to analyze feasibility of private alternatives: 25.8

Proposed implementation of private alternatives on a trial basis: 25.6

Allowed government departments to compete with the private sector in the bidding process: 23.0

Applied private alternatives to new services: 21.0

Kept the service complaint mechanism in-house: 21.0

Applied private alternatives to growing services: 20.4

Developed programs to minimize the effect on displaced public employees: 16.6

Surveyed citizens: 12.7

Established a citizens' advisory committee on private alternatives: 8.1

Provided ongoing opportunities for citizens to review contracts and service delivery: 8.1

Recommended changes in local laws: 7.4

Recommended changes in state laws: 6.7

Other: 6.7

Percentage reporting

surveys to monitor private service delivery—a drop from 31% in 2007 (not shown). This drop is surprising given the increased attention paid to citizen interaction and feedback in the best practice literature. Service quality and access can be harder to evaluate than cost and contract compliance, so local officials may need to increase attention to this area.

While the 2012 survey does not directly ask about evaluation of intergovernmental contracts, the ranking of obstacles (Figure 5-2) provides a clue that evaluation of service delivery agreements may face similar problems. When respondents were asked to describe obstacles to entering into partnerships with other governments for service provision, only 11% checked the "need to create new accountability structures." This could mean that such structures are easy to implement or are already in place, or that partnering jurisdictions

do not feel the need to monitor each other. Indeed, some research indicates that interjurisdictional agreements are built on a foundation of trust developed by local leaders in a regional social network.[7] The past three surveys have consistently found that "lack of adequate contract monitoring system" is also the lowest ranked challenge to privatization reported, and little monitoring of private service delivery contracts occurs. However, research shows that monitoring and evaluation are major challenges in contracting out to for-profit, nonprofit, and other government actors.[8] Costs of monitoring are high, and with intermunicipal contracting, weak sanctions make accountability difficult to ensure.[9] Thus, the continued low attention given to monitoring is cause for concern.

One mechanism that local governments use to address contract failure is insourcing—that is,

Figure 5-5 Evaluating Private Service Delivery, 2012

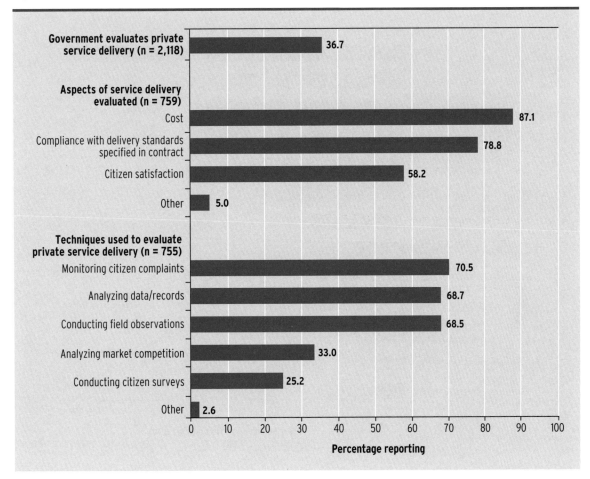

contracting back in-house those services that were previously contracted out. Insourcing is as common as outsourcing.[10] It gives government leaders a way to manage markets and maintain competition and benchmarking in the market over time. Eighteen percent of respondents to the 2012 survey reported insourcing; the reasons given were insufficient cost savings (53%), unsatisfactory service quality (51%), improvements in local government efficiency (30%), successful proposal by in-house staff (23%), and political support to bring the work back in-house (15%) (not shown). Problems with contract specification (10%), monitoring (13%), and lack of competitive bidders (7%), however, are the lowest-ranked reasons for reversals.

Alternative Sources of Revenue

As has been noted, one of the motivators for ASD is to save money. However, academic research does not find lower costs with private delivery.[11] The emerging literature on intermunicipal cooperation raises a similar concern. Economies of scale are exhausted

for many public services by the time a community reaches 25,000 in population.[12] Clearly, the motivations for cooperation extend beyond cost savings to regional coordination, an important issue in service delivery. However, these findings raise further questions about what local governments can do to balance their budgets and still meet citizen demands for services.

The second new question on the 2012 survey asked whether local governments finance service delivery through various alternative funding mechanisms, and it provided a list of 13 options. (Because property taxes are the primary source of local government revenue, they were left off the list.) Not surprisingly, user fees are the most common alternative source of revenue for jurisdictions (82%), while development projects fees—development review fees (52%), local impact fees/developer exactions (37%), and payments in lieu of taxes (32%)—are used to varying degrees (Figure 5-6). Nearly half the respondents reported levying hotel occupancy taxes (46%). Despite the pressures of the Great Recession,

Figure 5-6 Alternative Sources of Revenue

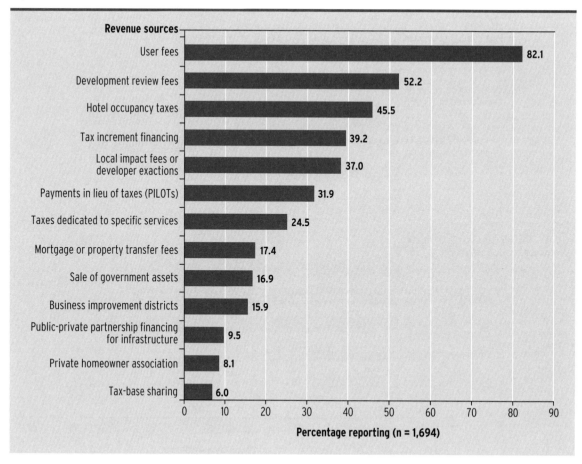

only 17% of respondents reported selling off public assets to raise money, and just 16% reported new efforts to promote additional voluntary taxation, such as business improvement districts.

Conclusion

ICMA's 2012 ASD survey reconfirms the important role of intermunicipal cooperation as an ASD strategy. As local government leaders have grown comfortable with privatization and understand the instances in which it can or cannot be useful, they are now looking for new places for reform, and intermunicipal contracting is gaining attention. Intermunicipal contracting allows local leaders to achieve economies of scale and promote service coordination across the metropolitan region but retain public sector control over service delivery. As a result, cooperation faces less opposition from local government employees, elected officials, labor unions, and citizens than does privatization.

Intermunicipal cooperation holds many advantages over privatization, but it shares a major concern. Just as the vast majority of private service delivery contracts go unmonitored by local governments, responses on the survey indicate that the same may hold true for intergovernmental partnerships. This general lack of oversight, on both private contracts and interjurisdictional ones, is cause for concern.

Local government leaders remain creative as they seek to find efficiencies in service provision and additional ways to raise revenue. Some of this innovation is likely in response to increased pressure on municipalities and counties since the recession. The 2009 *Municipal Year Book* article about the 2007 ASD survey described the increased emphasis on cooperation as a new form of "cooperative competition."[13] With the 2012 survey we see even more emphasis on the importance of cooperation in local government reform.

Notes

1 For comparisons with prior years, see Mildred E. Warner and Amir Hefetz, "Cooperative Competition: Alternative Service Delivery, 2002—2007," in *The Municipal Year Book 2009* (Washington, D.C.: ICMA Press, 2009), 11–20.

2 The 2012 ASD survey was funded by the U.S. Department of Agriculture National Institute for Food and Agriculture Grant #2011-68006-30793.

3 A metropolitan area contains a core urban area of 50,000 or more in population, and a micropolitan area contains an urban core of at least 10,000 (but less than 50,000) in population. Each metro or micro area consists of one or more counties, and includes the counties containing the core urban area as well as any adjacent counties that have a high degree of social and economic integration (as measured by commuting to work) with the urban core. Nonmetropolitan areas include both micropolitan and non-core-based statistical areas (non-CBSAs) (classified here as "other"); see Office of Management and Budget (2013), census.gov/population/metro/. The U.S. Census Bureau list of principal cities can be found at census.gov/population/metro/files/lists/2013/List2.xls.

4 The ASD strategies of franchises, concessions, and volunteers received so few responses that they are not included in the analysis for this article.

5 Amir Hefetz, Mildred E. Warner, and Eran Vigoda-Gadot, "Privatization and Inter-Municipal Contracting: US Local Government Experience 1992—2007," *Environment and Planning C: Government and Policy* 30, no. 4 (2012): 675–692.

6 Mildred E. Warner and Lingwen Zheng, "Economic Development Strategies for Recessionary Times: 2009 Survey Results," in *The Municipal Year Book 2011* (Washington, D.C.: ICMA Press, 2011), 33–42.

7 Kurt Thurmaier and Curtis Wood, "Interlocal Agreements as Overlapping Social Networks: Picket-Fence Regionalism in Metropolitan Kansas City," *Public Administration Review* 62, no. 5 (2002): 585–598.

8 Amanda M. Girth et al., "Outsourcing Public Service Delivery: Management Responses in Noncompetitive Markets," *Public Administration Review* 72, no. 6 (2012): 887–900.

9 Mary K. Marvel and Howard P. Marvel, "Outsourcing Oversight: A Comparison of Monitoring for In-House and Contracted Services," *Public Administration Review* 67, no. 3 (2007): 521–530.

10 Mildred Warner and Amir Hefetz, "In-Sourcing and Outsourcing: The Dynamics of Privatization among US Municipalities 2002—2007," *Journal of the American Planning Association* 78, no 3 (2012): 313–327.

11 Germà Bel, Xavier Fageda, and Mildred E. Warner, "Is Private Production of Public Services Cheaper Than Public Production? A Meta-Regression Analysis of Solid Waste and Water Services," *Journal of Policy Analysis and Management* 29, no. 3 (2010): 553–577.

12 Marc Holzer and John C. Fry, *Shared Services and Municipal Consolidation: A Critical Analysis* (Alexandria, Va.: Public Technology Institute, 2011).

13 Warner and Hefetz, "Cooperative Competition."

6

Advancing Sustainable Communities through Civic Engagement and Performance Measurement

Tad McGalliard
ICMA

What is sustainability? More importantly, what is a sustainable community? While the term *sustainability* is often associated with the environment, this is only one aspect of building a sustainable community. There are countless definitions, each of which builds from the triple bottom line identified in the *Brundtland Report*[1]—namely, economic growth, environmental protection, and social equality. Put succinctly, a sustainable community is one that is able to consistently thrive over time. Decisions made today to improve a community do not have a deleterious impact on the ability of future generations to improve their surroundings. This simple new approach offers a positivist viewpoint that has launched a significant amount of action across the United States.

The Early Years of Sustainability Actions

Throughout the 1990s and 2000s, sustainability emerged as an important framework for inquiry and activity. Smart growth strategies began to formulate at the national, state, and local levels as a means of combating sprawl. Brownfields revitalization kick-started new forms of local action to turn abandoned factories and other potentially contaminated sites into viable

SELECTED FINDINGS

Civic engagement is a necessary ingredient in creating sustainable community policies, programs, partnerships, and plans; however, only 27% of respondents to ICMA's 2010 sustainability survey reported that a citizen's commission, committee, or task force had been appointed as part of the local sustainability planning effort.

As they maximize economies of scale, partnerships have proven to be an essential strategy in addressing the challenges inherent in creating sustainable communities. Project Hope in Dubuque, Iowa, a workforce development and educational attainment initiative for local residents, involves a network of organizations, including the city, the regional council of governments, the local development corporation, and city schools.

Minneapolis, Minnesota, measures the performance of its sustainability efforts across 26 indicators that are centered on a vision for the community's long-term future.

new uses, often with the support of grants from the U.S. Environmental Protection Agency. The U.S. Department of Housing and Urban Development (HUD) launched the Empowerment Zone programs in 1994. Sustainlane .com began to rank the 50 most populous cities for their use of sustainability practices, such as bicycling, rail transport, and alternative/renewable energy. Green building and LEED (Leadership in Energy & Environmental Design) rating systems were developed.

Additionally, national organizations and associations were forming, including ICLEI USA, the U.S. membership association within the International Council for Local Environmental Initiatives, in 1995, and Smart Growth America, dedicated to researching and promoting smart growth practices nationwide, in 2000. The absence of national leadership on climate change issues in the early 2000s led to advocacy by mayors and other elected officials. In 2007, ICMA members, building on more than 90 years of commitment to effective stewardship of natural resources, called sustainability the "issue of our age." Other local government professionals were likewise launching sustainability initiatives.

In his book *Taking Sustainable Cities Seriously,* Kent Portney reflects on the explosion of new ideas and efforts to create more sustainable communities that emerged in the 1990s:

> A brief perusal of activities identified under the rubric of sustainable communities turns up a variety of different kinds of activities and related geographic areas, from the clean water initiative in the Fox-Wolf Basin area of Wisconsin; to the regional sustainability initiatives in the Great Lakes Basin . . . ; to the creation of affordable housing and brownfields development . . . ; to eco-industrial parks; to all of the eco-villages, such as Eco-Village at Ithaca (NY) and Eco-Village Cleveland . . . ; eco-neighborhoods . . . ; and coastal zone management initiatives in Virginia. . . .[2]

Portney also notes that during this time, the number of cities "taking sustainability seriously" was a small fraternity of forward-looking jurisdictions. As ICMA survey data and other data sources seem to indicate, that small fraternity has grown fairly significantly in the first 13 years of the 21st century.[3] Nevertheless, it is clear that we are still in the early stages of sustainability becoming an established or prevailing practice in the United States.[4] (For an in-depth discussion of emerging, leading, and prevailing practices in the United States, see "Spreading Innovation," Chapter 7 in this volume of *The Municipal Year Book.*)

Since 2008, sustainability has been propelled by support at the federal level through programs such as the federal Partnership for Sustainable Communities and funding provided through the American Recovery and Reinvestment Act.[5] HUD's Sustainable Communities Regional Planning Grants support multijurisdictional efforts in regions across the United States; the U.S. Department of Transportation's Transportation Investment Generating Economic Recovery (TIGER) discretionary grant program provides resources for innovative multimodal transportation projects; and the U.S. Department of Energy's Energy Efficiency and Conservation Block Grants, provided directly to local governments, helped fund local sustainability plans and planning efforts, although the program ended after one cycle of funding.[6] Each of these federal programs has provided financial resources for local governments to use in actualizing sustainability plans, programs, and other interventions that had been in hibernation.

Another notable development in this period was the founding of the Urban Sustainability Directors Network, organized by a core group of sustainability practitioners working for local governments. As of 2013, the network had grown to 135 members and had secured a variety of funding sources to support local government sustainability efforts through two programs:

- The Innovation Fund, which assists members and their partners in collaborating to develop, test, and spread high-impact solutions for advancing urban sustainability
- The Local Sustainability Matching Fund, which helps fund partnerships between municipal- or county-level sustainability directors and local or place-based community foundations.[7]

Citing the need for a national baseline of local sustainability policies and programs, ICMA launched a national survey of local governments in 2010. What the survey reveals is that while there are some jurisdictions—for example, Austin, Texas; Boulder, Colorado; and Seattle, Washington—that have pursued the pathways of sustainability for some time, we are still in the early stages across much of the United States.[8]

So if it is finally time to start taking sustainability seriously, what are some of the leading practices that seriously committed local governments are undertaking to advance sustainability in their communities? And if the "right" approach to sustainability is the one that focuses on important local priorities and captures the attention of a community in a way that produces outcomes that make a difference, what are the tools and practices that local governments can use to establish, implement, measure, and manage sustainability in their communities? Two approaches appear to be practices of leading communities that have adopted sustainability as a framework: (1) civic engagement to identify priorities and develop nongovernmental partnerships and (2) indicators and measures to help manage performance. The following sections explore these two practice areas, with a special focus on activities in Dubuque, Iowa, and Minneapolis, Minnesota.

Civic Engagement to Identify Issues and Develop Partnerships

To get started on the pathway to sustainability, a local government needs to understand what its sustainability priorities are; determine the appropriate focus and scope of effort for the community; and identify those issues that mesh with the community's needs and character. As Joel Mills notes in his introduction to a special edition of the *National Civic Review,* "Each community has its own sense of exceptionalism in confronting sustainability issues."[9]

Engaging the local community with its elected and appointed leadership is essential to developing both an understanding of and a consensus on what issues are most important for sustainability. The need for a shared community education process is critical given the complexity of the concept. According to ICMA's survey research data, however, only 27% of the responding communities reported that a citizen's commission, committee, or task force had been appointed as part of the local sustainability planning effort.[10] But as the following text makes clear, the actions that *have* been taken to engage citizens in community sustainability are noteworthy.

Civic Engagement in Baltimore, Northampton, and Corvallis

In developing its sustainability strategy, for example, Baltimore, Maryland (pop. 621,342),[11] convened a number of sustainability meetings, including a Youth Advisory Group. This group hosted a one-day event that attracted more than 150 students from public and private schools, and provided time for young people to voice their concerns and priorities for a more sustainable Baltimore.[12]

Northampton, Massachusetts (pop. 28,592), used a 28-month community planning process to facilitate the development of its sustainability plan, which was published in January 2008. The citizen engagement aspect included nine focus groups and neighborhood meetings, which were organized to gather information on

- characteristics and community values that should guide Northampton
- social, economic, and physical changes that have most affected the community
- areas of conflict among various goals and visions for a sustainable Northampton

- Key areas of concern about sustainability
- Key actions, policies, or infrastructure improvements needed to support a sustainable vision.

Northampton also implemented a citizen survey that was distributed to every household in the jurisdiction and resulted in over 3,000 responses for a 35% response rate. The survey produced information across a range of topic areas, such as the environment, land use, economic development, housing, equity, and residence. A few months later, the city held two workshops, which gathered further input from constituents by allowing them to comment on the city's summary of its findings to date.[13]

In developing its sustainability action plan, Corvallis, Oregon (pop. 52,283), created an inclusive engagement process to gather input from community members. A communications team for the planning process used various electronic and print outreach tools to let citizens know about upcoming meetings and other events. Corvallis used four town hall meetings with several hundred people in attendance at each, during which organizers used electronic keypad polling to gather opinions about community priorities and helped give each of the attendees the opportunity to express an opinion, even if that simply meant registering a vote. In between each of those meetings, 12 work groups met to do background research and make preliminary recommendations on issues ranging from community inclusion to housing to water management.

Participatory Practices for Sustainable Dubuque

Dubuque, Iowa (pop. 58,155), has adopted sustainability as the overarching brand for the community. The city describes Sustainable Dubuque as "the lens through which city operations are developed and analyzed. Likewise, there are numerous community initiatives active . . . along with businesses that are finding ways to save money and improve their environment and community by implementing the principles that define *Sustainable Dubuque.*"[14]

Citizen engagement as a necessity of regional, community, or urban planning has had eras of prominence, but there were also times when decision making was concentrated and compartmentalized in the hands of experts. In today's world, however, the advent of new technologies and the speed with which information flows from source to mass distribution often ensure that citizens will be engaged formally or otherwise. Dubuque has long recognized the value of engaging citizens in planning and program development. Nearly 5,000 residents participated in the city's Vision 2000 community planning process, which helped to launch a revitalization effort that continues to this day.

Sustainability Sustainable Dubuque, like other initiatives in the city, was launched with grassroots and civic engagement to identify priority objectives and goals. It was led by a citizen task force that included representatives from a wide variety of local stakeholder organizations, such as the local government, schools, ecumenical organizations, businesses, and nonprofits. During the two-year process, the task force delivered community presentations and facilitated the completion of about 900 citizen surveys.

Dubuque2.0 was organized as a follow-on to the original Sustainable Dubuque initiative.[15] Led by the Community Foundation of Greater Dubuque (CFGD) and the local chamber of commerce, and funded by a grant from the Knight Foundation, Dubuque2.0 set up a dedicated website to involve community members from a variety of professions in conversations about strategies for embedding sustainability actions in their own lives. From this effort has evolved the Sustainable Dubuque Collaboration,[16] which aims to create a viable community-supported organization that will engage with residents, foster education and learning, leverage existing partnerships, and develop new partnerships toward the creation of a more sustainable community.

Visioning In 2005, the CFGD and the chamber of commerce kicked off Envision 2010, a grassroots effort to engage the community in a visioning process to identify transformative ideas for the future. The lengthy process tapped the creativity of nearly 13,000 residents; more than 2,300 ideas were submitted, and after a review process, 10 ideas for creating social and community vibrancy were selected. These included major economic redevelopment efforts, such as expanding revitalization of the city's waterfront and warehouse district with commercial, recreational, cultural, and mixed-use approaches; integrating a bilingual education curriculum for K-12 students; and creating a community health center. Each of the selected projects has been adopted by a local organizational champion, and many have progressed toward completion or major milestones.

Partnerships Partnerships with nonprofit organizations, neighborhood associations, community development corporations, and other local and regional institutions have proven to be an essential strategy in confronting the challenges inherent in creating more livable and sustainable communities. As local governments have sought innovative ways to deliver needed services and maintain adequate service levels in an era of reduced resources, formal and informal partnerships have become popular approaches for ensuring community and social vibrancy. According to findings from *Beyond Citizen Engagement,* attitudes about partnering to deliver needed services are generally positive if

certain variables can be identified, such as impacts on the community. Importantly, citizens and participating groups want to make sure that their involvement in a project is actually making a difference.[17]

Hand in hand with Dubuque's commitment to citizen engagement is a passion for partnerships that has flourished over the last 20 years. These partnerships, which have been formed with such key local institutions as the chamber of commerce and the CFGD, have coincided with the city's commitment to engage residents as well as its efforts to leverage resources from state, regional, national, and even international sources.

Dubuque has gained much international prestige from its partnership with IBM on the Smarter Sustainable Dubuque effort, which has applied smarter metering technology in several areas, including water and electricity. Importantly, several of the pilot projects in the effort have been designed with a firm commitment to all three legs of sustainability's bottom-line stool: the economy, the environment, and social equity. For example, the smarter water pilot project developed a cost-share program to help residents fix leaks that had been identified through participation in the program. Another key element of the partnership was the recognition that there will be pockets of residents—the elderly, for example—who are not comfortable using online technologies even though they may want to participate in the program. As a result, the partnership developed in-person forums and also trained public library employees to help program participants fully engage in the program.

Another strong partner in Dubuque's sustainability efforts has been the CFGD. Founded in 2001, Dubuque's community foundation is a relative newcomer, considering the 100-year history of similar organizations, yet the foundation has been integral in convening, funding, and partnering with a variety of efforts, such as

- Project Hope, a workforce development and educational attainment initiative that helps support local residents with life skills as well as employment and training opportunities. Project Hope involves a network of organizations, including the city, the regional council of governments, the local development corporation, and Dubuque schools.

- The Dubuque Green and Healthy Homes Initiative, which connects low- to moderate-income homeowners with resources and information on issues such as lead hazards and weatherization.

- Programming and initiatives focused on the region's young people.[18]

There appear to be several reasons why Dubuque is so successful at developing partnerships. First, it is a modestly sized city with an appropriately sized government delivering a typical suite of public services.

Partnering in service delivery, particularly in areas of community development, maximizes economies of scale. In Dubuque, equity shares of sustainability initiatives are spread out among local government, private organizations, and nonprofit owners—an aspect that is exceptionally important as local government financial resources are becoming increasingly constrained.

Second, there are nongovernmental organizations in Dubuque that willingly contribute financial and other resources to support partnership-based efforts. The CFGD and the Greater Dubuque Development Corporation both have been substantial supporters of efforts in areas such as workforce development, economic development, youth, and education.

Third, and probably most important, public participation has been actively cultivated. The planning processes that started after the local economy collapsed in the 1980s have built up a willingness among individuals, nonprofits, the business community, and other stakeholders to overcome the traditional obstacles that partnerships have faced, such as mistrust and issues of control and funding, and engage in a search for solutions to challenges from the street level to the larger metropolitan statistical area. The power of civic engagement as a precursor to effective partnerships is notably evident in Dubuque's continued success.

Performance Measurement and Sustainability

The focus on creating more sustainable communities is entering its third decade since the *Brundtland Report* was issued, and the small scattering of sustainability activities in evidence back then has since proliferated to the point where some local governments in the United States and around the world have started to devise tools and metrics to better understand the results of their sustainability policies and interventions.

Maureen Hart, one of the leading experts on performance measurement and sustainability indicators, notes that effective sustainable community indicators

- assess the carrying capacity of community capital
- are relevant, understandable, and usable by the community
- illustrate the links between the economy, the environment, and society
- focus on the long-range view
- advance local sustainability but not at the expense of others
- are based on reliable and timely data.[19]

However, according to ICMA research, only one in five communities has adopted a sustainability plan that also includes "specific targets or benchmarks."[20] Among the early adopters was Seattle, which developed a series of five indicator reports for the Puget Sound region; these reports have been widely recognized as helping to break ground on sustainability indicators.[21]

Sustainability Indicators in Texas and North Carolina

Since the late 1990s, the Central Texas Sustainability Indicators Project has been tracking "40 indicators, derived from nearly 200 measures, of regional health and well-being."[22] The project focuses on a five-county region, including a large part of the Austin Metropolitan Statistical Area. Measures are organized into nine categories: demographics, public safety, education and children, social equity, engagement, economy, environment, health, and land use and mobility. Beginning in 2012, the project stopped producing written reports and switched over to an entirely online system. The system presents graphs that illustrate trends in indicator data, such as whether the indicator is showing improvement or decline from the ideal state. It also provides information about the sources of data and the calculating tools that are used to assess the data around each indicator.

And although Charlotte and Mecklenburg County, North Carolina, have not had a formal sustainability or livability effort until very recently, the CharMeck Quality of Life initiative is a long-running program on community- and neighborhood-level indicators. As of 2012, the study encompassed more than 400 "neighborhood profile areas" across all the jurisdictions in Mecklenburg County. Topic areas evolve each year and have been expanded to cover an increasing number of issues related to a sustainable community.[23]

The STAR Community Rating System

The latest tool available for local governments to consider in measuring their progress toward sustainability goals is the STAR Community Rating System. Officially released in fall 2013 after many years of development and beta testing, STAR provides a framework that can indicate how well a community is progressing toward community-level goals and objectives. The framework is divided into seven thematic sustainability goal areas, each of which comprises five to seven objectives that are "the core areas that contain evaluation measures and metrics"[24] (Figure 6–1). Each objective uses two types of evaluation measures:

- Community-level outcomes: measurable, condition-level indicators that show community progress (e.g., reductions in energy use or increased transportation access)
- Local actions: The range of decisions, investments, programs, plans, and codes that move a community toward community-level outcomes.[25]

Figure 6-1 STAR Goals and Objectives

STAR goals						
Built environment	**Climate and energy**	**Economy and jobs**	**Education, arts, and community**	**Equity and empowerment**	**Health and safety**	**Natural systems**
Ambient noise and light Community water systems Compact and complete communities Housing affordability Infill and redevelopment Public spaces Transportation choices	Climate adaptation Greenhouse gas mitigation Greening the energy supply Industrial sector resource efficiency Resource efficient buildings Resource efficient public infrastructure Waste minimization	Business retention and development Green market development Local economy Quality jobs and living wages Targeted industry development Workforce readiness	Arts and culture Community cohesion Educational opportunity and attainment Historic preservation Social and cultural diversity	Civic engagement Civil and human rights Environmental justice Equitable services and access Human services Poverty prevention and alleviation	Active living Community health and health system Emergency prevention and response Food access and nutrition Indoor air quality Natural and human hazards Safe communities	Green infrastructure Invasive species Natural resource protection Outdoor air quality Water in the environment Working lands

(left margin label: STAR objectives)

Source: Star Communities, "The Rating System," starcommunities.org/rating-system/framework.

STAR may prove to be the most useful new tool developed to help communities assess how sustainable they are; nevertheless, some communities have long valued performance measurement and have developed their own good systems for assessing progress.

Measuring Performance in Minneapolis

For at least the last decade, Minneapolis, Minnesota (pop. 392,880), has been one of the leading jurisdictions seriously working to advance the concept of sustainability across the city's programmatic, policy, and partnership activities. The modern roadmap for its sustainability efforts started in 2003, when the city council passed a new resolution to create the Minneapolis sustainability program. Engagement efforts in 2004 helped craft a 50-year vision for the city that contains 13 primary guiding principles:

1. Minneapolis protects environmental resources and enhances environmental conditions.

2. Minneapolis maintains its position as one of the cities with strongest social connections in the U.S., embracing people of all colors and all new immigrants.

3. Minneapolis strengthens educational attainment for all students.

4. Minneapolis becomes a national leader in maintaining health, and in reducing health disparities.

5. The city achieves a secure climate of public safety.

6. Arts and culture are a vital core of daily learning and expression for all residents.

7. Minneapolis has an increasingly transparent process of governance.

8. Physical design of the city augments the potential for sustainability.

9. Minneapolis becomes a national leader in community wealth creation, and reduces disparities.

10. Minneapolis strengthens its business sector by clustering a strong group of locally owned, sustainable-production firms.

11. Minneapolis housing is green and affordable.

12. Minneapolis enhances its tax base through green taxation.

13. The city coordinates its sustainability efforts with the entire Metro region and the rest of the world.[26]

By proposing a series of 30 core indicators as well as more than a 100 background indicators, this same effort laid the groundwork for some of the performance measurement tools that would be developed later. The initial set of core indicators is presented in Figure 6–2.

Figure 6-2 Minneapolis's 30 Initial Core Indicators

Environment/ecology	Social equity	Economy
1. Diversity of macro-invertebrate species (insects, etc.) in lakes, streams, and rivers.	1. Transportation mode split (walking, bicycle, bus, light rail, car pool, single occupant vehicle) by percent.	1. Percentage of workers earning a livable wage (at a single job).
2. Diversity of native fish populations in lakes, streams, and rivers.	2. Average time and distance of commute for (a) residents and (b) commuters into city.	2. Aggregate wealth created by residents in the lowest income quartile.
3. Acres (and percentage) of permeable (absorbs rainfall) roof and soil surfaces.	3. Domestic abuse rates.	3. Percentage of Minnesota corporations with headquarters in Minneapolis.
4. Acres (and geographic balance) of leaf canopy in Minneapolis.	4. Percentage of babies born at adequate weight.	4. Number of city residents employed in the Twin Cities region's manufacturing and service industry clusters (health, printing and publishing, food, computer technology, etc.).
5. Acres of natural space in city that sustain natural ecological communities.	5. Infant mortality rates.	
6. Percentage of Mississippi River gorge acreage with adequate understory vegetation.	6. Reading test scores for third graders.	5. Dollars invested in research and development and implementation of "three E's" sustainability by Twin Cities corporations (as percentage of gross revenue).
	7. Achievement test scores (ACT/SAT) for high school juniors/seniors.	
	8. Graduation rate for students in Minneapolis Public Schools, by race.	
	9. Teen suicide rate.	6. Percentage of renewable energy used in city (municipality, private sector, households).
	10. Arrest, conviction and incarceration rates for males of color.	
	11. Number and percentage of gang-related homicides.	7. Percentage of available housing units that are "green" (green renovation, rehabilitation, and new construction) and that are affordable to the lowest income quartile.
	12. Health disparities involving STDs, diabetes, cardiovascular disease, obesity, HIV transmission, asthma, cancer (especially breast, cervical and prostate), by race/ethnicity/immigration.	
	13. Percentage of city residents who carry adequate health insurance.	8. Percentage of housing units that meet or exceed USEPA Energy Star criteria.
	14. Percentage of eligible voters who vote.	
	15. Number of people participating in faith-based neighborhood- and social-improvement initiatives for Minneapolis.	
	16. Percent of parents and students creating art through school and after-school programs.	

Source: Ken Meter, *Fifty-Year Vision and Indicators for a Sustainable Minneapolis* (Minneapolis, Minn.: Crossroads Resource Center, 2004), 7-9, crcworks
.org/indicators.pdf.

In 2006, the city released its first annual report on sustainability; the report included a set of indicators, some baseline data, and some reporting on each indicator. Each report since then has contained a rich portrait of information—indicators, targets, and trend analysis as well as city and community activities undertaken in support of the indicators and targets. For example, the *2011 Sustainability Report* lists the following activities, among others, as being undertaken in support of the city's local food indicator:

- Developed a draft urban agriculture policy plan
- Funded development of a local food resource network
- Eased the process for residential startup of community gardens.[27]

Today, Minneapolis measures the performance of its sustainability efforts across 26 indicators in three main clusters: "A Healthy Life," "Greenprint," and "A Vibrant Community" (Figure 6–3). These indicators are centered on a vision for the community's long-term future, and each addresses linkages among various issues related to it. The city council also approved 10-year targets for each indicator in order to set a numerical goal and provide a better focus for what is being measured.

More so than many governments, Minneapolis is providing its citizens with detailed information on the state of sustainability in the community. And importantly, its aggressive measurement of its sustainability program provides the basis for continuously improving, revising, and developing new policies, programs, plans, and partnerships to create a more sustainable community for the current and future generations.

Figure 6-3   City of Minneapolis Indicators and Targets

	Indicator	Target 1	Target 2	Target 3
A Healthy Life	Healthy infants	Reduce infant mortality rate	Reduce low birth weight infants	
	Teen pregnancy	Reduce teen pregnancy rate		
	HIV and gonorrhea	Reduce new HIV case rate	Reduce new gonorrhea case rate	
	Healthy weight	Increase healthy weight rate	Decrease obesity rate	
	Asthma	Reduce asthma-related hospitalizations		
	Lead poisoning	Test all 1- and 2-year-olds for lead	Inspect all homes of children with elevated blood lead levels	
Greenprint	Climate change	Reduce citywide greenhouse gas emissions	Reduce greenhouse gas emissions from municipal operations	
	Renewable energy	Permit 70 renewable energy projects annually	Increase municipal renewable energy	
	Air quality	Reduce criteria air pollution levels	Reduce all monitored air toxics	
	Tree canopy	Maintain the tree canopy	Plant at least 6,000 trees annually	
	Biking	Increase on-street lanes and off-street trails	Increase % of bike commuters	Increase the number of cyclists measured by bike counts
	Transportation alternatives	Reduce % of Minneapolis residents driving alone to work	Reduce % of Minneapolis workers driving alone to work	
	Airport noise	Reduce average noise levels		
	Stormwater	Reduce pollutants in runoff	Increase number of rain gardens	
	Healthy lakes, streams and rivers	Earn LAURI [Lake Aesthetic and User Recreation Index] ratings of 8 or higher in city lakes	Achieve zero beach closings	Prevent the spread and introduction of aquatic invasive species
	Green jobs	Achieve a net gain of green manufacturing or service companies	Achieve growth in green jobs	Create jobs through building retrofits
	Local food	Increase food producing gardens	Ensure all residents live within 1/4 mile of a healthy food choice	
	Waste reduction and recycling	Increase organics collection	Recover two-thirds of all recyclable materials	Collect recyclables at Hennepin County-Minneapolis facility

continued

Figure 6-3   City of Minneapolis Indicators and Targets

	Indicator	Target 1	Target 2	Target 3
A Vibrant Community	Brownfield sites	Clean up 170 brownfield sites		
	Violent crimes	Reduce the violent crime rate	Maintain a low homicide rate	
	Community engagement	Ensure meaningful opportunities for resident engagement	Increase participation in city boards by non-white members	
	Homelessness	End homelessness by 2016		
	Cost-burdened households	Reduce cost-burdened renter households	Reduce cost-burdened owner households	Produce affordable housing through city programs
	Employment and poverty	Reduce racial/ethnic disparities in unemployment	Reduce racial/ethnic disparities in poverty	
	Graduation rate	Increase the high school graduation rate		
	Arts and the economy	Increase creative sector workers	Increase jobs at arts and cultural organizations and companies	Increase the number of artists living in Minneapolis

Source: City of Minneapolis, *2012 Sustainability Report*, 4, minneapolismn.gov/sustainability/reports/sustainability_livingwell.

Conclusion

ICMA members have called sustainability the "issue of our age." Certainly, many other professionals in local government or working in partnership with government officials are also looking for, testing, and applying new approaches to meet the sustainability needs of the present without compromising the security of future generations. Two of the important questions that need answers are, How will we get to a more sustainable future and, maybe more importantly, how will we know when we are there? While continuously advancing technology is going to play a major role in whether communities, countries, and civilizations are able to succeed in the quest to become more sustainable, two of the golden rules of local government management—civic engagement and performance measurement—seem necessary to provide the vision and indicators needed for success.

"We the People" are the oft-quoted three words that open the preamble of the U.S. Constitution. We the People, if given the opportunity through effective engagement, can provide imaginative, acceptable, and effective ideas for new policies, programs, partnerships, and other interventions for creating more sustainable communities in the United States. As strategies from Dubuque and many other places indicate, civic engagement is a necessary element of envisioning and legitimizing any community sustainability effort.

The importance of indicators and performance measurement cannot be overstated. As Portney notes,

the advancement of many sustainability plans in communities is laying the foundation for places to measure over time how their policies and programs are bringing about positive changes. He suggests that there has been good progress in measuring such indicators as greenhouse gas emissions, energy usage, and other metrics with established quantitative standards, but that "measures of many other results are sorely lacking. [And] unless and until such measures are developed, a fuller understanding [of] the effectiveness of city sustainability policies will be evasive."[28] Great football coaches and players are constantly looking for ways to outsmart their opponents by trying to identify trends in behavior and weaknesses to exploit in the opposition's game plan. Communities like Minneapolis that are continually measuring a range of sustainability actions are engaged in similar game planning by looking within for the unsustainable characteristics that can be overcome with effective policies and programs as well as through partnerships with local nongovernmental organizations.

James Svara and others contend that sustainability at the local level in the United States is still in its infancy.[29] However, in some places, sustainability is growing into adolescence, nurtured by both effective civic engagement and the caloric intake of quantifiable data provided by effective indicators and performance measurement approaches. These essential building blocks are the foundation for achieving robust, sustainable communities in the United States.

Notes

1 Gro Harlem Brundtland, *Our Common Future* (Oxford: Oxford University Press, 1987), un-documents.net/our-common-future.pdf.

2 Kent Portney, *Taking Sustainable Cities Seriously: Economic Development, the Environment, and Quality of Life in American Cities,* 2nd ed. (Cambridge: MIT Press, 2013), 12.

3 See, for example, James H. Svara, "The Early Stage of Local Government Action to Promote Sustainability," in *The Municipal Year Book 2011* (Washington, D.C.: ICMA Press, 2011), 43–60; and George C. Homsy and Mildred Warner, "Off the Beaten Path: Sustainability Activities in Small Towns and Rural Municipalities," in *The Municipal Year Book 2012* (Washington, D.C.: ICMA Press, 2012), 53–61.

4 James Svara, Anna Read, and Evelina Moulder, *Breaking New Ground: Promoting Environmental and Energy Programs in Local Government* (Washington, D.C.: IBM Center for the Business of Government, 2011), businessofgovernment.org/sites/default/files/Promoting%20Environmental%20and%20Energy%20Programs%20in%20Local%20Government.pdf.

5 See Partnership for Sustainable Communities at sustainablecommunities.gov/.

6 See the U.S. Department of Housing and Urban Development, "Sustainable Communities Regional Planning Grants," at portal.hud.gov/hudportal/HUD?src = / program_offices/sustainable_housing_communities/ sustainable_communities_regional_planning_grants; U.S. Department of Transportation, TIGER Grants, at dot .gov/tiger; and the U.S. Department of Energy, Energy Efficiency and Conservation Block Grant Program, at www1.eere.energy.gov/wip/eecbg.html.

7 See the Urban Sustainability Directors Network at sustainablecommunities.gov/.

8 Svara, "Early Stage of Local Government Action."

9 Joel Mills, "The Civics of Sustainability," *National Civic Review* 99 (Fall 2010): 5.

10 "ICMA 2010 Sustainability Survey Results," icma .org/en/icma/knowledge_network/documents/kn/ Document/301646/ICMA_2010_Sustainability_Survey_ Results.

11 All populations are 2012 estimates from the U.S. Census Bureau, available at quickfacts.census.gov/qfd/index .html#.

12 City of Baltimore, *The Baltimore Sustainability Plan* (2010).

13 City of Northampton, *Sustainable Northampton, Comprehensive Plan* (2008).

14 Sustainable Dubuque, "About Sustainable Dubuque" (2014), sustainabledubuque.org/en/about_us/about_ sustainable_dubuque/.

15 FSG and Network Impact, *Dubuque2.0: How the Community Foundation of Greater Dubuque Used Environmental Information to Spark Citizen Action* (February 2013), icma.org/en/icma/knowledge_network/ documents/kn/Document/304684/Dubuque_20_How_ the_Community_Foundation_of_Greater_Dubuque_ Used_Environmental_Information_to_Spark_C.

16 Sustainable Dubuque, "Sustainable Dubuque Collaboration" (2014), sustainabledubuque.org/en/ about_us/sustainable_dubuque_collaboration/.

17 P. K. Kannan and Ai-Mei Chang, *Beyond Citizen Engagement: Involving the Public in Co-Delivering Government Services* (Washington, D.C.: IBM Center for the Business of Government, 2013), businessofgovernment.org/sites/ default/files/Beyond%20Citizen%20Engagement.pdf.

18 Nancy van Milligan, president/CEO of CFGD, interview by author, December 23, 2013.

19 Maureen Hart, *Guide to Sustainable Community Indicators,* 2nd ed. (Andover, Mass.: Hart Environmental Data, 1999), available at sustainablemeasures.com/ publications/the_book.

20 Svara, Read, and Moulder, *Breaking New Ground,* 5.

21 For more information, see sustainableseattle.org/.

22 For more information, see indicatorsproject.com/.

23 For more information, see charmeck.org/QOL/Pages/ default.aspx.

24 Star Communities, "The Rating System," starcommunities .org/rating-system/framework.

25 Ibid.

26 Ken Meter, *Fifty-Year Vision and Indicators for a Sustainable Minneapolis* (Minneapolis, Minn.: Crossroads Resource Center, 2004), 4, crcworks.org/indicators.pdf.

27 Minneapolis Living Well, *2011 Sustainability Report* (June 2011), 23, minneapolismn.gov/sustainability/ reports/sustainability_livingwell. For more information on Minneapolis Sustainability, go to minneapolismn .gov/sustainability/indicators.

28 Portney, *Taking Sustainable Cities Seriously,* 333.

29 Svara, Read, and Moulder, *Breaking New Ground.*

7

Spreading Innovation

David Swindell
Center for Urban Innovation, Arizona State University

Karen Thoreson
Alliance for Innovation

The Dewey Decimal System, created by Melvil Dewey while he was working for the Amherst College library, was first introduced in 1876, a time when most libraries were available only to privileged or wealthy patrons but not open to the general public. Before the system was developed, most books were assigned a permanent shelf position according height and date of acquisition.[1] The Dewey system made finding a particular book much easier and contributed to the development of public libraries. Today, more than 200,000 libraries in more than 135 countries use this classification system.[2]

Before municipal parks were created, *public* common spaces for the benefit of regular citizens were rare.[3] The roots of the municipal parks movement began to take hold in the 1830s in England. One of the early examples of these parks is Princes Park in Liverpool's suburb of Toxteth. Richard Vaughan Yates, an iron merchant, privately financed Princes Park in 1842 and hired Joseph Paxton to design it in a manner that incorporated open space for the benefit of the

This article was prepared with the assistance of students in the Marvin Andrews Fellowship Program. This program represents a partnership of the Alliance for Innovation, Arizona State University, and the Arizona City County Management Association to identify and educate promising future local government leaders. The research assistance provided by these student was part of their first-year internship.

SELECTED FINDINGS

More than two-thirds of the practices that local governments are adopting are described as *prevailing*, which suggests that most local government change endeavors are focused on "catching up" to recognized industry standards. About 25% of the practices have been described as *leading*, and only a small fraction have been deemed *emerging*.

Local governments have been engaging in the *prevailing* practice of recycling for more than 50 years. However, when Ft. Lauderdale, Florida, sought to expand its recycling program, it switched its collection method to single-stream recycling, hired new employees and vendors, and started a public relations campaign to educate residents on recycling techniques, exemplifying a *leading* practice in its aggressive goals and businesslike approach to the service.

In 2002 Washoe County, Nevada, consolidated its animal services with two nearby cities and partnered with the Nevada Humane Society (NHS) to pass a bond issue to fund a new regional shelter, use NHS volunteers to help locate owners, and expand the use of microchips and online services. This approach, an *emerging* practice at this time, is now a *leading* practice and is rapidly becoming a *prevailing* one.

townspeople and additional landscaping for natural beauty. In the early 1990s, cities in the United States began to build neighborhood parks—with the partial intention of Americanizing and integrating immigrants. Today, most American cities and towns have public parks where citizens can recreate, celebrate, and get closer to nature.

Prior to the 1960s, policing philosophy was dominated by a "problem-oriented" approach. Connections to the community were limited and reactive in nature. Community policing emerged in the late 1960s when two federally funded research projects in Kansas City, Missouri—the Preventive Patrol Study and the Rand Corporation's Investigation Experiment—found that police rarely responded to crimes in progress and were limited in their ability to influence crime levels. Community policing shifted the focus to proactive problem solving by developing partnerships and engaging with residents to earn their trust. Today, most modern police agencies blend community policing and problem-oriented policing for the most effective results.[4]

What do these three topical vignettes have in common? All three represent a sea change in how local governments deliver services to their residents. In each case, a different stimulus created the innovation that changed all assumptions about what the public wanted or needed:

- For public libraries, where residents can more easily browse stacks to find what they need while establishing a common shared organizational culture, it was a personal invention. No one had as yet identified as a problem the fact that libraries had limited access and needed special expertise to use them. Yet in the second edition of his classification system, Dewey wrote that he had received comments and criticisms from nearly 100 people who helped him improve the numbering system.

- For public parks, where all members of the community can recreate, access nature, and enjoy community celebrations such as the Fourth of July, the impetus was apparently self-interest: Yates to be viewed as a benefactor, Paxton to showcase his design ideas, and the city of Liverpool to be recognized on the larger world stage. Yet it was the area residents who were the ultimate beneficiaries of a beautiful, open, and well-designed public area.

- For improved public safety, where residents are considered neighborhood experts in helping the police prevent and solve crimes, the incentive for community policing came from federally funded research focused on improved police/community relations, better training for officers, increased diversity among the police ranks, and more equitable outcomes for poverty-challenged neighborhoods.

Each of these innovations had a geographic genesis and might have stayed limited to one location but for an array of factors that led to the diffusion of the ideas until each became integrated elements in—and standard operating procedure for—communities throughout the United States and abroad. This article explores what these factors are that lend themselves to promoting or inhibiting the diffusion of new ideas, and it illustrates these points with a series of innovations at different stages of the diffusion process.

Building the Crucibles for Innovations

At the Alliance for Innovation and the Center for Urban Innovation at Arizona State University, we speak about innovation as being any idea or action that (1) is new to a given organization and, when implemented, (2) produces a better result. The success of an innovation is reflected not only in the immediate effects on the organization in which it is implemented, but also in the extent to which the innovation is shared and adapted by other organizations. Since the concept of innovation includes the spread of the idea,[5] ideas that are not shared and disseminated for implementation will not amount to an innovation. Thus, those interested in helping to improve the operations of government must be mindful of the dual goals of creating innovative ideas and of spreading those ideas that lead to positive change overall.

Regarding these goals, there is the fundamental challenge inherent in the fact that innovative ideas cannot be mandated or scheduled. Some burst onto the stage following a profound insight into addressing a problem—a "eureka moment." Others may be small steps in improved performance or incremental changes to existing policies or operations. Many of the factors that prompt innovative ideas are serendipitous and often the culmination of many previous ideas synthesized into something new. It may require researchers undertaking investigations for practitioners to see how new findings might relate to their organizations' missions and operations.

Given how innovative ideas emerge, those who want to encourage innovation must focus on creating an environment—one that provides a fitting combination of resources, time, and culture of experimentation—within which these ideas can flourish. As Steve Jobs, the late leader of Apple, once noted: "Innovation has nothing to do with how many R&D dollars you have. . . . It's not about money. It's about the people you have, how you're led, and how much you get it."[6] While he may have been understating the importance of capital, his point focuses on the innovative environment that was emblematic of his leadership style.

On a larger level, the United States has in fact managed to engender a culture of experimentation and innovation for government services and policy development. In 1787, the process of negotiating a new constitutional arrangement for the new nation resulted in the now-familiar two-tiered system of government in which some responsibilities are assumed by the national government and others are ostensibly entrusted to the states. The Founders were aware that such a system would provide citizens with opportunities to pursue their varied interests in diverse ways. Through multiple experiments, policy innovations would compete in the "marketplace of ideas," and through this competition, superior ideas would be implemented in states and possibly become the foundation for national policy. This vision has given rise to the conception of the states as "laboratories of democracy."[7]

In recent years, there has been an explosion of scholarly research on the role of states as policy laboratories and incubators of new innovations.[8] But what has received less formal scholarly attention has been the increasingly important role of local governments and public administrators as the primary sources of public service innovations. Since 1978, when the national government began making significant cuts in federal support to the states, and especially as a result of the Great Recession, local governments have been increasingly left to their own devices to meet the challenges of protecting and serving citizens at the most basic level. And with about 90,000 local governments in the United States alone, a growing number of scholars are beginning to realize that the most exciting environment for studying innovations is actually at the local level.

So one important goal for those interested in making perpetual improvements to public service and policy is to foster and support an environment within which innovations can emerge through experimentation. With its federal system of governance, the United States is well positioned to provide such an environment, and local government administrators and entrepreneurial elected officials are similarly well positioned to take advantage of that environment and generate new ideas. But innovation is not simply about idea generation; it also involves the spread of ideas.

How Do Innovative Ideas Spread?

In 1962, sociologist Everett Rogers published the first edition of *Diffusion of Innovations*.[9] While his work focuses primarily on how individuals change their behaviors, the most recent diffusion work has extended his theories beyond the individual and applied them to private and public sector agencies.

In his work, Rogers notes that there are four contextual factors that influence the extent to which an innovative idea will spread:

1. The new idea (the innovative idea that is implemented and successfully generates a positive outcome)

2. Communication channels (the possible means by which awareness of the idea may spread)

3. Time (how long it takes to weigh the value of the possible innovation for implementation)

4. The social system (in the current context, local government managers, their local elected officials, and their organizational staff, all of whom are responsible for the policy or service at the center of the innovation).

These four factors are all required for innovative ideas to spread; however, there is no specific combination of factors that will make the difference between those ideas that are widely implemented and those that go nowhere. New ideas will resonate differently in different kinds of communities facing different types of leadership and different resource constraints.

As these factors identify the context for diffusion, Rogers differentiates them from the process through which an innovation may be adopted. For Rogers (and for most of the scholars in this field), adoption proceeds through five stages:

1. The *knowledge or awareness* stage, in which there is basic awareness of the innovative idea but insufficient interest to seek additional information

2. The *persuasion* stage, in which interest reaches the point of motivating the decision maker to seek additional information about the innovative idea

3. The *decision* stage, in which the decision maker evaluates the benefits versus the costs of the innovation for his or her organization before deciding whether to adopt it

4. The *implementation* stage, in which the innovation is tested and evaluated for its utility to the organization

5. The *confirmation* stage, in which the evaluation determines whether the innovation becomes standard operating procedure.

Others have taken Rogers's work, extended his framework, and elaborated on it through observations of policy and service delivery experiments around the world. Of particular interest here are the mechanisms through which diffusion actually occurs, which is a challenging phenomenon to study in terms of tracing the paths by which new ideas are communicated. One of the more influential studies in recent years to focus on diffusion at the local level has identified four such mechanisms:[10]

1. *Learning.* Policy makers learn from other governments that are experimenting with new ideas to see what is successful and what they might import into their own organizations.

2. *Economic competition.* Governments are often in competition with one another and will adopt new ideas in accordance with the positive or negative effects those ideas have had on the jurisdictions with which they compete.

3. *Imitation.* Imitators focus not on the innovation itself but on another government that is doing the innovating and that they want to be like.

4. *Coercion.* Direct coercion to adopt an innovation may come about through legislative or economic authority (such as a mandate or grant).

Together, these contextual factors, stages, and mechanisms explain both the environment within which new ideas emerge and the likelihood that those ideas may be implemented and shared. Some innovations "catch on" when these elements align and the appropriate mechanisms facilitate increasingly widespread adoption; others "die on the vine," even though they may be superior in terms of efficiency or effectiveness. Rogers's 1962 work provides a conceptual illustration of the diffusion process, starting from the point where the new policy or practice is limited to one or a small number of implementers. As word spreads, other jurisdictions experiment with the innovation. If the innovation continues proving out, more jurisdictions learn about it and adopt it with increasing frequency until it becomes the norm. Once that happens, the number of new implementers begins to decline and the innovation nears a saturation point. But as that happens, newer innovations are under way to improve upon the new norm, and the process continues.

ICMA, the Alliance for Innovation (previously known as the Innovation Groups), and the Center for Urban Innovation, as well as numerous other professional organizations, are part of the array of mechanisms in this process. They help facilitate idea development, test new ideas, evaluate the effectiveness of those ideas, disseminate the results, and provide training for those decision makers who want to learn about the innovations and adopt or tailor them for their own jurisdictions. But the primary criterion that is likely to determine the success or appropriateness of a policy or practice in a new jurisdiction lies in the nature of the policy or practice itself. The next section describes 19 innovations to highlight the different stages at which they currently exist in the diffusion process.

Past, Current, and Future Innovative Local Government Practices

For the past 35 years, the Alliance for Innovation has focused on identifying successful new practices that local governments are using and/or on promoting those that produce great results. Six years ago, it began to conduct in-person or online sessions with groups of local government practitioners, asking them not only to report what new practices they were pursuing but also to describe those practices as *emerging, leading,* or *prevailing.*

- *Emerging.* An emerging practice is a new activity that has just begun to be tested in a few localities. Emerging practices are often pilot projects because the results of the effort are uncertain and the risk of failure is high. Typically, a local government will have very few emerging practices under consideration and only in the departments that are led by early adopters or risk-tolerant staff.

- *Leading.* A leading practice is a new practice that has been tested in a number of local governments and found to produce good results. Forward-thinking local governments are often on the lookout for leading practices that have been successful elsewhere.

- *Prevailing.* A prevailing practice is one that has proven to be useful and might be considered to be a state of the practice. Even though such a practice is not considered to be risky, a local government still needs to make changes in order to adopt it, and so many communities have not adopted what might be considered an industry standard.

The informal polls conducted with local government participants (in conference sessions, workshops, online meetings, etc.) have produced interesting results. First, in approximately 95% of the cases, the participants have agreed on how a certain practice should be described, demonstrating common awareness across multiple jurisdictions and staff as to which new practices have been proven and which are still being tested. Second, participants have described more than two-thirds of the practices being adopted by their local governments as *prevailing.* This suggests that most new local government change endeavors are focused on "catching up" to recognized industry standards. About 25% of the practices have been described as *leading,* and only a small fraction have been deemed *emerging.* Lastly, any disagreements about the categorization have been primarily based on regional differences rather than on size of community, form of government, or economic resources. This is not surprising in that regionally, local governments have different challenges: coastal cities need sophisticated hurricane disaster plans, northern cities need snow removal expertise, arid southwestern communities might focus more intently on promoting xeriscape (i.e., landscaping and gardening designed to reduce or eliminate the need for irrigation), and so forth.

What is clear is that new practices mature through these categories. Over the years, some emerging practices move to wider adoption and others are abandoned, either because they do not produce the desired result(s) or because they are too specialized to be widely adopted. Generally, results from the Alliance's research lend additional support to Rogers's work. However, the degree of support varies according to the type of innovations under consideration. The following case studies demonstrate that maturation process in specific topic areas.

Organizational Change

All organizations are called on to change periodically, but dramatic change within an organization is pretty rare. The fiscal crisis of 2008 and the ensuring years provided the impetus for courageous organizations to "advance" rather than retreat in the face of a severe economic downturn.

In 2010, **Phoenix, Arizona** (pop. 1,488,750),[11] faced a $200 million budgetary shortfall. Among other strategies, it undertook a citywide organizational review to eliminate layers of supervision, broaden the span of control (i.e., the number of employees under a single supervisor), streamline service delivery, and reduce inefficiencies. Span of control reviews are certainly not new; that on its own would be classified as a *prevailing* practice. However, the sheer scope of this project across all departments (comprising nearly 12,500 employees) and the results it achieved make this certainly a *leading* practice. Through a comprehensive effort, the city reached the lowest per capita employee-to-population ratio since 1970 and increased its span of control from 1 to 5.3 in 2010 to 1 to 8.1 in 2012.

City leaders in **Las Vegas, Nevada** (pop. 596,424), faced equally challenging budget reductions in 2010 but developed a different set of initiatives to address their problem. Las Vegas combined an organization-wide Fundamental Service Review, which was an internal "audit" of how its services matched up with the city council's goals, with a "Your City Your Way" externally focused program that sought input from citizens on service priorities. This *leading* practice resulted in a roadmap for service reductions and departmental consolidations in response to the fiscal challenges confronting the city.

Not all internal change efforts are driven by budget. Notably, two organizations in 2013 rethought their engagement strategies with their community constituents and/or their employees. Although **Wellington, Florida** (pop. 58,679), also made substantial organizational changes to cope with revenue losses during the recession, the village chose to use the crisis to focus on its employees through a comprehensive program of retraining and professional development. The program, titled "Academies of Wellington," includes four components: Leadership Academy, Wellington Experience, Practical Application Series, and Technology Series. Taken together, these new competency-based programs are an *emerging* practice that seeks to improve upon the traditional "cutback" approach to recessionary pressures by fostering a culture that enables employees to gain new skills and competencies.

Brooklyn Park, Minnesota (pop. 77,752), where ethnic demographics have shifted dramatically over the past two decades, took public participation to a new level by asking community members to write a job description for their new community engagement coordinator. This generated contributions from 16 citizens, creating ownership and excitement about the job. This clearly *emerging* practice advanced transparency and better connected the new coordinator with the community.

Animal Control/Animal Shelters

Less than a decade ago, most publically funded animal control services operated on principles that were primarily punitive in nature. A resident who lost a pet would have to pay a fine and could quite possibly lose the animal altogether through euthanasia. But change began to occur in the mid-2000s. Instead of warring with animal rescue groups over high fees, overcrowded shelter conditions, and short-hold terms for lost pets, shelters entered into partnerships with those groups to find owners, increase rates of adoption and fostering, and implement microchip technology for the broadest segment of the pet population.

Washoe County, Nevada (pop. 429,908), was one of the first jurisdictions nationally to pursue this *emerging* practice. In 2002, the county consolidated its animal services with two nearby cities and partnered with the Nevada Humane Society (NHS). Together, they successfully passed a bond issue to fund a new regional shelter, use NHS volunteers to help locate owners, and stepped up their use of technology with microchips and expanded online services.

What was a groundbreaking change in 2002 has now become a *leading* practice with progressive public shelters. In 2012 the Alliance for Innovation received case study submissions from **Manatee County, Florida** (pop. 333,895), and **San Antonio, Texas** (pop. 1,382,951), both of which detailed their journeys to achieve some of Washoe County's results. Manatee County shelter staff rallied around the philosophy that Nathan Winograd espoused in his 2007 book *Redemption: The Myth of Pet Overpopulation and the No Kill Revolution in America.*[12] Staff set a goal of a 90% save rate for its sheltered animal population, improving their performance toward meeting that goal by 2% each month since 2011. San Antonio began revamping its animal control processes to increase the live release rate for sheltered pets and decrease the stray animal population in the city. Although the initiative began in 2007, critics deemed it a failure by 2011 because it lacked clear goals and targeted resources. So San Antonio regrouped, formed strategic partnerships with the animal welfare community, and by early 2012 had improved its live release rate from 40% to 66%.

Sustainability

ICMA has been promoting sustainable practices since 2007, and many local governments had been pursuing "green" service delivery for years before that. While most local governments engage in rather simplistic and low-level sustainable activities that will not achieve the wider goals of long-term sustainability,[13] a smaller number have undertaken more aggressive initiatives.

In 2012, **Fort Collins, Colorado** (pop. 148,612), set out to reduce greenhouse gas emissions by 20% by 2020. One of the first initiatives it undertook was a free bike loan program called the Fort Collins Bike Library. Nonprofit organizations help to provide city staff with repairs and maintenance on the bikes, and enthusiastic cyclists volunteer daily at three stations to check out bikes and offer route advice. Anyone, even tourists, can borrow a bike at no cost. While bike sharing for a fee is becoming more common in larger communities across North America, Fort Collins's program of providing the bikes for free is certainly a *leading* practice.

By 2012, **Fort Lauderdale, Florida** (pop. 170,747), already had the largest municipal recycling program in Broward County. But innovative strategies were needed to increase recycling tonnages from single-family residences, and improve accessibility for multifamily complexes and users of public spaces. So the city converted its residential curbside program to single-stream recycling (i.e., all materials are fully commingled rather than sorted out), distributed 40,000 wheeled carts, and launched a robust marketing effort to promote the new program—and was rewarded with a 41% increase in recycled tonnage. In 2013, it designed and deployed new co-collection containers for use in traditional (e.g., bus stops) and nontraditional (e.g., baseball dugouts) public spaces; these containers maintain a small footprint and maximize procurement and collection efficiencies. In 2014, the city launched "Get in the Green,"

offering rebates of up to $1,000 to multifamily properties that initiate or substantially increase recycling among their tenants. All three programs follow a strategy of incentives, communication, and compliance and rely on detained work plans to ensure success. Local governments have been running recycling programs for more than 50 years, so this is clearly a *prevailing* practice. However, Fort Lauderdale's program exemplifies a *leading* practice in its aggressive goals and businesslike approach to sustainability.

The high mountainous terrain where **Flagstaff, Arizona** (pop. 67,468), is located experienced major weather-related damage in 2011 from extreme drought, reduced snowpack, soaring temperatures, fire-related forest damage, and resulting flooding. These simultaneous conditions caused city leaders to worry about the long-term impact of climate change. To assess the area's vulnerability and associated risk, the city commissioned a study called "Municipal Resiliency and Preparedness." As an innovative and *emerging* practice, this study demonstrates a more formal commitment to preparing for weather-related events, and it guides local policy regarding the placement and reinforcement of city facilities and services.

Social Media

In 2010 the city of **Eau Claire, Wisconsin** (pop. 66,966), began using social media tools such as Facebook, Twitter, YouTube, and Blogger to interact with citizens and the news media. Departments use these tools to publish information about schedule changes and community events as well as to recruit volunteers. There is a small cost to set up the platforms, but through these tools, Eau Claire has enjoyed improved response time and greater website traffic. While use of some social media is now a *prevailing* practice in local government, Eau Claire has shown an impressive depth of use for each platform, resulting in increased citizen engagement.

The village manager of **Schaumberg, Illinois** (pop. 74,781), recognized that with the rapid adoption of mobile devices and social networks, citizens were expecting their local government to be available 24/7. That expectation—along with the fact that with 60% of the village's workforce eligible for retirement, a younger, more technologically savvy workforce was entering the ranks—led the manager to create a new communications platform for departments and employees that essentially functions like an internal social network. The software portal integrates the village's intranet page as a wiki, enabling employees to access all of the village's applications and programs in one place and to submit comments and ideas on all of the village's projects, regardless of what department they work in. This software portal has substantially increased the transparency of the village's work, sped up business execution, and reduced the need for in-person meetings. It has also made the meetings that do occur more productive because participants can access information and thus tend to be better prepared. Social media used as an internal communication tool may be commonplace in the private, nonwork environment, but within a local government it is an *emerging* practice.

As is the case for many municipalities, **Dallas, Texas** (pop. 1,241,162), is required by state and federal law to redraw its district lines every 10 years. Historically, redistricting has been a contentious and highly political event with limited public involvement. Deciding to increase resident participation in the process, city staff acquired an online software solution that allowed residents to submit their own redistricting maps via the Internet. With simple instructions in both English and Spanish, the software was available to anyone who had Internet access; it was also installed on public library computers. After weeks of public submissions, the Dallas Redistricting Commission met to review each map for compliance with legal requirements and then selected three for additional public comments. Following more public hearings, a final recommendation went to the city council, and the mayor signed the finalized map one week later. While local redistricting may forever remain a politically sensitive issue, allowing the public to participate helped the process remain fair and transparent. With this *emerging* practice, municipal redistricting took a step forward.

Economic Development

In 2011, **Avondale, Arizona** (pop. 78,256), entered into a professional services agreement with the Gangplank Collective to manage a collaborative workspace for technology-focused businesses and entrepreneurs. Gangplank serves as an incubator for tech start-ups by providing affordable space, mentoring, connection to talent, and potential funding sources. It also promotes civic engagement in the community as it conducts free weekly meetings on topics of interest to the business community. While public-private partnerships have become a *prevailing* practice, the focus on the technology sector and the community engagement aspect of this agreement make it a *leading* practice.

Arvada, Colorado (pop. 109,745), which is part of the larger, nonprofit Arvada Economic Development Association (AEDA), has worked for more than a decade to promote a culture of economic development by encouraging all city employees to participate in the Economic Development Team. (In 2012 more than 90% of Arvada's workforce was actively involved.) The AEDA attends city department staff meetings to discuss economic development issues, challenging each department to help seek new businesses and retain existing ones. This *leading* practice is about the successful way in which AEDA has engaged all city employees and thus made its small team huge in terms of people power and economic impact.

Virginia Beach, Virginia (pop. 447,021), is one of the first localities in the United States to officially assert that early childhood education is a workforce issue rather than a social or educational one. Recognizing that businesses are competing globally for talent, Virginia Beach's Department of Economic Development created the GrowSmart program.[14] Focusing on the first five years of a child's life, the program seeks to promote healthy development, improve school readiness, and increase the quality of local child care centers. One of the early results was an increase in the number of women- and minority-owned businesses, which were often new child care centers and preschools. This program is an example of a community willing to take the long view on return on investment. It is an *emerging* practice, and time will tell what results it produces.

Neighborhood Enhancement

In 2008, a number of neighborhoods in **Cincinnati, Ohio** (pop. 296,550), were run down, plagued by high crime and many boarded-up, vacant buildings. To address these problems, Cincinnati's leaders collaborated with private businesses and community volunteers to form the Neighborhood Enhancement Program (NEP),[15] a comprehensive approach to reduce crime, increase property values, improve local businesses, and enhance community pride. NEP used crime statistics, reports of graffiti litter, and other code violation data to identify where the city could allocate more resources. Because NEP required data-driven results to establish a baseline from which to evaluate progress, the city joined forces with the nonprofit group Keep Cincinnati Beautiful to measure existing conditions and clean up litter on the streets; it also partnered with the Hamilton County Sheriff's Office and the Ohio Attorney General's Office to reduce illegal gang activity. As a result of these partnerships, NEP focus areas had much lower crime, fewer code violations, and a measurable reduction in litter. While programs like NEP are becoming more common in local government, what makes NEP a *leading* practice is its reliance on data to measure success and the fruitful partnerships that city leaders developed with community groups.

In 2009, **Philadelphia, Pennsylvania** (pop. 1,547,607), faced a growing problem of high crime, blight, and loss of trust in the community. Many residents felt abandoned by government. In response, the city completely reorganized its police department, and to coordinate efforts in these challenged neighborhoods, it also brought other city departments under the direct supervision of the mayor's office. In this model, known as Public Service Areas (PSA), city representatives met with residents to determine what specific concerns needed to be addressed. Together, residents and staff worked with churches and community groups to repair potholes, clean up litter, demolish vacant buildings, and provide new children's programs. In one pilot community, crime was reduced by 17%, which led the city to expand the effort to all high-crime neighborhoods. Relying on residents to set their own agenda and participate in the solution is an *emerging* practice, enabling citizens to become coproducers of improved city services.

In 2003, city leaders in **Tucson, Arizona** (pop. 524,295), were grappling with the recurrent problem of slums. Slum conditions existed across the city, but officials avoided instituting any changes because they feared failure and public backlash over stricter code enforcement. After a top management change, however, the city created a team of inspectors from several departments, such as community services, fire, police, planning, and public works. The elected officials focused on eliminating or clarifying confusing sections of the city code so that building standards could be more easily communicated and enforced. To garner support for increased enforcement, they also instituted a media campaign, which soon resulted in citizens reporting code violations; landlords and homeowners associations became involved as well. Slum conditions began to decrease, and citizen groups endorsed the program. Cross-departmental teams were an *emerging* practice at the time but have since become a *leading* practice in progressive local governments.

Lessons Learned

The above cases offer a partial illustration of the wide array of policy and practice innovations currently under consideration and development across communities of different sizes and in different regions of the country. These 19 cases also illustrate the different stages of diffusion through which innovative ideas pass as some move toward more comprehensive adoption as standard practice.

Additionally, the cases exemplify seven lessons derived from Charles Shipan and Craig Volden's extensive review of research on an even wider array of policy innovation diffusion situations. These lessons (quoted in italics) bear highlighting as they relate to the discussion here:[16]

1. *Policy diffusion is not (merely) the geographic clustering of similar policies.* As previously noted, certain regions excel in particular practices. Local governments in Florida, for instance, have sophisticated disaster plans in place to evacuate residents during hurricane season. However, although geographic proximity probably still plays a role in diffusion, the importance of that role has diminished with technological advances in communication channels.

2. *Governments compete with one another.* Competition among local governments varies considerably by region and within metropolitan areas. An innovative idea in one jurisdiction will influence a competing jurisdiction's policy choices related to that idea, as can be seen from the examples provided in the section "Neighborhood Enhancement" above. Larger cities in the United States monitor each other's approach and progress in combating high crime and improving impoverished neighborhoods.

3. *Politics and government capabilities are important to diffusion.* As Rogers notes, a good idea is certainly critical for an innovation's diffusion, but local politics and government capacity are external factors that have a significant impact on whether an innovation is adopted and implemented by another organization. For example, a local government like Flagstaff may find it preferable to address sustainability in terms of "resiliency" rather than use more politically charged language such as "climate change." In Dallas, those charged with redistricting recognized that politics had damaged previous efforts to redraw the district maps, but by opening up the process to a broad group of residents, organizers were able to deflect criticisms that the redistricting board members were exercising personal political agendas.

4. *Policy diffusion depends on the policies themselves.* While external factors influence adoption of an innovation, so too does the internal nature of the innovation itself in terms of its observability, complexity, compatibility, trialability (whether it can be experimented with on a limited basis initially), and relative advantage over existing policy or practice. The cases presented under "Animal Control/Animal Shelters" are good examples of how external pressures (animal rights advocates) have combined with internal interests (staff wanting to reduce costs and the use of euthanasia, and increase adoption rates) to dramatically change the policies from punitive to proactive.

5. *Decentralization is crucial for policy diffusion.* Decision makers at higher levels of government often pursue standardized policy innovations, but such efforts can stifle innovation and diffusion at lower levels of government. Decentralized jurisdictional or organizational decision making increases the likelihood that successful new policies and practices will spread. Schaumburg, through its internal social media tools, and Arvada, which empowers employees throughout the organization to contribute to economic development, are both excellent examples of decision makers recognizing the power of decentralizing both information and policy actions.

6. *Policy diffusion is not always beneficial.* Although competition between governments incentivizes continual innovation, policy diffusion is not always good for every government unit: implementation of untested innovations is perilous, and an innovation applied in one jurisdiction will not necessarily fit the needs or context of another jurisdiction. As described above in the section "Organizational Development," Phoenix and Las Vegas experienced some of the country's most precipitous revenue declines during the Great Recession, but they chose very different paths to address organizational change. Likewise, Brooklyn Park's demographic changes demanded the unique solution of allowing community members to develop a city job description for the community engagement coordinator. Other communities would not necessarily benefit from the adoption of such an approach.

7. *Governments learn from each other.* Governments compete with one another, but they also collaborate and learn from each other through a myriad of information exchange forums, such as those provided by ICMA and the Alliance for Innovation. The Alliance has been sponsoring the Transforming Local Government conference for 20 years, the sole purpose of which is to bring forward new ideas and innovations that local governments have developed and to share them with other practitioners.

These general lessons and the cases above illustrate the mechanisms through which innovative ideas spread. The challenge for those who feel that innovation can benefit local governments and quality of life lies in how to facilitate the spread of ideas that are appropriate for different types of jurisdictions.

Our Roles

ICMA, the Alliance for Innovation, and the Center for Urban Innovation at Arizona State University, as well as other organizations, have three critical roles to play in this overall process of supporting the continual improvement of government.

First, organizations like these have the time and resources to examine past experiments (failures and successes) across the public, private, and nonprofit sectors in order to develop innovative ideas that can aid local jurisdictions. A current example of this is the Local Government Research Collaborative, led by ICMA, the Alliance, and the Center for Urban Innovation. More than 20 local governments joined the collaborative and contributed money to a research fund, which supports efforts by university scholars to investigate and develop new practices and policy options that the local governments can consider testing in their communities. After the innovative ideas have been evaluated and modified, they can be packaged and shared through ICMA's Center for Management Strategies and the Alliance's networks to facilitate diffusion.

Second, these same organizations can continue to solicit and collect information on current practices and new ideas from jurisdictions in order to track those practices that are emerging, prevailing, and leading. Lessons learned from these experiments can then be shared through publications directed at administrators and elected officials as well as through professional conferences, where participants can share their experiences implementing new policies and practices. Such information sharing can highlight the kinds of contextual and internal characteristics that might contribute to success or failure, thereby helping others learn if and how they might best adapt new ideas to their own jurisdictions.

Finally, scholars need to expand the focus of their policy diffusion research. Historically, research on policy innovation and diffusion has centered on the adoption decision. But as Rogers's framework illustrates, adoption is only halfway through the process. Researchers should be expanding their work to include a better understanding and evaluation of implementation. As Shipan and Volden note, organizations that blindly imitate innovations that have yet to be evaluated run risks. University researchers can bring their intellectual talents to bear on evaluating new policies and practices and applying them to local problems. They can also provide additional resources through their students, thereby contributing not only to the talent engaged in the evaluations but also to the applied learning experiences for students facing real-world evaluation challenges that can directly affect a community's quality of life.

While university researchers can be a valuable resource for evaluation, local governments cannot ignore this responsibility themselves. All too often, new practices are not evaluated because of time or resource constraints.[17] As a result, it isn't possible to know whether the innovation was at the root of any change in performance or quality of life, nor can lessons be derived from the experiment and shared with peer jurisdictions.

Developing, collecting, and warehousing experiments in new policies and practices, working with communities willing to try new ideas, working with researchers to evaluate experiments, working to improve upon the experiments, disseminating the results, and training those interested in adopting innovative changes in their communities are all important contributions that organizations like ICMA and the Alliance can provide to help facilitate the complete diffusion process. And working with universities committed to applied service and education provides an avenue for many local jurisdictions to access additional talent in aiding in the innovation process.

Notes

1 Wayne Wiegand, *Irrepressible Reformer: A Biography of Melvil Dewey* (Chicago: ALA Editions, 1996).

2 Kathleen Fox and Justin Friello, "Happy Birthday, Melvil Dewey!" New York Society Library, December 9, 2013, nysoclib.org/blog/happy-birthday-melvil-dewey.

3 David Thorpe, "A History of Greenspace and Parks," December 28, 2013, davidthorpe.info/parkhistory/municipalparks.html; and Princes Park Development, "History," December 28, 2013, princes-park-mansions.org.uk/index/history.

4 Wesley Skogan and Kathleen Frydl, eds., *Fairness and Effectiveness in Policing: The Evidence* (Washington, D.C.: National Academies Press, 2003); and Ronald Clark and John Eck, *Crime Analysis for Problem Solvers in 60 Small Steps* (Washington, D.C.: U.S. Department of Justice, 2005).

5 Charles Shipan and Craig Volden stress this aspect in their definition of policy diffusion as "one government's policy choices being influenced by the choices of other governments." See Charles Shipan and Craig Volden, "Policy Diffusion: Seven Lessons for Scholars and Practitioners," *Public Administration Review* 72, no. 6 (2012): 788, deepblue.lib.umich.edu/bitstream/handle/2027.42/94496/puar2610.pdf?sequence=1.

6 Brent Schlender, "The Three Faces of Steve," *Fortune* 138, no. 9 (November 1998): 96, money.cnn.com/magazines/fortune/fortune_archive/1998/11/09/250880/.

7 David Osborne, *Laboratories of Democracy* (Boston: Harvard Business School Press, 1990).

8 For an excellent example of this line of state-level inquiry, see Graeme Boushey, *Policy Diffusion Dynamics in America* (New York: Cambridge University Press, 2010).

9 See Everett Rogers, *Diffusion of Innovations,* 5th ed. (New York: Free Press, 2003).

10 Charles Shipan and Craig Volden, "The Mechanisms of Policy Diffusion," *American Journal of Political Science* 52, no. 4 (2008): 840–857.

11 All populations are 2012 estimates from the U.S. Census Bureau, available at quickfacts.census.gov/qfd/index.html#.

12 Nathan J. Winograd, *Redemption: The Myth of Pet Overpopulation and the No Kill Revolution in America* (New Almaden, Calif.: Almaden Books, 2007).

13 James Svara, "The Early State of Local Government Action to Promote Sustainability," *The Municipal Year Book 2011* (Washington, D.C.: ICMA Press, 2011).

14 City of Virginia Beach, "Virginia Beach GrowSmart Program Wins National Innovation Award" (April 11, 2013), vbgov.com/news/pages/selected.aspx?release=1382.

15 City of Cincinnati "Neighborhood Enhancement Program (2014), cincinnati-oh.gov/community-development/neighborhood-development/nep/.

16 Shipan and Volden, "Policy Diffusion," 789–792. The lessons are presented here in a different order than they appear in the published article.

17 Cheryl Hilvert and David Swindell, "Collaborative Service Delivery: What Every Local Government Manager Should Know," *State and Local Government Review* 45, no. 4 (2013).

8

CAO Salary and Compensation: Stability Continues

Evelina R. Moulder
ICMA

There is always interest in the compensation of public employees, whether related to pensions and benefits or to actual salaries. Yet identifying a "typical" salary and benefits for a city or county manager or chief appointed official (CAO) is difficult because of the many variables that have an impact on the compensation package.

According to the "ICMA Guidelines for Compensation," the compensation of local government managers should be "fair, reasonable, transparent, and based on comparable public salaries nationally and regionally."[1] But what is fair and reasonable? CAOs are the chief appointed professional managers and administrators in cities, counties, towns, and villages. If the CAO is a city, county, or town manager, he or she serves as the chief executive officer (CEO) of a major enterprise, with more lines of business than most comparably sized private companies. If the CAO works for a mayor or county executive, he or she serves as chief operating officer, again with substantial executive responsibilities for a highly complex organization. Additionally, the actual range of services for which the CAO is responsible varies widely.

While ICMA recommends that compensation benchmarks be established in accordance with comparable local government and/or public sector agencies, there is no consensus to date on what external

SELECTED FINDINGS

The overall median base salary for chief appointed officials (CAOs) overall is $105,000. Base salary is generally related to population size of the local government; however, even within each population category and within the same geographic region, the specifics are unique.

Forty-one percent of CAOs, as well as a majority of those in local governments with a population of 25,000 and over, reported that their base salaries are publicly available on the local government website.

In a majority of cases overall, benefit packages for CAOs are calculated in the same manner as for other employees of the local government.

positions are appropriate for benchmarking CAO pay. ICMA guidelines are broad, stating that "compensation should be based on the position requirements, the complexity of the job reflected in the composition of the organization and community, the leadership needed, labor market conditions, cost of living in the community, and the organization's ability to pay."[2]

Examining new data from a 2013 national survey of local government executives, this article looks at compensation issues for city, county, and town managers and administrators in local governments with the council-manager plan, and at the equivalent appointed positions in local governments with the mayor-council, town meeting, or representative town meeting plan. Judging from the results of this survey, it would be inaccurate to provide an unqualified, relevant amount of pay for the "average" CAO; there *is* no average CAO any more than there is an average city, county, or town. Responses show that pay practices vary widely according to the size, location, and philosophy of each local government.

Survey Methodology

The 2013 *ICMA Compensation Survey for Local Government Chief Appointed Officials* was sent to all local governments in the ICMA database for which ICMA has a name in the CAO position. The survey was designed to collect information on compensation for CAOs that would reflect the norms around the country, and to examine practices in relation to the principles contained within the "ICMA Guidelines for Compensation."

The initial survey was mailed in April 2013, and a follow-up survey was later mailed to nonrespondents. It was clear from some of the responses that clerks or elected officials were reporting for themselves, in which case those records were excluded from the final analysis. With those records excluded, the survey response rate was 41%, with 3,168 surveys submitted from among 7,739 mailed (Table 8–1).

Base Salary

It is not possible to determine from the survey what the base salary benchmark should be for the CAO in any specific jurisdiction. In brief, the "ICMA Guidelines" recommend that the following factors be considered in establishing CAO pay:

- Scope of services provided
- Requirements of the job
- Experience needed to successfully perform
- Market pay for comparable public sector executives
- Local government's financial position
- The individual CAO's credentials, experience, and expertise.

Base salary is generally related to population size of the local government; however, even within each population category and within the same geographic regions, the specifics are unique. Arguably, CAOs in smaller local governments may have a breadth of hands-on responsibility uncommon in large communities,

Table 8-1 Survey Response

Classification	No. of municipalities/ counties[a] surveyed (A)	Respondents No.	Respondents % of (A)
Total	7,739	3,168	41
Population group			
Over 1,000,000	33	10	30
500,000-1,000,000	68	24	35
250,000-499,999	130	49	38
100,000-249,999	352	158	45
50,000-99,999	620	271	44
25,000-49,999	972	404	42
10,000-24,999	1,731	726	42
5,000-9,999	1,428	572	40
2,500-4,999	1,299	491	38
Under 2,500	1,106	463	42
Geographic region			
Northeast	1,687	570	34
North-Central	2,112	961	46
South	2,531	970	38
West	1,408	666	47
Geographic division			
New England	740	282	38
Mid-Atlantic	947	288	30
East North-Central	1,211	531	44
West North-Central	907	432	48
South Atlantic	1,498	646	43
East South-Central	304	76	25
West South-Central	728	248	34
Mountain	481	231	48
Pacific Coast	923	434	47
Metro status			
Metropolitan Statistical Area	4,221	1,819	43
Micropolitan Statistical Area	1,215	509	42
New England City and Town Area	409	155	38
Undesignated	1,894	685	36
Form of government			
Mayor-council	2,060	734	36
Council-manager	3,912	1,856	47
Commission	76	32	42
Town meeting	308	120	39
Representative town meeting	49	17	35
County commission	351	61	17
Council-administrator (manager)	668	254	38
Council-elected executive	223	58	26
Unknown	92	36	39

a For a definition of terms, please see "Inside the *Year Book*," xxi-xxiv.

The Principles

Compensation and personnel matters should be guided by the core principles of the ICMA Code of Ethics. ICMA affirms that the standard practice for establishing the compensation of local government managers be fair, reasonable, transparent, and based on comparable public salaries nationally and regionally. ICMA members should act with integrity in all personal and professional matters in order to merit the trust of elected officials, the public and employees. Local government managers have an ethical responsibility to be clear about what is being requested and to avoid excessive compensation.

Elected officials perform a critical governance role providing oversight of the management of the organization. To that end, they must be engaged in establishing the process for determining the compensation for all executives appointed by the governing body.

Compensation should be based on the position requirements, the complexity of the job reflected in the composition of the organization and community, the leadership needed, labor market conditions, cost of living in the community, and the organization's ability to pay.

Source: "ICMA Guidelines for Compensation" (2010), 1, icma.org/Documents/Document/Document/302085.

Table 8-2 Median Salaries, in Total and by Population, 2013

Population	Overall median salary ($)
Total	105,000
Over 1,000,000	252,500
500,000-1,000,000	183,250
250,000-499,999	180,250
100,000-249,999	167,000
50,000-99,999	155,000
25,000-49,999	137,000
10,000-24,999	116,295
5,000-9,999	95,500
2,500-4,999	79,000
Under 2,500	62,500

and managers in large communities typically bring to their positions extensive experience acquired in smaller communities. A small community may have a strong financial capacity while a large city may have a weak financial position, or vice versa. This reality is reflected in the wide variation in base pay.

To ensure that respondents reported the same information, survey instructions defined *base salary* as follows:

This amount is not necessarily your taxable income. It is your salary before any pre-tax contributions are deducted to arrive at taxable income. For example, if your salary is $250,000 and you put $17,000 in pre-tax dollars into a retirement account, your base salary is $250,000.

Survey results show that the overall median salary is $105,000, which is slightly higher than the median shown in the 2012 ICMA salary survey data ($103,000). By population groupings, the median amounts for 2013 are shown in Table 8-2.

As Figure 8-1 shows, the median salary increases steadily among the population groups. The median is used instead of the mean, or average, because it is not as influenced by outliers as the average salary can be; nonetheless, the variance is significant. Maximum salaries show more variation among the population groups and are influenced by many factors, such as manager experience and tenure; particular characteristics of the locality; cost of living; median income in the locality; services delivered; and breadth of responsibility, such as for schools, public hospitals, airports, and ports. Maximum salaries do not show a correlation to populations but rise and fall across the population categories. Appendix Tables 8-A1 and 8-A2 show the mean, median, minimum, and maximum salaries for cities and counties, respectively, within each state by population group.

When the median salaries of 2013 are compared with those reported in 2012,[3] the data show that the salaries overall have increased only slightly (Figure 8-2). The exceptions are in the 500,000–1,000,000 population group, in which the median salaries decreased by $7,159, and in the 250,000–499,000 and under-2,500 population groups, in which they decreased by $1,615 and just $500, respectively.

Base Salary Documentation

Documentation of base salary is important for providing transparency to taxpayers and shielding CAOs from accusations of trying to hide their compensation. Asked whether their base salaries are documented in contracts or letters of agreement with the appointing authority, 72% of respondents overall responded in the affirmative (not shown).

The most notable variation occurs when the data are arrayed by form of government, with 79% of respondents serving in council-manager governments and 58% of those in mayor-council governments reporting base salary documentation. In the former case, the full council is normally responsible for setting compensation, while in the latter case, compensation may be negotiated between only the mayor and the CAO. But while 79% is a high percentage replying that base salary is documented, there are no obvious reasons in a council-manager form of government for the percentage to be less than 100%.

Figure 8-1   Base Salary by Population Group

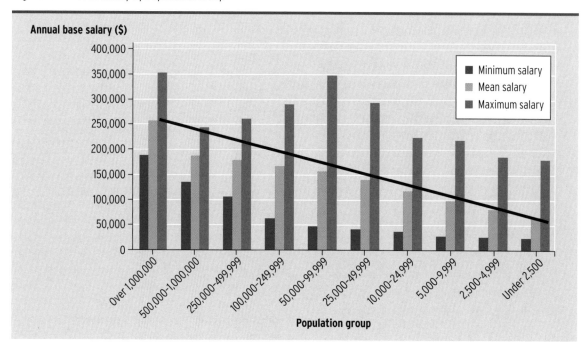

Figure 8-2   Comparison of Median CAO Salaries, 2012 and 2013

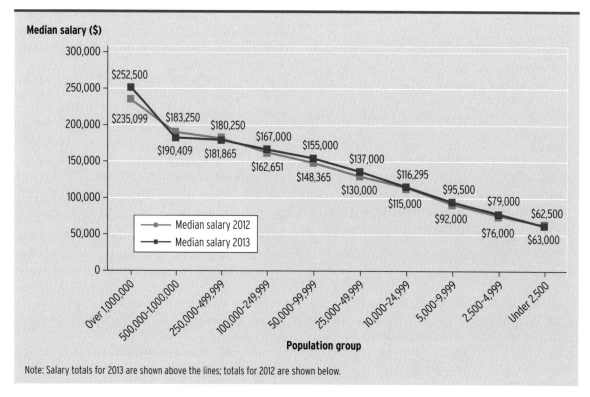

Note: Salary totals for 2013 are shown above the lines; totals for 2012 are shown below.

Base Salary Publicly Accessible on the Local Government Website

While salaries are a matter of public record, they are not always easy for the public to access. For maximum transparency, 41% of respondents overall, as well as a majority of CAOs in local governments with a population of 25,000 or greater, reported that their base salaries are publicly available on the local government website (Figure 8–3).

Compensation beyond Base Salary

Beyond base pay, the only additional compensation that is common practice is car allowance (50% reporting) (Figure 8–4). A few respondents wrote in other types of compensation, such as life insurance, country club membership, longevity pay, and ICMA membership.

Salary and Performance Review

Annual performance evaluations of the manager/CAO can benefit both the manager and the governing body, identifying both successes and missed opportunities as well as future goals and objectives. The review process offers an occasion for discussion among all parties and can help the governing body avoid some of the pitfalls of unclear direction. A majority of all respondents reported an annual performance evaluation (76%), regardless of whether compensation is considered during that process (Table 8–3).

Transparency

1. Local government managers should provide their total compensation package to the governing body when requesting compensation changes so that the governing body has a comprehensive view of the compensation package.

2. In the interest of fairness and transparency, there should be full disclosure to the governing body, prior to formal consideration and approval, of the potential cost of any benefit changes negotiated during employment.

3. When the terms and conditions of employment are being renegotiated with the employer and at the end when the employment is being terminated, ICMA members have a duty to advise the elected officials to seek legal advice.

4. In the interests of transparency, the salary plan and salary ranges for local government positions, including that of the manager, should be publicly accessible on the agency's website.

Source: "ICMA Guidelines for Compensation" (2010), 3, icma.org/Documents/Document/Document/302085.

Figure 8-3   Base Salary Publicly Available on Website

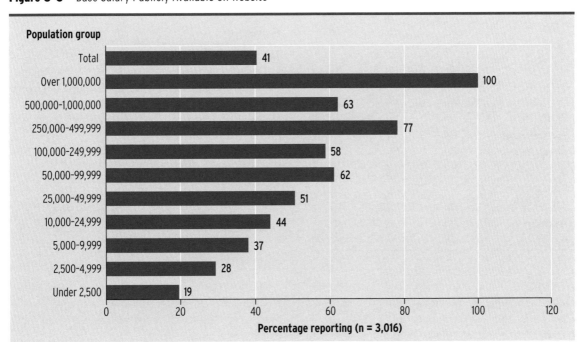

Figure 8-4 Compensation beyond Base Salary

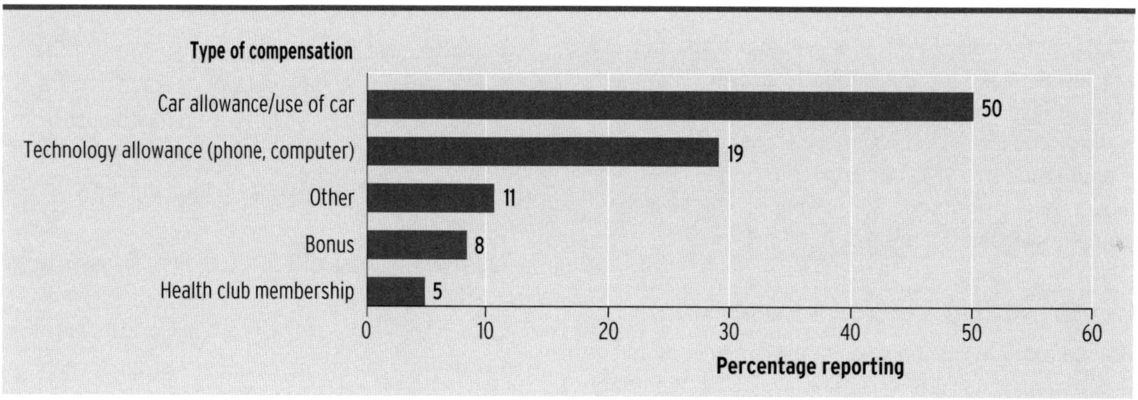

Table 8-3 Annual Performance Evaluation

	Total	Annual performance evaluation occurs	
		No.	%
Total	3,092	2,359	76
Population group			
Over 1,000,000	9	8	89
500,000-1,000,000	22	17	77
250,000-499,999	48	33	69
100,000-249,999	153	123	80
50,000-99,999	265	219	83
25,000-49,999	393	318	81
10,000-24,999	707	538	76
5,000-9,999	559	417	75
2,500-4,999	485	367	76
Under 2,500	451	319	71
Geographic division			
New England	280	238	85
Mid-Atlantic	284	139	49
East North-Central	520	378	73
West North-Central	424	356	84
South Atlantic	626	476	76
East South-Central	74	43	58
West South-Central	241	192	80
Mountain	224	186	83
Pacific Coast	419	351	84

While a majority of respondents also reported having annual salary reviews (67%), 20% indicated other frequencies of salary review while 15% reported no salary review at all (Figure 8–5). Consistent with the "ICMA Guidelines" concerning transparency, 90% of respondents indicated that their total compensation package is available to all members of the governing body (not shown).

Pay Decreases and Furlough Days

Overall, 11% of respondents reported cuts in base pay since December 2007, and of note is the high percentage in Pacific Coast localities (26%) (not shown). One California city manager cut his own pay in order to fund raises for two department heads.[4]

Furlough days were reported by 4% overall, which is lower by 6 percentage points than the percentage reporting furlough days since April 2012. The median number of furlough days is seven, up from the six reported in 2012 (not shown).

Benefits

The survey collected information on benefits provided to CAOs, with attention given to how those benefits are calculated—that is, whether they are calculated using the same process used to calculate the benefits for other employees. The following definition was provided to survey respondents:

> "The same" does not necessarily mean the same dollar amount; it means that the benefit is determined in the same manner, e.g., if health insurance premiums paid by the employee are based [on] type of coverage, is that how your premium contribution is calculated?

In every instance, a majority of respondents reported that their benefits are calculated in the same manner as the benefits are calculated for other employees (Figure 8–6).

Figure 8-5 Frequency of Salary Review

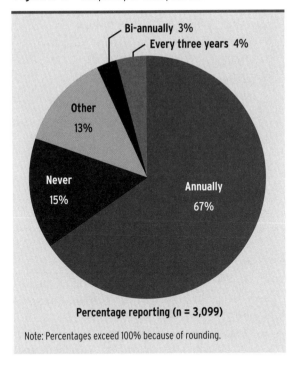

Percentage reporting (n = 3,099)

Note: Percentages exceed 100% because of rounding.

Employment Contracts/Agreements

Seventy-nine percent of CAOs reported having an employment agreement or contract (not shown), although there is noticeable variation between the percentages reported in mayor-council localities (67%) and those in council-manager (86%) localities. In 95% of the cases where an employment agreement or contract is in place, the agreement documents the CAO's full compensation. In addition, respondents reported that the agreement

- was approved in a public session (96%)
- is available to the public upon request (98%)
- is posted on the local government website (16%).

The facts that an employment agreement is typically approved in a public session and is available to the public upon request reflect the value of transparency to the public.

Severance Benefits

Because CAOs serve at the pleasure of elected officials, their positions can be more vulnerable to political shifts

Figure 8-6 Benefits Calculated in the Same Manner as for Other Employees

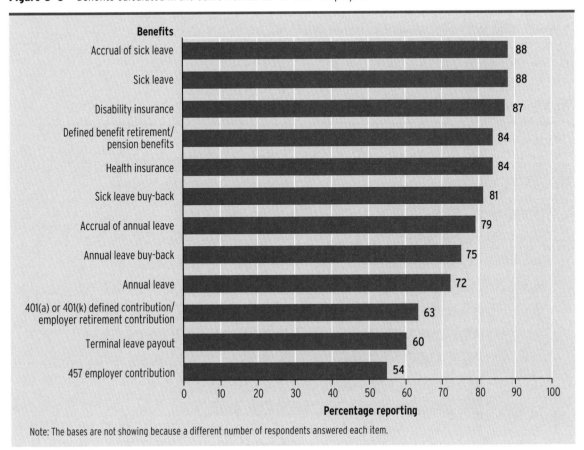

Note: The bases are not showing because a different number of respondents answered each item.

than those of other professions. To financially buffer CAOs from the consequences of suddenly finding themselves without a job, severance benefits are particularly important. Overall, 78% of respondents reported that they are eligible to receive severance pay (Figure 8–7).

Of those who have an employment agreement, 84% reported that the severance pay is specified in their contracts (not shown). For the plurality of respondents (45%) and for all population groups except the very smallest, the amount of severance pay reported is typically up to six months (Figure 8–8), although the ICMA model employment agreement recommends one year.

Summary

In summary, the following findings reflect the current situation:

- Base salaries are generally correlated to the size of the local government, but variations are extremely broad, distorting the value of a calculated mean or average.

- The CAO base salary is documented, the total compensation package is available to all members of the governing body, and, in a majority of jurisdictions with populations of 25,000 or more, the base salary is posted on the local government's website.

- Most CAOs receive an annual salary review and an annual performance review.

- Most CAOs receive a car allowance.

- Typical benefit packages for CAOs, usually calculated for the CAO in the same manner as for other local government employees, include
  - health insurance
  - disability insurance
  - annual leave
  - sick leave
  - accrual of annual leave
  - accrual of sick leave
  - annual leave buy-back
  - sick leave buy-back
  - terminal leave payout
  - defined benefit retirement/pension benefits
  - 401(a) or 401(k) defined contribution employer retirement contribution
  - 457 employer retirement contribution.

- CAOs have an employment agreement or contract that is approved in a public session and made available to the public upon request.

- CAOs are eligible to receive severance pay, which is specified in the employment agreement and, most commonly, amounts to either six months or a year of pay.

In addition to the prevalent practices, the survey revealed that a number of CAOs in larger jurisdictions have taken pay reductions and furlough days since December 2007.

Figure 8-7   Eligible for Severance Pay

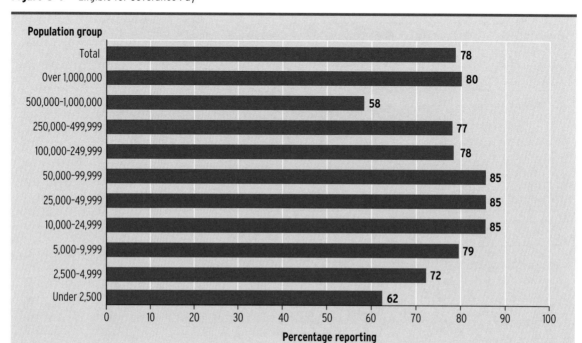

Population group	Percentage reporting
Total	78
Over 1,000,000	80
500,000-1,000,000	58
250,000-499,999	77
100,000-249,999	78
50,000-99,999	85
25,000-49,999	85
10,000-24,999	85
5,000-9,999	79
2,500-4,999	72
Under 2,500	62

Figure 8-8 Amount of Severance Pay for CAOs Eligible to Receive It

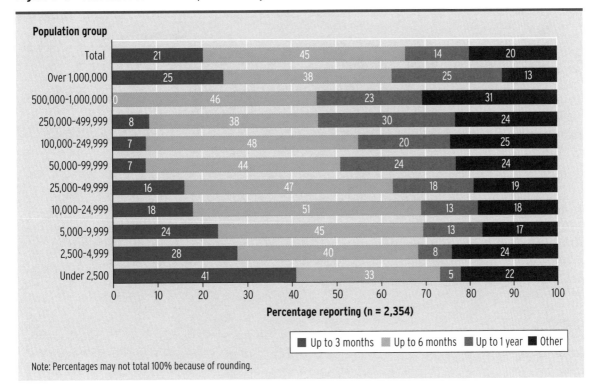

Note: Percentages may not total 100% because of rounding.

Results of the 2013 *ICMA Compensation Survey for Local Government Chief Appointed Officials* serve several purposes. Survey data demonstrate the impossibility of establishing actual salary benchmarks outside of a specific market; however, survey data do establish the norms for compensation practices across local governments.

There will always be variations based on characteristics of the local government, including its financial condition and service provisions, and on characteristics of the CAO, such as tenure, experience, and education. Nonetheless, with data on what the majority of respondents report, norms can be established, providing a framework for elected officials when determining compensation packages in conjunction with the "General Compensation Guidelines for all Employees" (see sidebar).

Notes

1 "ICMA Guidelines for Compensation" (2010), 1, icma .org/Documents/Document/Document/302085.

2 Ibid.

3 Evelina R. Moulder and Ron Carlee, "CAO Salary and Compensation: Stability Is the Trend," in *The Municipal Year Book 2013* (Washington, D.C.: ICMA Press, 2013), 102.

4 "San Leandro City Manager Cuts His Own Salary to Give Raises to Two Executives," *CaliforniaCityNews.org*, November 28, 2012, californiacitynews.org/2012/11/san-leandro-city-manager-cuts-his-own-salary-give-raises-two-executives.html (accessed 11/25/2013).

General Compensation Guidelines for all Employees

1. Each local government should establish benchmark agencies which are determined using set criteria, such as, but not limited to
   - Close geographic proximity
   - Similarity with regard to the nature of the services provided
   - Similarity in employer size/population size
   - Similarity in the socio-economic makeup of the population
   - Other similar employers in the immediate area

2. The local government should develop appropriate compensation levels that are in line with their labor market. Doing so will enable the organization to establish and maintain a reputation as a competitive, fair, and equitable employer as well as a good steward of public funds.

3. When considering any salary or benefit changes, the immediate and anticipated long-term financial resources of the organization always should be taken into account.

4. Appropriate financial practices should be followed to both disclose and properly fund any related future liability to the local government.

Source: "ICMA Guidelines for Compensation" (2010), 3, icma.org/ Documents/Document/Document/302085.

Appendix Table 8-A1 City Salaries by Population Group within States

State	No. reporting	Annual base salary			
		Minimum ($)	Mean ($)	Median ($)	Maximum ($)
Alabama					
Total	8	68,370	113,260	100,000	167,668
50,000-99,999	1	167,668	167,668	167,668	167,668
10,000-24,999	3	94,000	114,642	100,000	149,926
5,000-9,999	2	68,370	69,185	69,185	70,000
Under 2,500	2	142,854	142,854	142,854	142,854
Alaska					
Total	18	48,000	103,599	105,000	160,000
25,000-49,999	2	102,000	123,500	123,500	145,000
5,000-9,999	3	90,000	123,333	125,000	155,000
2,500-4,999	5	105,000	119,000	116,500	138,000
Under 2,500	8	48,000	80,654	70,000	160,000
Arizona					
Total	35	70,000	137,173	134,000	225,000
500,000-1,000,000	1	202,000	202,000	202,000	202,000
250,000-499,999	1	225,000	225,000	225,000	225,000
100,000-249,999	2	190,000	197,500	197,500	205,000
50,000-99,999	5	130,000	162,252	172,000	183,000
25,000-49,999	7	119,051	146,146	148,000	163,968
10,000-24,999	8	81,500	130,065	130,900	181,400
5,000-9,999	5	98,000	110,270	103,263	136,552
2,500-4,999	4	70,000	86,000	87,500	99,000
Under 2,500	2	78,000	91,000	91,000	104,000
Arkansas					
Total	3	114,466	146,989	149,500	177,000
100,000-249,999	1	177,000	177,000	177,000	177,000
50,000-99,999	1	149,500	149,500	149,500	149,500
10,000-24,999	1	114,466	114,466	114,466	114,466
California					
Total	214	73,000	188,249	197,000	350,000
Over 1,000,000	1	236,467	236,467	236,467	236,467
250,000-499,999	3	170,000	214,000	214,000	258,000
100,000-249,999	22	190,000	227,738	224,000	292,520
50,000-99,999	60	150,150	208,765	201,000	350,000
25,000-49,999	53	139,000	200,505	201,942	296,000
10,000-24,999	39	90,000	161,147	166,300	210,000
5,000-9,999	23	100,788	145,821	145,000	220,000
2,500-4,999	11	86,800	136,853	135,000	187,554
Under 2,500	2	73,000	126,500	126,500	180,000

continued

Appendix Table 8-A1   City Salaries by Population Group within States

State	No. reporting	Annual base salary			
		Minimum ($)	Mean ($)	Median ($)	Maximum ($)
Colorado					
Total	82	52,069	122,238	120,000	219,759
250,000-499,999	1	186,850	186,850	186,850	186,850
100,000-249,999	5	191,200	206,836	207,063	219,759
50,000-99,999	4	133,985	169,525	170,779	202,558
25,000-49,999	7	127,000	149,890	155,000	177,531
10,000-24,999	12	104,000	135,605	132,500	171,438
5,000-9,999	18	83,000	120,211	120,000	173,763
2,500-4,999	8	70,000	108,944	108,000	149,159
Under 2,500	27	52,069	86,641	75,000	151,198
Connecticut					
Total	25	40,000	124,659	126,736	183,000
100,000-249,999	1	115,085	115,085	115,085	115,085
50,000-99,999	1	183,000	183,000	183,000	183,000
25,000-49,999	10	116,000	134,569	132,600	157,260
10,000-24,999	9	84,589	126,350	130,000	143,990
5,000-9,999	2	80,683	85,443	85,443	90,203
2,500-4,999	2	40,000	40,000	40,000	40,000
Delaware					
Total	14	55,000	83,940	78,130	136,650
25,000-49,999	1	118,000	118,000	118,000	118,000
10,000-24,999	1	111,300	111,300	111,300	111,300
5,000-9,999	3	83,000	105,097	95,641	136,650
2,500-4,999	1	64,509	64,509	64,509	64,509
Under 2,500	8	55,000	70,758	74,275	86,250
Florida					
Total	137	41,000	128,505	128,750	275,000
500,000-1,000,000	1	210,000	210,000	210,000	210,000
100,000-249,999	7	149,000	190,300	178,400	275,000
50,000-99,999	17	120,000	176,192	175,000	251,639
25,000-49,999	11	135,000	164,692	166,500	196,000
10,000-24,999	40	98,350	137,911	135,000	206,618
5,000-9,999	22	74,900	113,129	105,106	189,000
2,500-4,999	15	65,000	99,575	94,555	144,385
Under 2,500	24	41,000	72,797	74,000	110,680
Georgia					
Total	70	48,000	106,895	110,000	185,000
100,000-249,999	2	139,323	159,162	159,162	179,000
50,000-99,999	5	127,500	148,445	139,900	181,579
25,000-49,999	9	110,000	136,474	140,500	166,226
10,000-24,999	19	80,000	121,478	124,783	185,000
5,000-9,999	12	72,529	99,932	98,125	130,000
2,500-4,999	14	55,342	79,100	78,900	104,000
Under 2,500	9	48,000	62,904	61,000	85,250

continued

Appendix Table 8-A1   City Salaries by Population Group within States

State	No. reporting	Annual base salary			
		Minimum ($)	Mean ($)	Median ($)	Maximum ($)
Idaho					
Total	7	82,000	107,634	110,780	125,000
25,000-49,999	1	120,000	120,000	120,000	120,000
10,000-24,999	2	110,780	114,254	114,254	117,728
5,000-9,999	2	82,000	91,216	91,216	100,432
2,500-4,999	1	97,500	97,500	97,500	97,500
Under 2,500	1	125,000	125,000	125,000	125,000
Illinois					
Total	137	56,000	129,953	130,321	238,818
100,000-249,999	4	89,900	155,636	174,043	184,560
50,000-99,999	12	108,000	172,141	172,150	238,818
25,000-49,999	26	105,000	157,617	158,000	206,191
10,000-24,999	46	70,000	129,634	127,000	223,000
5,000-9,999	29	56,000	107,987	99,803	195,000
2,500-4,999	15	56,000	96,594	89,078	137,500
Under 2,500	5	63,128	100,242	87,125	182,000
Indiana					
Total	8	60,000	82,417	70,000	126,000
10,000-24,999	5	73,000	102,167	107,500	126,000
2,500-4,999	2	61,000	64,000	64,000	67,000
Under 2,500	1	60,000	60,000	60,000	60,000
Iowa					
Total	84	42,000	91,456	83,084	209,930
100,000-249,999	1	208,710	208,710	208,710	208,710
50,000-99,999	3	155,000	178,310	170,000	209,930
25,000-49,999	4	117,000	145,484	144,967	175,000
10,000-24,999	11	92,251	124,604	121,150	162,475
5,000-9,999	27	64,517	94,411	94,760	120,000
2,500-4,999	16	54,000	73,050	72,933	98,272
Under 2,500	22	42,000	57,018	55,085	78,409
Kansas					
Total	67	50,000	93,942	86,670	182,644
100,000-249,999	2	180,000	181,322	181,322	182,644
50,000-99,999	2	140,000	150,265	150,265	160,530
25,000-49,999	4	129,421	136,399	133,883	148,409
10,000-24,999	12	88,649	111,169	113,352	134,605
5,000-9,999	11	80,000	95,197	97,850	109,000
2,500-4,999	18	53,000	82,181	84,440	116,000
Under 2,500	18	50,000	67,396	68,305	85,490

continued

Appendix Table 8-A1   City Salaries by Population Group within States

State	No. reporting	Annual base salary			
		Minimum ($)	Mean ($)	Median ($)	Maximum ($)
Kentucky					
Total	13	40,000	104,744	111,153	139,500
50,000-99,999	1	139,500	139,500	139,500	139,500
25,000-49,999	3	119,392	129,464	132,000	137,000
10,000-24,999	4	101,700	113,713	115,577	122,000
5,000-9,999	2	72,500	81,338	81,338	90,176
2,500-4,999	2	81,000	88,124	88,124	95,248
Under 2,500	1	40,000	40,000	40,000	40,000
Maine					
Total	88	25,000	68,265	65,000	117,689
25,000-49,999	1	116,000	116,000	116,000	116,000
10,000-24,999	7	83,636	104,888	107,750	117,689
5,000-9,999	21	53,000	83,716	82,000	117,667
2,500-4,999	23	44,365	63,267	63,564	94,665
Under 2,500	36	25,000	54,495	50,000	114,703
Maryland					
Total	30	64,000	104,759	92,160	204,973
50,000-99,999	2	165,000	184,987	184,987	204,973
25,000-49,999	4	95,599	131,466	146,800	152,000
10,000-24,999	4	85,838	115,960	116,000	146,000
5,000-9,999	5	85,000	100,927	99,000	128,480
2,500-4,999	9	68,224	78,853	79,040	91,881
Under 2,500	6	64,000	87,784	87,000	120,483
Massachusetts					
Total	87	41,809	122,031	124,000	187,703
50,000-99,999	3	118,000	153,663	169,588	173,400
25,000-49,999	15	107,300	148,293	150,000	187,703
10,000-24,999	34	92,978	132,551	133,706	162,400
5,000-9,999	20	71,000	107,052	107,850	158,000
2,500-4,999	11	55,364	98,011	100,000	150,000
Under 2,500	4	41,809	64,484	61,500	93,125
Michigan					
Total	138	39,750	87,909	87,264	152,000
100,000-249,999	3	137,217	142,406	145,000	145,000
50,000-99,999	6	123,500	140,583	142,000	152,000
25,000-49,999	10	94,000	113,951	113,000	138,346
10,000-24,999	27	81,000	100,927	98,077	139,000
5,000-9,999	26	62,500	93,389	93,000	132,095
2,500-4,999	33	50,000	77,179	74,250	112,100
Under 2,500	33	39,750	60,252	58,450	91,092

continued

Appendix Table 8-A1 City Salaries by Population Group within States

State	No. reporting	Annual base salary			
		Minimum ($)	Mean ($)	Median ($)	Maximum ($)
Minnesota					
Total	113	45,000	98,276	97,000	165,780
100,000-249,999	1	165,780	165,780	165,780	165,780
50,000-99,999	5	143,900	147,119	144,800	154,000
25,000-49,999	10	112,771	131,591	131,810	156,000
10,000-24,999	29	86,471	114,840	116,640	144,304
5,000-9,999	13	84,843	100,963	105,040	114,000
2,500-4,999	31	64,500	86,097	84,998	108,600
Under 2,500	24	45,000	65,392	65,000	88,786
Mississippi					
Total	5	57,165	85,305	81,000	136,000
25,000-49,999	3	81,000	101,453	87,360	136,000
10,000-24,999	1	57,165	57,165	57,165	57,165
5,000-9,999	1	65,000	65,000	65,000	65,000
Missouri					
Total	82	37,500	95,916	92,000	205,000
250,000-499,999	1	205,000	205,000	205,000	205,000
100,000-249,999	2	151,000	174,621	174,621	198,242
50,000-99,999	3	131,000	157,000	150,000	190,000
25,000-49,999	8	122,000	141,562	135,387	178,500
10,000-24,999	19	65,000	105,559	108,000	155,900
5,000-9,999	17	42,500	87,244	86,000	144,816
2,500-4,999	21	47,800	74,628	71,935	120,000
Under 2,500	11	37,500	55,705	55,000	74,419
Montana					
Total	8	43,000	97,948	109,580	130,000
100,00-249,999	1	130,000	130,000	130,000	130,000
50,000-99,999	2	105,859	110,430	110,430	115,000
25,000-49,999	1	119,600	119,600	119,600	119,600
5,000-9,999	2	87,325	100,313	100,313	113,300
2,500-4,999	2	43,000	56,250	56,250	69,500
Nebraska					
Total	33	41,974	84,185	81,702	132,000
25,000-49,999	1	110,000	110,000	110,000	110,000
10,000-24,999	8	102,000	120,057	125,000	132,000
5,000-9,999	8	70,000	89,085	92,384	104,000
2,500-4,999	5	74,000	83,408	81,702	101,580
Under 2,500	11	41,974	56,244	54,000	75,000
Nevada					
Total	6	72,300	152,912	158,297	196,540
500,000-1,000,000	1	178,000	178,000	178,000	178,000
100,000-249,999	1	193,640	193,640	193,640	193,640
50,000-99,999	2	138,593	167,567	167,567	196,540
5,000-9,999	1	138,400	138,400	138,400	138,400
2,500-4,999	1	72,300	72,300	72,300	72,300

continued

Appendix Table 8-A1   City Salaries by Population Group within States

State	No. reporting	Annual base salary			
		Minimum ($)	Mean ($)	Median ($)	Maximum ($)
New Hampshire					
Total	44	27,688	82,943	76,065	143,168
25,000-49,999	2	133,000	138,084	138,084	143,168
10,000-24,999	8	90,000	112,777	107,713	143,000
5,000-9,999	14	59,000	82,233	85,953	108,150
2,500-4,999	12	37,500	69,165	70,834	96,400
Under 2,500	8	27,688	61,141	60,279	89,793
New Jersey					
Total	57	35,215	131,038	133,442	198,750
250,000-499,999	1	180,000	180,000	180,000	180,000
100,000-249,999	1	135,937	135,937	135,937	135,937
50,000-99,999	2	95,000	146,875	146,875	198,750
25,000-49,999	13	120,000	153,145	159,500	180,000
10,000-24,999	22	75,000	128,859	133,442	170,000
5,000-9,999	11	65,000	120,080	125,078	158,159
2,500-4,999	6	35,215	104,582	109,750	149,000
Under 2,500	1	107,430	107,430	107,430	107,430
New Mexico					
Total	16	75,500	110,094	104,100	166,500
500,000-1,000,000	1	145,600	145,600	145,600	145,600
50,000-99,999	2	150,000	158,250	158,250	166,500
25,000-49,999	3	113,484	126,161	125,000	140,000
10,000-24,999	3	82,000	98,324	101,400	111,571
5,000-9,999	5	77,252	93,290	101,000	105,200
Under 2,500	2	75,500	79,750	79,750	84,000
New York					
Total	26	65,900	127,966	114,803	214,000
25,000-49,999	4	112,000	142,812	140,000	179,247
10,000-24,999	8	83,000	148,057	146,053	214,000
5,000-9,999	7	77,845	121,719	120,118	166,872
2,500-4,999	6	65,900	99,134	86,000	158,769
Under 2,500	1	89,490	89,490	89,490	89,490
North Carolina					
Total	123	36,820	95,860	85,000	245,000
500,000-1,000,000	1	245,000	245,000	245,000	245,000
100,000-249,999	6	166,634	181,200	180,000	200,000
50,000-99,999	4	135,000	155,563	160,000	171,690
25,000-49,999	8	119,263	142,378	140,296	162,916
10,000-24,999	23	78,000	116,305	115,019	139,050
5,000-9,999	17	65,000	86,572	91,000	110,323
2,500-4,999	32	42,840	77,526	78,859	118,500
Under 2,500	32	36,820	67,183	61,826	127,000

continued

Appendix Table 8-A1 City Salaries by Population Group within States

State	No. reporting	Annual base salary			
		Minimum ($)	Mean ($)	Median ($)	Maximum ($)
North Dakota					
Total	7	38,200	107,362	114,109	163,000
100,000-249,999	1	163,000	163,000	163,000	163,000
25,000-49,999	2	129,210	132,105	132,105	135,000
10,000-24,999	2	99,008	99,008	99,008	99,008
5,000-9,999	1	79,752	79,752	79,752	79,752
Under 2,500	1	38,200	38,200	38,200	38,200
Ohio					
Total	99	30,000	99,521	94,650	255,000
250,000-499,999	1	255,000	255,000	255,000	255,000
100,000-249,999	1	155,000	155,000	155,000	155,000
50,000-99,999	6	95,000	128,956	130,000	173,000
25,000-49,999	16	65,000	118,391	117,583	183,602
10,000-24,999	25	61,000	102,132	106,621	154,127
5,000-9,999	24	61,800	96,422	94,113	138,226
2,500-4,999	18	30,000	78,241	75,096	121,306
Under 2,500	8	35,000	57,039	53,872	96,000
Oklahoma					
Total	47	54,312	107,059	104,064	229,407
500,000-1,000,000	1	229,407	229,407	229,407	229,407
250,000-499,999	1	145,000	145,000	145,000	145,000
50,000-99,999	4	127,000	145,833	150,613	155,107
25,000-49,999	5	114,000	125,605	123,372	144,282
10,000-24,999	15	72,000	115,453	112,000	151,000
5,000-9,999	10	78,000	94,119	95,882	115,000
2,500-4,999	9	57,800	72,636	70,000	96,013
Under 2,500	2	54,312	59,651	59,651	64,990
Oregon					
Total	105	24,624	85,389	78,600	182,561
100,000-249,999	1	182,561	182,561	182,561	182,561
50,000-99,999	6	128,000	143,729	145,008	155,293
25,000-49,999	4	130,000	143,125	139,250	164,000
10,000-24,999	16	96,132	123,562	125,000	144,000
5,000-9,999	14	78,000	97,421	100,077	117,282
2,500-4,999	14	60,000	80,261	80,912	101,345
Under 2,500	50	24,624	54,697	55,666	100,290
Pennsylvania					
Total	178	32,500	86,632	85,561	207,049
100,000-249,999	1	96,500	96,500	96,500	96,500
50,000-99,999	1	207,049	207,049	207,049	207,049
25,000-49,999	12	85,000	117,679	116,750	182,000
10,000-24,999	64	59,500	101,073	100,913	157,185
5,000-9,999	51	45,000	76,294	75,000	115,900
2,500-4,999	36	32,500	69,168	70,000	95,692
Under 2,500	13	36,500	57,947	51,625	95,000

continued

Appendix Table 8-A1 City Salaries by Population Group within States

State	No. reporting	Minimum ($)	Mean ($)	Median ($)	Maximum ($)
			Annual base salary		
Rhode Island					
Total	7	100,940	121,484	118,620	155,725
25,000-49,999	4	115,239	129,491	123,500	155,725
10,000-24,999	1	100,940	100,940	100,940	100,940
5,000-9,999	2	110,000	110,000	110,000	110,000
South Carolina					
Total	30	40,000	96,150	94,500	170,793
50,000-99,999	1	139,252	139,252	139,252	139,252
25,000-49,999	2	170,000	170,397	170,397	170,793
10,000-24,999	6	95,981	111,770	107,500	131,304
5,000-9,999	9	69,000	86,871	87,500	116,900
2,500-4,999	8	60,000	79,697	80,000	109,428
Under 2,500	4	40,000	74,491	77,481	103,000
South Dakota					
Total	12	50,000	88,429	80,392	134,172
25,000-49,999	1	132,000	132,000	132,000	132,000
10,000-24,999	4	106,007	118,393	115,000	134,172
5,000-9,999	1	85,000	85,000	85,000	85,000
2,500-4,999	2	60,000	68,500	68,500	77,000
Under 2,500	4	50,000	65,886	66,576	80,392
Tennessee					
Total	38	43,084	97,224	94,328	160,000
100,000-249,999	1	155,219	155,219	155,219	155,219
50,000-99,999	3	108,165	134,055	134,000	160,000
25,000-49,999	8	86,494	125,214	134,000	150,000
10,000-24,999	9	55,000	91,471	86,091	117,000
5,000-9,999	4	79,190	101,506	94,500	137,835
2,500-4,999	7	45,000	72,232	71,733	98,655
Under 2,500	6	43,084	51,521	53,500	56,000
Texas					
Total	187	33,987	125,289	120,000	355,000
Over 1,000,000	2	304,773	329,887	329,887	355,000
500,000-1,000,000	1	238,000	238,000	238,000	238,000
250,000-499,999	2	226,000	236,500	236,500	247,000
100,000-249,999	9	172,516	207,760	206,000	239,551
50,000-99,999	10	150,000	185,556	170,000	250,000
25,000-49,999	27	102,000	156,635	150,275	215,000
10,000-24,999	36	76,125	133,792	130,000	226,200
5,000-9,999	38	70,500	115,945	114,500	175,000
2,500-4,999	37	55,600	86,286	83,000	156,125
Under 2,500	25	33,987	70,807	68,100	169,983

continued

Appendix Table 8-A1   City Salaries by Population Group within States

State	No. reporting	Annual base salary			
		Minimum ($)	Mean ($)	Median ($)	Maximum ($)
Utah					
Total	34	45,000	109,320	109,817	154,611
100,000–249,999	2	131,588	135,794	135,794	140,000
50,000–99,999	4	134,000	139,550	138,100	148,000
25,000–49,999	7	106,000	125,909	124,000	154,611
10,000–24,999	12	82,136	104,500	104,000	124,000
5,000–9,999	5	45,000	92,479	88,752	128,000
2,500–4,999	2	69,500	69,750	69,750	70,000
Under 2,500	2	65,000	72,500	72,500	80,000
Vermont					
Total	26	27,000	71,933	69,750	107,679
10,000–24,999	2	93,000	100,340	100,340	107,679
5,000–9,999	6	67,500	87,148	90,000	102,000
2,500–4,999	11	27,000	66,293	67,000	104,872
Under 2,500	7	32,900	61,811	63,680	93,000
Virginia					
Total	67	43,000	117,793	106,142	245,000
250,000–499,999	1	228,360	228,360	228,360	228,360
100,000–249,999	5	178,000	207,500	203,500	245,000
50,000–99,999	4	126,840	160,088	167,755	178,000
25,000–49,999	4	157,590	163,823	165,350	167,000
10,000–24,999	13	111,000	144,522	148,070	172,094
5,000–9,999	14	75,000	102,208	103,000	140,000
2,500–4,999	14	58,526	87,515	87,923	106,195
Under 2,500	12	43,000	69,783	74,025	97,850
Washington					
Total	58	40,327	128,689	127,812	221,208
100,000–249,999	1	221,208	221,208	221,208	221,208
50,000–99,999	5	147,000	157,112	152,000	175,000
25,000–49,999	6	143,592	154,350	149,448	180,610
10,000–24,999	21	116,000	136,579	134,516	166,392
5,000–9,999	13	92,700	119,725	120,000	151,368
2,500–4,999	3	89,352	102,809	104,076	115,000
Under 2,500	9	40,327	83,673	87,053	117,745
West Virginia					
Total	7	50,000	89,116	89,000	141,813
50,000–99,999	1	141,813	141,813	141,813	141,813
10,000–24,999	1	95,000	95,000	95,000	95,000
5,000–9,999	4	65,000	84,250	84,500	103,000
2,500–4,999	1	50,000	50,000	50,000	50,000

continued

Appendix Table 8-A1   City Salaries by Population Group within States

State	No. reporting	Annual base salary Minimum ($)	Mean ($)	Median ($)	Maximum ($)
Wisconsin					
Total	86	58,000	90,902	90,605	140,000
50,000-99,999	3	120,000	129,167	127,500	140,000
25,000-49,999	4	118,000	125,209	124,418	134,000
10,000-24,999	21	79,187	103,193	101,000	122,500
5,000-9,999	27	66,000	87,348	90,000	114,900
2,500-4,999	17	68,806	82,954	77,805	140,000
Under 2,500	14	58,000	72,156	67,856	105,000
Wyoming					
Total	7	51,500	120,061	130,000	183,000
50,000-99,999	1	183,000	183,000	183,000	183,000
25,000-49,999	1	141,882	141,882	141,882	141,882
10,000-24,999	2	101,745	115,873	115,873	130,000
5,000-9,999	2	95,500	116,150	116,150	136,800
Under 2,500	1	51,500	51,500	51,500	51,500

Appendix Table 8-A2 County Salaries by Population Group within States

State	No. reporting	Annual base salary			
		Minimum ($)	Mean ($)	Median ($)	Maximum ($)
Alabama					
Total	4	42,000	62,600	55,356	97,688
50,000-99,999	2	65,312	81,500	81,500	97,688
25,000-49,999	1	42,000	42,000	42,000	42,000
10,000-24,999	1	45,400	45,400	45,400	45,400
Alaska					
Total	2	134,680	154,840	154,840	175,000
50,000-99,999	1	175,000	175,000	175,000	175,000
2,500-4,999	1	134,680	134,680	134,680	134,680
Arizona					
Total	5	113,400	151,480	160,000	168,000
100,000-249,999	4	151,000	161,000	162,500	168,000
50,000-99,999	1	113,400	113,400	113,400	113,400
California					
Total	17	103,000	189,187	180,000	262,932
Over 1,000,000	2	245,000	252,500	252,500	260,000
500,000-1,000,000	1	210,168	210,168	210,168	210,168
250,000-499,999	5	180,000	218,678	215,384	262,932
100,000-249,999	2	172,380	196,690	196,690	221,000
50,000-99,999	3	150,000	158,831	160,000	166,493
25,000-49,999	1	156,000	156,000	156,000	156,000
10,000-24,999	3	103,000	127,249	118,746	160,000
Colorado					
Total	17	31,572	110,225	120,000	160,000
500,000-1,000,000	2	148,000	149,000	149,000	150,000
250,000-499,999	2	141,231	150,616	150,616	160,000
50,000-99,999	1	155,000	155,000	155,000	155,000
10,000-24,999	6	80,000	115,000	117,000	150,000
5,000-9,999	4	52,716	84,929	83,500	120,000
2,500-4,999	1	58,300	58,300	58,300	58,300
Under 2,500	1	31,572	31,572	31,572	31,572
Delaware					
Total	1	120,800	120,800	120,800	120,800
100,000-249,999	1	120,800	120,800	120,800	120,800
Florida					
Total	30	70,000	156,794	155,000	290,000
Over 1,000,000	1	290,000	290,000	290,000	290,000
500,000-1,000,000	4	180,000	192,875	183,250	225,000
250,000-499,999	7	165,000	186,589	187,004	203,549
100,000-249,999	8	122,500	150,371	146,320	193,000
50,000-99,999	4	120,000	134,251	134,637	147,730
25,000-49,999	4	70,000	98,405	101,309	121,000
10,000-24,999	2	75,600	75,600	75,600	75,600

continued

Appendix Table 8-A2 County Salaries by Population Group within States

State	No. reporting	Annual base salary			
		Minimum ($)	Mean ($)	Median ($)	Maximum ($)
Georgia					
Total	27	55,000	104,588	92,951	175,000
100,000-249,999	4	138,000	150,750	145,000	175,000
50,000-99,999	5	126,000	133,830	135,000	140,000
25,000-49,999	10	55,000	94,582	90,476	146,000
10,000-24,999	7	60,000	74,486	75,000	92,131
5,000-9,999	1	64,480	64,480	64,480	64,480
Hawaii					
Total	1	126,385	126,385	126,385	126,385
100,000-249,999	1	126,385	126,385	126,385	126,385
Illinois					
Total	9	57,632	125,908	120,000	240,000
500,000-1,000,000	1	240,000	240,000	240,000	240,000
250,000-499,999	1	160,000	160,000	160,000	160,000
100,000-249,999	4	110,000	129,400	126,300	155,000
50,000-99,999	1	57,632	57,632	57,632	57,632
25,000-49,999	1	79,000	79,000	79,000	79,000
10,000-24,999	1	78,937	78,937	78,937	78,937
Indiana					
Total	3	47,750	57,631	50,495	74,648
50,000-99,999	3	47,750	57,631	50,495	74,648
Iowa					
Total	2	91,534	134,005	134,005	176,475
100,000-249,000	1	176,475	176,475	176,475	176,475
25,000-49,999	1	91,534	91,534	91,534	91,534
Kansas					
Total	9	75,000	107,670	94,556	178,597
250,000-499,999	1	178,597	178,597	178,597	178,597
100,000-249,999	1	135,678	135,678	135,678	135,678
25,000-49,999	5	89,000	99,951	94,556	111,400
10,000-24,999	1	75,000	75,000	75,000	75,000
5,000-9,999	1	80,000	80,000	80,000	80,000
Kentucky					
Total	3	32,000	71,093	46,000	135,278
100,000-249,999	1	135,278	135,278	135,278	135,278
25,000-49,999	1	46,000	46,000	46,000	46,000
2,500-4,999	1	32,000	32,000	32,000	32,000
Louisiana					
Total	4	38,000	97,250	95,000	161,000
100,000-249,999	2	110,000	135,500	135,500	161,000
50,000-99,999	1	80,000	80,000	80,000	80,000
10,0002-4,999	1	38,000	38,000	38,000	38,000

continued

Appendix Table 8-A2   County Salaries by Population Group within States

State	No. reporting	Annual base salary			
		Minimum ($)	Mean ($)	Median ($)	Maximum ($)
Maine					
Total	5	54,000	73,305	66,475	107,266
250,000-499,999	1	107,266	107,266	107,266	107,266
25,000-49,999	3	58,885	68,419	66,475	79,898
Under 2,500	1	54,000	54,000	54,000	54,000
Maryland					
Total	8	100,000	138,628	137,500	193,000
500,000-1,000,000	1	193,000	193,000	193,000	193,000
100,000-249,999	4	105,000	134,006	128,812	173,400
25,000-49,999	2	100,000	122,500	122,500	145,000
10,000-24,999	1	135,000	135,000	135,000	135,000
Michigan					
Total	22	56,000	100,501	92,500	157,558
500,000-1,000,000	1	157,558	157,558	157,558	157,558
250,000-499,999	1	155,000	155,000	155,000	155,000
100,000-249,999	4	105,414	117,028	115,690	131,316
50,000-99,999	6	80,000	101,694	97,800	122,763
25,000-49,999	7	70,189	84,854	83,000	101,478
10,000-24,999	3	56,000	75,407	77,220	93,000
Minnesota					
Total	16	65,268	122,709	116,000	190,000
Over 1,000,000	1	190,000	190,000	190,000	190,000
100,000-249,999	3	160,000	163,919	164,756	167,000
50,000-99,999	3	105,000	120,380	109,000	147,139
25,000-49,999	4	105,602	116,577	116,000	128,128
10,000-24,999	4	65,268	90,503	90,371	116,000
5,000-9,999	1	86,000	86,000	86,000	86,000
Mississippi					
Total	3	79,483	116,879	135,000	136,154
25,000-49,999	2	79,483	107,242	107,242	135,000
10,000-24,999	1	136,154	136,154	136,154	136,154
Missouri					
Total	2	36,000	72,235	72,235	108,470
250,000-499,999	1	108,470	108,470	108,470	108,470
5,000-9,999	1	36,000	36,000	36,000	36,000
Montana					
Total	2	99,980	104,990	104,990	110,000
50,000-99,999	2	99,980	104,990	104,990	110,000
Nebraska					
Total	2	129,000	130,489	130,489	131,977
250,000-499,999	1	131,977	131,977	131,977	131,977
100,000-249,999	1	129,000	129,000	129,000	129,000

continued

Appendix Table 8-A2   County Salaries by Population Group within States

State	No. reporting	Annual base salary			
		Minimum ($)	Mean ($)	Median ($)	Maximum ($)
Nevada					
Total	3	120,265	175,101	201,781	203,258
Over 1,000,000	1	203,258	203,258	203,258	203,258
250,000-499,999	1	201,781	201,781	201,781	201,781
10,000-24,999	1	120,265	120,265	120,265	120,265
New Jersey					
Total	4	164,487	186,299	192,000	196,707
500,000-1,000,000	1	164,487	164,487	164,487	164,487
250,000-499,999	3	188,000	193,569	196,000	196,707
New Mexico					
Total	6	76,908	125,252	128,611	163,380
500,000-1,000,000	1	148,000	148,000	148,000	148,000
100,000-249,999	1	157,000	157,000	157,000	157,000
50,000-99,999	1	163,380	163,380	163,380	163,380
25,000-49,999	2	97,000	103,111	103,111	109,222
5,000-9,999	1	76,908	76,908	76,908	76,908
New York					
Total	13	89,000	109,051	108,000	131,167
100,000-249,999	2	116,667	123,917	123,917	131,167
50,000-99,999	7	94,744	110,678	108,000	130,000
25,000-49,999	3	89,000	95,597	91,590	106,200
10,000-24,999	1	108,300	108,300	108,300	108,300
North Carolina					
Total	40	61,200	131,947	128,498	239,000
500,000-1,000,000	1	239,000	239,000	239,000	239,000
250,000-499,999	3	169,645	183,548	183,000	198,000
100,000-249,999	12	115,000	161,897	161,171	220,000
50,000-99,999	11	92,319	116,228	116,004	138,000
25,000-49,999	7	71,400	105,184	104,651	130,571
10,000-24,999	6	61,200	81,368	81,158	100,000
Ohio					
Total	9	55,990	106,072	115,000	175,000
500,000-1,000,000	1	175,000	175,000	175,000	175,000
250,000-499,999	1	125,000	125,000	125,000	125,000
100,000-249,999	4	98,000	117,666	120,000	132,662
50,000-99,999	1	66,000	66,000	66,000	66,000
25,000-49,999	2	55,990	58,995	58,995	62,000
Oregon					
Total	9	76,234	125,887	130,449	152,000
250,000-499,999	2	152,000	152,000	152,000	152,000
100,000-249,999	2	143,000	144,500	144,500	146,000
50,000-99,999	1	128,340	128,340	128,340	128,340
25,000-49,999	2	76,234	98,387	98,387	120,540
10,000-24,999	2	108,421	120,490	120,490	132,558

continued

Appendix Table 8–A2   County Salaries by Population Group within States

State	No. reporting	Minimum ($)	Mean ($)	Median ($)	Maximum ($)
		|—————————— Annual base salary ——————————|			
Pennsylvania					
Total	7	64,000	97,831	94,000	140,000
500,000–1,000,000	1	140,000	140,000	140,000	140,000
250,000–499,999	2	110,000	117,297	117,297	124,594
100,000–249,999	2	64,000	79,000	79,000	94,000
50,000–99,999	2	70,221	76,111	76,111	82,000
South Carolina					
Total	12	68,000	120,917	113,000	180,000
250,000–499,999	2	151,500	165,750	165,750	180,000
100,000–249,999	3	107,000	124,083	130,000	135,250
50,000–99,999	4	103,000	121,000	113,000	155,000
25,000–49,999	1	68,000	68,000	68,000	68,000
10,000–24,999	2	92,358	97,628	97,628	102,897
South Dakota					
Total	1	73,286	73,286	73,286	73,286
10,000–24,999	1	73,286	73,286	73,286	73,286
Tennessee					
Total	2	108,470	122,410	122,410	136,350
500,000–1,000,000	1	136,350	136,350	136,350	136,350
250,000–499,999	1	108,470	108,470	108,470	108,470
Texas					
Total	5	52,191	125,776	65,207	233,000
Over 1,000,000	1	233,000	233,000	233,000	233,000
500,000–1,000,000	1	216,657	216,657	216,657	216,657
50,000–99,000	1	61,826	61,826	61,826	61,826
10,000–24,999	1	52,191	52,191	52,191	52,191
5,000–9,999	1	65,207	65,207	65,207	65,207
Utah					
Total	2	76,000	105,000	105,000	134,000
25,000–49,999	1	134,000	134,000	134,000	134,000
10,000–24,999	1	76,000	76,000	76,000	76,000
Virginia					
Total	39	60,000	130,752	125,557	269,847
Over 1,000,000	1	269,847	269,847	269,847	269,847
100,000–249,999	1	169,000	169,000	169,000	169,000
50,000–99,999	8	126,000	167,840	170,500	220,000
25,000–49,999	12	94,554	134,170	134,679	185,400
10,000–24,999	12	60,000	100,852	100,873	123,123
5,000–9,999	4	68,000	101,322	93,012	151,265
2,500–4,999	1	92,201	92,201	92,201	92,201

continued

Appendix Table 8-A2 County Salaries by Population Group within States

State	No. reporting	Annual base salary			
		Minimum ($)	Mean ($)	Median ($)	Maximum ($)
Washington					
Total	4	111,514	134,808	124,991	177,735
250,000-499,999	1	177,735	177,735	177,735	177,735
50,000-99,999	2	111,514	120,748	120,748	129,981
10,000-24,999	1	120,000	120,000	120,000	120,000
West Virginia					
Total	4	28,656	73,303	74,028	116,500
100,000-249,999	2	88,055	102,278	102,278	116,500
50,000-99,999	1	60,000	60,000	60,000	60,000
5,000-9,999	1	28,656	28,656	28,656	28,656
Wisconsin					
Total	16	89,000	111,715	99,427	165,376
100,000-249,999	2	144,891	155,134	155,134	165,376
50,000-99,999	3	113,000	136,500	136,500	160,000
25,000-49,999	7	91,660	101,074	97,465	115,000
10,000-24,999	4	89,000	91,077	90,111	94,120
Wyoming					
Total	1	120,000	120,000	120,000	120,000
10,000-24,999	1	120,000	120,000	120,000	120,000

9

Police and Fire Personnel, Salaries, and Expenditures for 2013

Evelina R. Moulder
ICMA

Continuing the trend identified in 2010 when police and fire departments, like other local government departments, saw their budgets reduced, police and fire expenditures in 2013 continue to be a concern in some communities. There is hope that as the housing market continues to strengthen, property tax revenues may slowly increase. In August 2013, the national median price rose 11.7% from a year ago.[1]

As Figure 9–1 shows, of the 299 municipalities that responded to the survey each year from 2009 to 2013, the average number of sworn police officers is comparatively high in 2009 and then decreases gradually but consistently through 2011. In 2012 and 2013, there is a gradual increase. For fire services, the decreases and increases are slight in the average number of staff.

The statistics in this annual article are not intended to be used for benchmarking, which requires that many factors be considered to identify localities of similar characteristics, such as population density, vulnerability to natural disasters, and the like. Rather, these statistics are meant to provide a general picture of police and fire personnel and expenditures for each year.

Methodology

The data in this research were collected from responses to ICMA's annual *Police and Fire Personnel, Salaries, and Expenditures* survey, which was mailed in February 2013 to 4,227 municipalities with populations of 10,000 or more (Table 9–1). A second survey was sent to those local governments that did not respond

SELECTED FINDINGS

The average entrance salaries are $45,664 for police and $40,887 for fire personnel. The average maximum salaries for police and fire personnel are $64,897 and $57,091, respectively.

The average maximum salary including longevity pay for police officers is $72,084; for fire personnel, it is $65,074. These salaries vary significantly by geographic division: For police and fire, East South-Central cities show the lowest average maximums. For police, the Mid-Atlantic and Pacific Coast cities show the highest. For fire, the Pacific Coast cities show the highest.

Average overtime expenditures are $517,520 for police and $527,235 for fire departments.

The average per capita total departmental expenditures are $224.22 for police and $136.04 for fire departments.

to the first. Respondents had a choice of completing and submitting the survey on the web or by mail. A total of 1,342 jurisdictions submitted surveys for an overall response rate of 32%, which is close to last year's response rate (33%), with a slightly smaller percentage of municipalities under 50,000 population responding in 2013.

Figure 9-1 Average Numbers of Sworn Police and Firefighters, 2009–2013

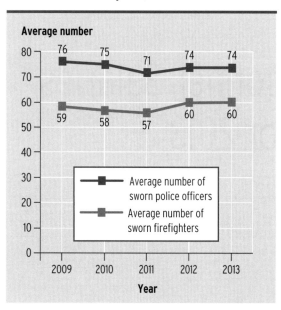

Table 9-1 Survey Response

Classification	No. of municipalities[a] surveyed (A)	Respondents No.	% of (A)
Total	4,227	1,342	32
Population group			
Over 1,000,000	9	4	44
500,000–1,000,000	25	5	20
250,000–499,999	44	16	36
100,000–249,999	236	81	34
50,000–99,999	549	169	31
25,000–49,999	1,029	315	31
10,000–24,999	2,335	750	32
Geographic region			
Northeast	1,101	234	21
North-Central	1,448	489	34
South	972	348	36
West	706	271	38
Geographic division			
New England	363	82	23
Mid-Atlantic	738	152	21
East North-Central	1,158	362	31
West North-Central	291	128	44
South Atlantic	442	183	41
East South-Central	195	44	23
West South-Central	334	120	36
Mountain	205	86	42
Pacific Coast	501	185	37

a   For a definition of terms, please see "Inside the *Year Book*," xxi–xxiv.

The survey response patterns are presented in Table 9–1 by population group, geographic region, and geographic division. The response pattern varies by population size, with a high of 44% in cities with a population over 1,000,000. By geographic division, the pattern reveals that Mid-Atlantic, New England, and East South-Central jurisdictions were the least likely to complete the questionnaire (all showing about 21%–23%), while South Atlantic, Mountain, and West North-Central jurisdictions were the most likely to do so (41%, 42%, and 44%, respectively).

Administration

Respondents were asked several questions about service provision and delivery. Eighty-eight percent of the jurisdictions responding to the 2013 survey indicated that they provide police services, and 79% reported that they provide fire services (not shown)—percentages that decreased in 2013 but had remained almost identical for several prior years. Twenty-one jurisdictions reported having a public safety department. To be counted among these respondents, a city had to report "public safety department" as the type of service for both police and fire (see the sidebar on page 115).

These data on cities that provide police and fire services do not necessarily mean that all these cities actually deliver each service. Six percent of jurisdictions reported contracting with another government for police service delivery (Figure 9–2); the highest percentage of cities reporting this arrangement is in the Pacific Coast division (20%) (not shown). Among the 151 cities that

do not provide police services, 137 answered the question about how the services *are* provided; of those, a majority (76), all of which are under 250,000 in population, reported that the county provides the service (not shown). Thirteen cities reported a regional police service; 6 reported a special district.

Of the cities that provide fire protection services, a majority (61%) reported having a full-time paid or a full-time and part-time paid fire department, 17% reported a combination of paid and volunteer fire personnel, 13% reported an all-volunteer fire department, and the remaining cities said they contract out for such services or provide them in some other way (Figure 9–2). Among the 278 cities that do not provide fire services, 258 provided information on how the services *are* provided, and of those,

Cities Reporting a Public Safety Department (Consolidated Police and Fire)

Ceres, CA	Oak Park, MI
Sunnyvale, CA	Mexico, MO
Steamboat Springs, CO	Sikeston, MO
Bainbridge, GA	Columbus, OH
Blackman Township, MI	Aiken, SC
East Grand Rapids, MI	Cayce, SC
Escanaba, MI	North Myrtle Beach, SC
Farmington, MI	Spartanburg, SC
Grand Haven, MI	Mitchell, SD
Gross Pointe Park, MI	San Benito, TX
Holland, MI	

50% reported that services are provided by a special district, and 21% indicated that the county provides the service (not shown). Regional fire services were reported by 9%.

Personnel

The average size of the full-time paid workforce for both police and fire departments is shown in Table 9–2. The data include both uniformed and civilian, or nonuniformed, personnel. The average number of total police department employees reported, 105, represents a decrease over the average number reported in 2012, which was 135. Using the average number of personnel per capita normalizes the data, and when the per capita per 1,000 population is calculated, the average drops slightly for police (from 2.38 in 2012 to 2.26 in 2013). As for fire personnel, the average number reported is 72, compared with 77 in 2012; and the average number of full-time paid personnel per capita per 1,000 population is 1.47, down slightly from 1.51 in 2012.

As with all averages in this article, these fluctuate depending on which cities report information each year. One difference this year is that the District of Columbia did not respond to the survey, although it responded last year. Because the District is home to federal buildings, including the White House and Congress, where protests, parades, and other activities occur, it requires higher levels of staffing than other municipalities in the population group 500,000–1,000,000. These different needs skew the staffing and expenditure data for the small number of cities (eight) reporting from that group. This year, only five cities in that population group responded, and the staffing levels are lower and in line with the other per capita staffing figures for cities.

Figure 9-2   Type of Service, 2013

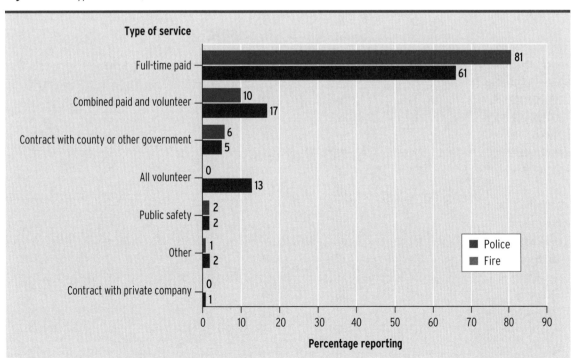

The average numbers of full-time police personnel in the other population categories in 2013 have decreased somewhat from the 2012 figures.

The patterns for fire departments are somewhat different from those for police departments (Table 9–2). Cities over 1,000,000 population and those with a population of 250,000–499,999 show higher average numbers of full-time personnel than in 2012. The remaining groups tend to show lower average numbers of full-time personnel. On the other hand, per capita figures per 1,000 population for full-time paid fire personnel are higher in 2013 than in 2012 for all population groups except those of 500,000–1,000,000 and those below 49,999.

The cross-sectional pattern by geographic division indicates that municipalities in the Mountain and West South-Central divisions have the highest average numbers of full-time police employees (213 and 200, respectively) and that those in the Mid-Atlantic and New England divisions have the lowest (48 and 50, respectively) (Table 9–2). Regarding full-time paid fire employees, the highest average numbers are also in the Mountain and West South-Central divisions (138 and

107, respectively), and the lowest average numbers are also in the Mid-Atlantic and New England divisions (42 and 41, respectively).

For police departments, the South Atlantic division shows the highest average number of full-time paid personnel per 1,000 population (3.12), while the lowest is in the Mid-Atlantic division (1.86). For fire, the highest average number of full-time paid personnel per 1,000 population is in the East South-Central division (2.19), followed by the South Atlantic division (2.01), while the lowest is in the West North-Central division (1.03), followed closely by the Mid-Atlantic division (1.06).

Figure 9–3 shows the changes over 10 years in the average numbers of full-time employees per 1,000 population for both services.

Table 9–3 presents the average numbers of full-time uniformed, or sworn, personnel in police and fire departments as of January 1, 2013. Among reporting cities, these numbers are 83 for police departments and 71 for fire departments, lower than the 2012 averages. For the three cities reporting with over 1,000,000 in population, the average number of sworn police personnel reported in 2013 is 3,025, which is lower than the 3,117 reported

Table 9-2 Full-Time Paid Personnel, 2013

	Police			Fire		
Classification	No. of cities reporting	Mean	Per capita per 1,000 population	No. of cities reporting	Mean	Per capita per 1,000 population
Total	1,046	105	2.26	782	72	1.47
Population group						
Over 1,000,000	3	3,765	2.85	2	1,998	1.53
500,000-1,000,000	3	1,830	2.66	4	983	1.46
250,000-499,999	15	950	2.78	14	524	1.52
100,000-249,999	59	322	2.13	54	185	1.26
50,000-99,999	131	143	2.07	118	96	1.41
25,000-49,999	251	77	2.23	194	51	1.48
10,000-24,999	584	36	2.30	396	24	1.51
Geographic division						
New England	76	50	2.09	61	41	1.60
Mid-Atlantic	107	48	1.86	35	42	1.06
East North-Central	244	67	2.04	203	51	1.34
West North-Central	114	68	2.07	86	43	1.03
South Atlantic	149	128	3.12	123	87	2.01
East South-Central	36	78	2.81	34	62	2.19
West South-Central	113	200	2.45	106	107	1.60
Mountain	74	213	2.30	56	138	1.24
Pacific Coast	133	120	1.91	78	82	1.18

Figure 9-3   Police and Fire Trends in Employees per 1,000 Population, 2002-2012

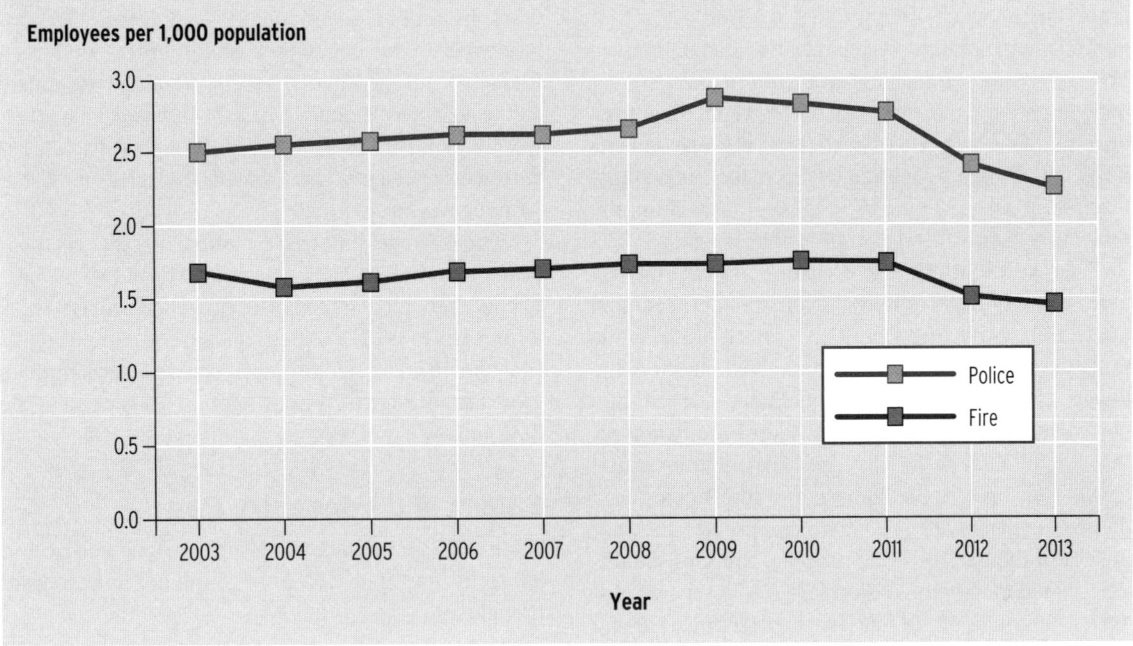

Table 9-3   Uniformed Sworn Personnel, 2013

	Police			Fire		
Classification	No. of cities reporting	Mean	Per capita per 1,000 population	No. of cities reporting	Mean	Per capita per 1,000 population
Total	1,004	83	1.81	749	71	1.42
Population group						
Over 1,000,000	3	3,025	2.31	3	1,736	1.33
500,000-1,000,000	3	1,456	2.10	4	913	1.34
250,000-499,999	15	741	2.16	14	492	1.43
100,000-249,999	59	237	1.57	54	164	1.12
50,000-99,999	128	106	1.55	119	91	1.33
25,000-49,999	243	61	1.76	188	50	1.43
10,000-24,999	553	30	1.91	367	24	1.48
Geographic division						
New England	71	43	1.79	58	41	1.55
Mid-Atlantic	96	44	1.64	30	49	1.15
East North-Central	233	56	1.69	186	51	1.33
West North-Central	111	55	1.67	80	43	1.04
South Atlantic	144	101	2.53	122	82	1.89
East South-Central	36	63	2.30	34	60	2.14
West South-Central	109	164	1.85	107	118	1.49
Mountain	74	155	1.71	55	122	1.13
Pacific Coast	130	85	1.37	77	71	1.06

in 2012. The figures per capita per 1,000 population show a high of 2.31 for the over-1,000,000 population group and a low of 1.55 for cities of 50,000–99,999.

It is important to recognize that fluctuations in averages within population groups from year to year depend on the population size of the responding jurisdictions. If, in a given year, most of the respondents have populations at the high end of the range—that is, closer to 249,999 than to 100,000—that will usually result in a higher average number of personnel.

The West South-Central division shows the highest average number of full-time sworn police personnel (164), followed by the Mountain division (155), while the Mid-Atlantic and New England divisions show the lowest (44 and 43, respectively) (Table 9–3). When per capita per 1,000 population figures are reviewed, the South Atlantic (2.53) and East South-Central (2.30) divisions are the highest, and the Pacific Coast division is the lowest (1.37), which was also the case in 2011 and 2012. For fire personnel, the West South-Central and Mountain divisions again show the highest average numbers of full-time sworn personnel (118 and 122, respectively), while the New England and West North-Central divisions show the lowest (41 and 43, respectively). As for per capita per 1,000 population figures, the East South-Central division shows the highest average number of uniformed fire personnel (2.14), followed by the South Atlantic division (1.89), while the Pacific Coast and West North-Central divisions show the lowest (1.06 and 1.04, respectively).

Staffing Requirements for Fire Personnel

All seven reporting jurisdictions with a population of 500,000 and over reported minimum staffing requirements, as did 78% of reporting jurisdictions overall (not shown). The responses by geographic division indicate that the majority of jurisdictions in all areas of the country except the Mid-Atlantic division have a minimum requirement, and that more than 90% of cities in the South Atlantic and East South-Central divisions have requirements or policies advising minimum staffing per shift.

The average minimum staffing for apparatus—pumpers, ladders, and other equipment—is shown in Table 9–4. For pumpers, ladders, and rescue units, the average minimum crew is generally higher among larger cities.

Hours Worked per Shift

Several questions were asked regarding the average number of hours worked per week and per shift for both services. The results, which are not displayed,

are as expected. Approximately 73% of jurisdictions reported that their police department employees work 40 hours a week, and 19% reported a 42-hour workweek. The remainder show other workweek hours. Fire departments had more varied responses to the workweek question: 36% indicated that their workweek is 56 hours, and only 6% reported a 40-hour workweek. Twenty-two percent reported a 50- to 54-hour workweek in 2013.

The average number of hours worked per shift also varies between the services. Thirty-two percent of the cities indicated that their police officers work 8-hour shifts, and 56% reported 10- or 12-hour shifts (not shown). Fire departments, on the other hand, are most likely to have 24-hour shifts (76%), close to the 78% in 2012.

Salary and Longevity Pay

Tables 9–5 through 9–8 present various salary and longevity pay data for full-time police officers and firefighters.

Minimum and Maximum Salaries

Tables 9–5 and 9–6 present detailed entrance and maximum salary data for police officers and firefighters, respectively, as well as the average number of years required for each to reach the maximum. In addition to the measures of central tendency (mean and median) for the salary data, the first and third quartiles are included to indicate the degree of dispersion. The annual base salaries are the entrance salaries paid to sworn police officers or firefighters within their first 12 months of employment. Each reported amount excludes uniform allowances, holiday pay, hazardous duty pay, and any other form of additional compensation. The maximum is the highest annual base salary paid to uniformed personnel who do not hold any promotional rank.

The median entrance salary for police personnel in 2013 is $44,764 and the mean is $45,664 (Table 9–5). The median maximum salary for police is $62,681 and the mean is $64,897. The entrance salaries for firefighters tend to be lower than those for police, with a median of $40,128 and a mean of $40,887 (Table 9–6). The maximum fire salary median and mean are $55,866 and $57,091, respectively. For both police and fire personnel, the mean is higher than the median for both entrance and maximum salaries. This indicates that some higher salaries are positively skewing the mean.

The highest average entrance salaries for both police and fire personnel are found in the Pacific Coast division. The highest average maximum salary for police personnel is found in the Mid-Atlantic division, followed by the Pacific Coast division. For fire

Table 9-4 Minimum Crew per Fire Apparatus, 2013

	Pumpers		Ladders		Rescue units	
Classification	No. of cities reporting	Average minimum crew	No. of cities reporting	Average minimum crew	No. of cities reporting	Average minimum crew
Total	528	3.1	481	3.0	392	2.5
Population group						
Over 1,000,000	3	4.0	3	4.3	2	2.0
500,000-1,000,000	4	4.0	4	4.0	4	3.3
250,000-499,999	12	3.7	12	3.7	8	2.9
100,000-249,999	46	3.3	45	3.3	31	2.5
50,000-99,999	101	3.3	100	3.1	72	2.4
25,000-49,999	132	3.0	120	2.9	94	2.3
10,000-24,999	230	3.0	197	2.9	181	2.6
Geographic division						
New England	34	3.0	32	2.6	27	2.4
Mid-Atlantic	41	3.4	39	3.3	35	3.2
East North-Central	105	3.0	95	2.8	88	2.4
West North-Central	54	3.3	49	3.2	43	2.7
South Atlantic	92	3.0	84	2.8	67	2.3
East South-Central	25	3.0	23	3.0	20	2.5
West South-Central	78	3.2	71	3.1	49	2.5
Mountain	37	3.4	35	3.4	21	2.3
Pacific Coast	62	3.0	53	3.1	42	2.3

Table 9-5 Police Officers' Annual Base Salary, January 1, 2013

	Entrance salary				Maximum salary				No. of years to reach maximum	
Classification	No. of cities reporting	Mean ($)	First quartile ($)	Median ($)	Third quartile ($)	No. of cities reporting	Mean ($)	First quartile ($)	Median ($)	Third quartile ($)	No. of cities reporting	Mean
Total	1,031	45,664	37,404	44,764	51,718	1,006	64,897	53,108	62,681	73,683	796	8
Population group												
Over 1,000,000	3	43,554	42,212	42,941	44,590	3	69,133	67,486	69,921	71,174	3	14
500,000-1,000,000	3	48,468	46,608	47,216	49,702	3	70,405	66,961	72,322	74,808	2	10
250,000-499,999	16	48,737	41,670	48,313	53,462	16	69,017	64,009	66,942	73,791	14	9
100,000-249,999	59	51,808	40,222	49,400	58,916	56	73,604	60,956	70,887	82,662	47	9
50,000-99,999	128	50,164	41,953	48,436	56,600	127	68,188	57,380	68,652	79,298	102	8
25,000-49,999	253	46,559	37,893	45,084	52,416	245	66,625	55,100	63,030	77,400	175	8
10,000-24,999	569	43,527	36,513	43,347	49,466	556	62,336	50,668	59,760	70,180	453	8
Geographic division												
New England	73	45,673	41,589	45,784	48,889	72	59,899	53,789	57,213	65,382	67	9
Mid-Atlantic	103	49,716	41,370	47,896	56,156	102	84,022	70,445	82,816	95,994	104	7
East North-Central	242	48,025	42,570	48,024	52,974	239	66,129	57,376	64,766	76,566	221	7
West North-Central	111	41,001	35,277	41,891	45,940	108	56,450	48,238	56,652	64,829	84	8
South Atlantic	147	36,541	32,459	35,556	39,625	140	59,287	48,049	54,386	61,894	54	12
East South-Central	37	31,984	28,853	32,261	35,447	34	46,963	39,358	48,122	52,714	27	14
West South-Central	114	39,999	33,912	39,999	45,498	108	54,539	45,223	53,546	63,919	77	10
Mountain	69	44,596	37,447	43,597	50,500	70	60,471	54,604	61,190	71,849	50	10
Pacific Coast	135	61,185	52,122	59,750	68,133	133	78,811	66,456	77,136	87,396	112	5

Table 9-6 Firefighters' Annual Base Salary, January 1, 2013

Classification	Entrance salary					Maximum salary					No. of years to reach maximum	
	No. of cities reporting	Mean ($)	First quartile ($)	Median ($)	Third quartile ($)	No. of cities reporting	Mean ($)	First quartile ($)	Median ($)	Third quartile ($)	No. of cities reporting	Mean
Total	744	40,887	33,397	40,128	48,052	720	57,091	46,777	55,866	65,704	547	8
Population group												
Over 1,000,000	3	46,567	44,626	46,312	48,380	3	64,843	62,454	65,532	67,576	3	15
500,000-1,000,000	4	45,807	43,943	45,619	47,483	4	65,884	61,398	65,800	70,286	3	9
250,000-499,999	13	45,755	40,778	47,653	50,834	14	64,322	59,732	64,316	68,365	12	9
100,000-249,999	51	47,931	38,888	48,944	54,124	50	65,839	58,801	63,658	73,359	42	8
50,000-99,999	113	45,728	38,000	44,084	52,248	111	63,344	54,508	62,289	71,960	87	8
25,000-49,999	188	41,863	34,249	40,216	47,567	182	58,912	50,384	56,641	66,266	128	8
10,000-24,999	372	37,689	31,287	37,833	44,278	356	52,534	42,056	50,898	60,594	272	8
Geographic division												
New England	60	42,649	37,375	43,446	47,119	59	56,077	49,244	55,184	58,538	52	8
Mid-Atlantic	33	37,600	35,951	39,190	42,100	31	62,980	55,160	63,658	78,773	29	8
East North-Central	188	44,845	40,038	43,872	50,832	183	60,705	51,908	60,663	68,654	163	6
West North-Central	71	34,990	30,156	35,643	43,958	72	51,628	41,739	50,290	57,769	58	8
South Atlantic	122	32,560	28,812	32,514	34,958	116	49,501	43,345	48,664	55,789	41	12
East South-Central	36	31,381	27,452	32,064	34,519	33	45,795	38,313	48,039	52,561	25	15
West South-Central	107	38,385	32,092	37,852	44,092	99	51,840	42,816	52,447	61,310	72	9
Mountain	49	41,268	36,521	41,160	46,747	49	58,757	53,280	58,711	66,156	37	9
Pacific Coast	78	57,358	49,899	56,526	63,110	78	73,771	65,386	73,674	82,998	70	5

personnel, the highest average maximum salary is in the Pacific Coast division. The lowest average entrance and maximum salaries for both police personnel and firefighters are found in the East South-Central division. For both services, the difference between the highest and lowest average entrance salaries among the geographic divisions is substantial: $29,201 for police and $25,977 for fire. The difference between the highest and lowest average maximum salaries among the geographic divisions for police is $37,059, compared with $27,976 for firefighters.

For both police and fire services, an average of eight years of service is required to reach the maximum salary—identical to 2012.

Longevity Pay

Longevity pay is defined as compensation beyond the regular maximum salary based on number of years of service. Longevity serves as an economic incentive to decrease employee turnover and reward those employees who have already achieved the maximum salary and now have limited opportunities for promo-

tion. Longevity pay can be administered in several ways: a flat dollar amount, a percentage of the base salary, a percentage of the maximum pay, or a step increase in the basic salary plan.

Tables 9-7 and 9-8 show a range of longevity pay data for police and firefighter personnel, respectively. The tables cover whether personnel can receive longevity pay, the maximum salary they can receive including longevity pay, and the average number of years of service that is required for them to receive longevity pay.

Sixty percent of all police departments reporting have a system that awards longevity pay to their personnel (Table 9-7). The West South-Central and Mid-Atlantic divisions show the highest percentages of cities with longevity pay for police personnel (88% and 89%, respectively).

The average maximum salary including longevity pay for police officers is $72,084. The figures range from a low of $68,240 for cities with populations of 10,000–24,999 to a high of $94,709 for cities with populations of 100,000–249,999. Geographic divisions show

Table 9-7 Longevity Pay for Police Officers, January 1, 2013

Classification	No. of cities reporting (A)	Personnel can receive longevity pay				Maximum salary including longevity pay					No. of years of service to receive longevity pay	
		Yes		No		No. of cities reporting	Mean ($)	First quartile ($)	Median ($)	Third quartile ($)	No. of cities reporting	Mean
		No.	% of (A)	No.	% of (A)							
Total	1,045	627	60	418	40	479	72,084	57,552	68,057	81,654	617	6
Population group												
Over 1,000,000	3	3	100	0	0	3	83,034	73,774	76,426	88,991	3	3
500,000-1,000,000	3	2	67	1	33	2	76,158	74,990	76,158	77,325	2	4
250,000-499,999	16	10	63	6	38	9	68,970	68,194	70,779	73,399	11	8
100,000-249,999	59	35	59	24	41	29	94,709	66,130	82,577	100,169	34	7
50,000-99,999	129	74	57	55	43	61	77,138	64,578	74,931	86,384	73	7
25,000-49,999	254	147	58	107	42	112	72,385	57,671	66,145	82,038	144	6
10,000-24,999	581	356	61	225	39	263	68,240	55,028	64,927	77,707	350	6
Geographic division												
New England	76	53	70	23	30	44	64,134	57,234	61,884	69,768	52	7
Mid-Atlantic	111	99	89	12	11	75	91,084	75,136	87,156	100,476	92	6
East North-Central	244	166	68	78	32	134	68,922	58,976	66,562	79,516	167	6
West North-Central	111	56	51	55	50	44	65,816	57,378	64,994	74,397	57	6
South Atlantic	147	55	37	92	63	37	64,648	49,806	59,077	75,335	49	6
East South-Central	40	19	48	21	53	12	48,223	42,481	49,594	54,220	20	6
West South-Central	111	98	88	13	12	61	64,317	47,863	57,138	66,598	97	2
Mountain	73	22	30	51	70	17	67,340	61,377	68,505	73,399	22	5
Pacific Coast	132	59	45	73	55	55	85,545	70,706	85,428	98,004	61	11

a clear disparity in this regard. Once again, cities in the East South-Central division show the lowest average maximum at $48,223, while the highest average maximums are $91,084 for Mid-Atlantic and $85,545 for Pacific Coast jurisdictions. Cost of living is certainly a factor to consider. The median home prices in the central United States are much lower than they are on the East and West Coasts.

The longevity pay patterns for firefighters (Table 9–8) show that 56% of jurisdictions overall reported longevity pay for fire personnel, including 88% of jurisdictions in the West South-Central division (the high) and 34% of jurisdictions in the Mountain and 39% in the Pacific Coast divisions (the low).

The average maximum salary with longevity pay for firefighters is $65,074. Among population groups, the 30 cities reporting with populations 100,000–249,999 show the highest average maximum salary with longevity pay ($89,643). Geographically, Pacific Coast jurisdictions show the highest average maximum salary with longevity pay ($87,177), and East

South-Central communities again show the lowest ($46,754).

Overall, the length of service required for both police and firefighters to receive longevity pay is six years, which is almost identical to the numbers reported every year since 2006. However, the number of years varies somewhat within the classification categories. In the Pacific Coast division, for example, both groups of personnel serve a well-above-average number of years (11 for police and 11 for fire) to qualify for longevity pay.

Expenditures

Respondents were asked to provide expenditure (not budget) figures for their police and fire departments' most recently completed fiscal year. The items include salaries and wages for all department personnel, contributions for employee benefits, capital outlays, and all other departmental expenditures. Average expenditures are presented in Tables 9–9 through 9–16. Per capita expenditures are shown in addition to average

Table 9-8   Longevity Pay for Firefighters, January 1, 2013

	Personnel can receive longevity pay				Maximum salary including longevity pay					No. of years of service to receive longevity pay	
	No. of cities reporting (A)	Yes		No		No. of cities reporting	Mean ($)	First quartile ($)	Median ($)	Third quartile ($)	No. of cities reporting	Mean
Classification		No.	% of (A)	No.	% of (A)							
Total	830	463	56	367	44	363	65,074	52,170	61,838	73,400	465	6
Population group												
Over 1,000,000	3	3	100	0	0	3	78,784	70,176	70,821	83,410	3	4
500,000-1,000,000	4	3	75	1	25	3	74,649	69,878	70,304	77,246	3	7
250,000-499,999	14	9	64	5	36	9	66,327	61,434	68,505	69,565	9	6
100,000-249,999	54	33	61	21	39	30	89,643	62,279	70,278	90,222	33	6
50,000-99,999	119	72	61	47	40	59	71,238	61,192	70,042	80,074	69	5
25,000-49,999	198	111	56	87	44	95	65,520	54,085	62,113	75,166	113	7
10,000-24,999	438	232	53	206	47	164	57,609	46,741	55,570	66,654	235	5
Geographic division												
New England	68	47	69	21	31	36	61,109	53,082	57,278	67,116	46	8
Mid-Atlantic	54	24	44	30	56	19	69,857	58,874	66,023	81,961	24	6
East North-Central	211	141	67	70	33	118	66,033	55,904	64,866	73,456	144	7
West North-Central	90	37	41	53	59	29	60,823	52,543	56,637	63,883	42	7
South Atlantic	120	48	40	72	60	37	58,762	45,919	54,181	66,277	45	6
East South-Central	39	19	49	20	51	13	46,754	39,563	48,967	52,252	20	7
West South-Central	109	96	88	13	12	63	63,075	45,462	56,427	65,070	96	2
Mountain	56	19	34	37	66	17	63,564	62,599	67,675	72,995	16	6
Pacific Coast	83	32	39	51	61	31	87,177	75,625	83,745	97,542	32	11

expenditures. Again, per capita presentations are useful because they normalize the information.

Salaries and Wages

Part of ICMA's process of reviewing survey results is to design logic checks that will identify problematic values. One logic check is that total expenditures for salaries and wages must be greater than the minimum salary for police (or fire) sworn personnel multiplied by the number of sworn personnel reported. For those jurisdictions reporting total expenditures for salaries and wages below that amount, the total amount of salary and wage expenditures was removed.

Table 9–9 shows the average per capita expenditure for civilian and uniformed police personnel in 2013 to be $153.06, a slight decrease from 2012. As population decreases, average per capita expenditures also generally decrease. The exception here is for cities with a population of 250,000–499,999, where the average per capita is $220.29. This is in contrast to 2012, when the population group with the highest

average per capita was that of 500,000–1,000,000. The cities responding in 2012 differed from those responding in 2013 in those population groups, which probably explains some of the difference.

Overall, the spread of average per capita salary and wage expenditures among population groups is much greater for police departments than for fire departments ($70.37 vs. $35.51). The average per capita police expenditures show a low of $149.92 in cities of 25,000–49,999 in population and a high of $220.29 in cities of 250,000–499,999 in population (Table 9–9). For firefighters, the average per capita expenditures range from a low of $81.09 in cities with populations of 250,000–499,999 to a high of $108.95 in cities with populations of 50,000–99,999.

Geographically, Pacific Coast jurisdictions show the highest average per capita salary and wage expenditures for police personnel ($174.47) and for firefighters ($136.93). Cities in the West North-Central and East South-Central divisions show the lowest for police ($125.49 and $125.59, respectively). The West

Table 9-9 Expenditures for Salaries and Wages (Civilian and Uniformed), 2013

	Police			Fire		
Classification	No. of cities reporting	Mean ($)	Per capita ($)	No. of cities reporting	Mean ($)	Per capita ($)
Total	951	6,732,045	153.06	749	3,917,385	95.32
Population group						
Over 1,000,000	0	0	0	0	0	0
500,000-1,000,000	3	130,748,748	185.61	1	42,870,489	73.44
250,000-499,999	13	76,671,503	220.29	6	27,827,974	81.09
100,000-249,999	54	24,321,034	156.50	47	14,159,866	95.60
50,000-99,999	115	10,658,254	153.61	110	7,551,719	108.95
25,000-49,999	220	5,208,968	149.92	173	3,752,813	106.27
10,000-24,999	546	2,432,585	152.09	412	1,404,960	87.32
Geographic division						
New England	70	3,915,894	153.66	63	3,009,498	107.08
Mid-Atlantic	98	3,982,441	164.69	43	2,492,886	65.16
East North-Central	227	5,147,758	151.80	198	2,936,869	99.85
West North-Central	105	4,478,419	125.49	87	2,021,948	53.22
South Atlantic	135	6,859,421	171.62	114	4,284,365	105.83
East South-Central	35	3,469,995	125.59	34	3,009,799	107.72
West South-Central	100	9,804,123	133.51	90	4,355,011	88.11
Mountain	63	12,064,713	151.21	51	6,710,259	85.15
Pacific Coast	118	11,110,571	174.47	69	8,043,394	136.93

North-Central division shows the lowest average per capita for fire personnel ($53.22).

Social Security and Retirement Benefits

The average expenditures for municipal contributions to federal Social Security and other employee retirement programs are reported in Table 9–10. These expenditures are for both uniformed and civilian personnel. The table shows combined retirement and Social Security contributions because some states opt out of Social Security programs for local government employees, relying instead on employee-sponsored retirement programs. Zeros have been removed from the calculations because although zero is a legitimate answer, it skews the averages. There is always extensive variation in these reported amounts, which often do not seem realistic in relation to the number of employees.

The average per capita expenditure for employee Social Security and retirement benefits for police departments in 2013 ($33.70) is almost identical to the 2012 amount ($33.87). Among the population groups, the highest average police per capita expenditure for Social Security and retirement ($49.71) is for the over-1,000,000 population group. Geographically, the highest average police department per capita expenditure for these benefits is found in the Pacific Coast division ($50.98); the lowest is in the West North-Central division ($21.72).

The average per capita expenditure for employee Social Security and retirement benefits reported for fire departments in 2013 is $22.38 (Table 9–10), compared with $22.24 in 2012. The per capita amounts fluctuate somewhat among the population groups. Among the geographic divisions the fluctuation is more pronounced. The highest average fire department per capita expenditure for Social Security and retirement benefits is in the Pacific Coast division ($32.36), and the lowest is again in the West North-Central division ($11.12).

Health, Hospitalization, Disability, and Life Insurance

Table 9–11 shows the average total municipal contributions for health, hospitalization, disability, and life insurance programs. The mean per capita expenditures for 2013 are almost identical to last year's for police,

Table 9-10 Total Municipal Contributions to Social Security and State/City-Administered Employee Retirement Systems, 2013

	Police			Fire		
Classification	No. of cities reporting	Mean ($)	Per capita ($)	No. of cities reporting	Mean ($)	Per capita ($)
Total	906	1,785,202	33.70	708	1,310,029	22.38
Population group						
Over 1,000,000	3	65,604,895	49.71	3	34,758,957	26.59
500,000-1,000,000	3	26,107,744	37.87	4	19,232,557	28.88
250,000-499,999	13	14,890,451	43.56	12	8,910,586	26.09
100,000-249,999	53	6,223,282	40.70	47	3,866,356	24.91
50,000-99,999	117	2,714,976	38.11	109	1,848,434	26.50
25,000-49,999	209	1,174,036	33.24	165	828,095	23.32
10,000-24,999	508	503,582	31.76	368	324,818	20.18
Geographic division						
New England	46	955,933	30.98	36	790,791	22.11
Mid-Atlantic	86	946,673	37.44	31	1,086,971	23.50
East North-Central	216	1,107,059	33.78	187	947,385	24.96
West North-Central	102	879,284	21.72	85	561,568	11.12
South Atlantic	138	1,433,861	36.33	115	1,302,154	26.79
East South-Central	35	784,120	27.78	33	722,373	24.66
West South-Central	105	2,978,896	25.15	102	1,800,494	16.13
Mountain	63	3,706,415	29.87	48	2,567,410	18.10
Pacific Coast	115	3,405,126	50.98	71	2,253,097	32.36

and there is an increase to $18.57 for fire, above the 2012 amount of $17.84.

Total Personnel Expenditures

Table 9–12 shows the total personnel expenditures for civilian and uniformed employees for both police and fire services. These data represent total salaries and wages; contributions for federal Social Security and other retirement programs; and contributions to health, hospitalization, disability, and life insurance programs. To be included in this table, the jurisdiction had to provide each of these expenditures. Those that reported an amount of zero were excluded from the table. Again, although zero is a legitimate amount, it negatively skews the average.

For fire services in particular, the workforce composition affects personnel expenditures. Departments that rely heavily on volunteers have significantly lower personnel expenditures than those that use paid staff. The amounts reported are for all departments, regardless of whether they rely on volunteers.

The mean per capita personnel expenditures are $206.28 for police and $126.86 for fire. For police departments, the per capita figures are generally lower among the smaller population groups. One exception is the population group over 1,000,000, in which only three cities reported and the average per capita is $81.00. Among the geographic divisions, the high for police is in the Pacific Coast division ($246.73), and the low is in the West North-Central division ($166.63).

For fire departments, the mean per capita personnel expenditures vary among population groups, from a low of $43.42 in the cities reporting with over 1,000,000 population to a high of $146.48 in cities with a population of 50,000–99,999. Geographically, the average per capita high is seen in the Pacific Coast division ($181.62), and the low is again seen in the West North-Central ($72.57) division.

Overtime Expenditures

At the request of some local governments, a new question was added in the 2010 survey to address overtime expenditures (Table 9–13). The reported 2013 per capita average overtime expenditures are $10.50 for police departments and $8.96 for fire departments. Overtime expenditures for fire personnel show more

Table 9-11 Total Municipal Contributions for Health, Hospitalization, Disability, and Life Insurance Programs, 2013

Classification	Police No. of cities reporting	Mean ($)	Per capita ($)	Fire No. of cities reporting	Mean ($)	Per capita ($)
Total	883	1,358,393	28.58	699	946,291	18.57
Population group						
Over 1,000,000	3	42,093,144	31.29	3	22,652,254	16.82
500,000-1,000,000	3	25,186,965	34.98	4	16,176,739	23.38
250,000-499,999	12	11,843,992	33.78	11	5,752,540	16.56
100,000-249,999	51	4,001,084	26.56	43	2,373,371	15.69
50,000-99,999	118	1,915,715	27.71	109	1,353,695	19.44
25,000-49,999	204	977,797	28.09	162	675,426	19.45
10,000-24,999	492	459,172	29.03	367	290,162	18.29
Geographic division						
New England	46	973,793	35.79	37	859,408	26.90
Mid-Atlantic	84	695,056	34.18	36	358,997	15.25
East North-Central	210	1,111,507	31.70	187	844,064	21.43
West North-Central	99	707,237	21.25	81	444,898	10.91
South Atlantic	136	1,081,703	26.57	113	740,331	18.74
East South-Central	34	651,943	24.09	33	556,407	20.76
West South-Central	99	2,181,497	20.87	97	1,272,116	13.69
Mountain	60	2,544,302	26.06	46	2,019,379	15.65
Pacific Coast	115	2,216,915	33.90	69	1,515,269	24.56

variation than those for police among population groups, and both services show noticeable variation among the geographic divisions.

As with all police and fire expenditures, it is important to consider population density and other factors before making definitive comparisons. A community with high manufacturing activity may pose a higher risk for fire, resulting in more overtime, and a community may have high levels of gang activity that influence the need for police overtime. In addition, for some communities, paying overtime is less costly than hiring additional personnel because of the cost of benefits.

Capital Outlays

Table 9-14 (see page 128) shows departmental expenditures for capital outlays. These outlays include the purchase and replacement of equipment, the purchase of land and existing structures, and construction. The amounts include the capital expenditures within individual departmental budgets as well as those expenditures included in citywide capital budgets designated for departmental programs or equipment.

Total capital outlay expenditures may fluctuate dramatically from one year to the next for both police and fire departments. This is because the cost of individual capital projects varies widely among communities as well as within the same community over time. Whereas the number of employees, which relates to population size, determines personnel expenditures, fire equipment such as pumpers will cost the same regardless of the size of the community. Thus, the per capita cost for the pumpers will necessarily be higher among cities with fewer people.

The 2013 average municipal expenditures for capital outlays per capita are $8.49 for police, an increase from the $7.62 shown in 2012, and $10.19 for fire, which is above the 2012 figure of $7.93. For police, the highest average capital outlay per capita ($11.41) is in the population group 25,000–49,999. Geographically, the highest average capital outlay per capita for police services is in the West North-Central division ($13.68); for fire services, the highest are in the East South-Central and Mid-Atlantic divisions ($15.54 and $15.32, respectively). For police services, the lowest average capital outlay per capita is in the Pacific Coast

Table 9-12 Total Personnel Expenditures, 2013

	Police			Fire		
Classification	No. of cities reporting	Mean ($)	Per capita ($)	No. of cities reporting	Mean ($)	Per capita ($)
Total	976	9,445,727	206.28	790	5,725,417	126.86
Population group						
Over 1,000,000	3	107,698,038	81.00	3	57,411,211	43.42
500,000-1,000,000	3	182,043,457	258.47	4	46,126,918	70.62
250,000-499,999	13	102,494,869	295.03	12	28,097,735	81.81
100,000-249,999	57	32,407,457	209.87	50	18,985,748	126.77
50,000-99,999	122	14,503,325	208.15	116	10,170,010	146.48
25,000-49,999	223	7,133,709	204.75	177	5,058,142	143.40
10,000-24,999	555	3,261,124	204.42	428	1,880,528	117.09
Geographic division						
New England	70	5,184,000	197.53	62	4,030,079	137.70
Mid-Atlantic	98	5,408,957	226.85	52	2,957,963	78.45
East North-Central	231	7,104,253	209.57	205	4,470,737	138.76
West North-Central	105	5,999,403	166.63	89	2,917,747	72.57
South Atlantic	140	9,078,615	227.11	117	6,169,425	147.55
East South-Central	36	4,751,669	171.86	35	4,129,512	147.47
West South-Central	105	14,372,996	171.99	102	6,852,908	106.89
Mountain	68	16,856,458	190.76	54	10,339,820	109.84
Pacific Coast	123	15,915,301	246.73	74	11,074,562	181.62

division ($4.52); for fire, it is in the New England division ($5.45).

Other Expenditures

Table 9–15 (see page 129) presents the data for all other departmental expenditures not accounted for in the previous tables. These include ongoing maintenance, utilities, fuel, supplies, and other miscellaneous items. The average per capita expenditures reported for 2013 are $37.95 for police, an increase from 2012, and $25.10 for fire, also an increase from the 2012 average per capita expenditure.

Total Department Expenditures

Table 9–16 (see page 130) shows the combined personnel, capital outlay, and all other departmental expenditures. The average per capita figures for 2013 are $224.22 and $136.04 for police and fire, respectively—decreases for both services from totals reported in 2012.

Total expenditures are not included for those localities in which the sum of expenditures reported (salaries and wages, employee benefit contributions, capital outlays, and other expenses) differs from the amount reported for total expenditures by more than $100. Most of the variations were by thousands of dollars. This same logic has been applied each year for the analysis.

Not all cities include the same expenditures in their budgets. Of the 685 jurisdictions providing information about services included in the fire department budget, 53% cited ambulance personnel and 54% cited ambulance equipment (not shown). Emergency medical technicians (EMTs) were included by 89%, and EMT equipment was included by 90%. This does not necessarily mean, however, that these are the only jurisdictions that provide EMT and ambulance services; these are just the cities that reported having these services in the fire department budget.

Table 9-13 Total Overtime Expenditures, 2013

	Police			Fire		
Classification	No. of cities reporting	Mean ($)	Per capita ($)	No. of cities reporting	Mean ($)	Per capita ($)
Total	945	517,520	10.50	684	527,235	8.96
Population group						
Over 1,000,000	3	10,379,452	7.79	3	11,748,695	9.14
500,000-1,000,000	3	7,744,313	10.90	4	8,341,048	12.96
250,000-499,999	13	5,845,905	16.95	12	4,125,863	12.44
100,000-249,999	54	1,872,176	12.27	48	1,408,307	8.79
50,000-99,999	117	773,631	10.89	108	736,319	10.44
25,000-49,999	219	374,173	10.88	166	292,053	8.51
10,000-24,999	536	158,828	9.95	343	136,753	8.56
Geographic division						
New England	70	404,383	16.88	53	495,370	17.22
Mid-Atlantic	92	313,566	12.12	26	732,449	8.48
East North-Central	221	382,002	10.99	175	261,127	7.83
West North-Central	104	238,921	6.51	68	112,987	3.64
South Atlantic	135	337,620	7.82	112	269,258	5.57
East South-Central	35	213,485	7.74	33	176,185	7.48
West South-Central	103	783,071	7.60	99	763,891	6.54
Mountain	65	867,148	8.95	47	1,075,504	8.76
Pacific Coast	120	1,104,659	15.28	71	1,405,709	20.37

Conclusion

This report has examined the cross-sectional and longitudinal patterns found in the responses to ICMA's annual *Police and Fire Personnel, Salaries, and Expenditures* survey. Most of the changes over time in police and fire employment and expenditures have been small, incremental shifts. It is not uncommon for one year to show increases and the next to show decreases in average expenditures.

Although using per capita figures instead of absolute numbers reduces the skew of the data, any analysis of the reported changes must control for population size of the responding jurisdictions. Another influential factor is a significant difference in the number reporting in any population group. Any major increase or decrease in that number can affect the average.

Notes

1 RealEstateABC.com, "Existing Home Sales—Report" (last updated October 21, 2013), realestateabc.com/outlook.htm (accessed November 13, 2013).

Table 9-14 Municipal Expenditures for Capital Outlays, 2013

Classification	Police			Fire		
	No. of cities reporting	Mean ($)	Per capita ($)	No. of cities reporting	Mean ($)	Per capita ($)
Total	812	306,036	8.49	603	375,995	10.19
Population group						
Over 1,000,000	3	4,125,168	2.87	2	7,532,478	6.11
500,000–1,000,000	2	5,352,954	6.82	3	4,242,440	5.57
250,000–499,999	9	2,393,164	6.94	9	2,501,140	7.37
100,000–249,999	42	633,008	4.25	38	706,487	4.92
50,000–99,999	108	361,722	5.22	90	489,022	7.64
25,000–49,999	191	400,462	11.41	152	296,994	8.47
10,000–24,999	457	135,100	8.50	309	195,537	12.58
Geographic division						
New England	56	154,145	6.90	41	166,096	5.45
Mid-Atlantic	77	104,322	5.68	36	270,609	15.32
East North-Central	187	304,618	8.78	168	302,073	9.60
West North-Central	100	322,033	13.68	72	236,292	9.83
South Atlantic	119	297,592	9.14	88	301,684	9.52
East South-Central	36	200,098	8.04	31	358,810	15.54
West South-Central	84	425,755	8.21	78	756,959	10.87
Mountain	59	624,732	9.59	40	473,072	11.15
Pacific Coast	94	291,807	4.52	49	546,425	8.91

Table 9-15   All Other Department Expenditures, 2013

Classification	Police			Fire		
	No. of cities reporting	Mean ($)	Per capita ($)	No. of cities reporting	Mean ($)	Per capita ($)
Total	922	1,880,007	37.95	749	1,167,318	25.10
Population group						
Over 1,000,000	3	56,670,262	42.60	3	27,795,620	19.93
500,000-1,000,000	3	36,080,519	51.68	4	13,279,170	20.17
250,000-499,999	12	13,170,780	37.91	11	8,285,087	22.50
100,000-249,999	53	6,383,071	44.61	47	2,973,361	20.85
50,000-99,999	116	3,106,354	44.42	105	1,690,591	25.06
25,000-49,999	213	1,498,332	42.77	172	1,037,505	30.45
10,000-24,999	522	535,020	33.77	407	370,935	23.50
Geographic division						
New England	68	509,154	22.29	60	404,582	17.54
Mid-Atlantic	92	363,703	19.05	58	325,066	15.53
East North-Central	212	1,189,884	34.86	184	939,932	29.31
West North-Central	101	1,104,669	29.66	85	562,524	18.78
South Atlantic	135	1,632,541	45.13	111	1,342,180	27.54
East South-Central	35	1,293,081	56.16	34	766,118	32.84
West South-Central	99	3,321,000	28.59	96	1,220,934	18.31
Mountain	67	3,994,500	41.49	52	2,979,223	23.12
Pacific Coast	113	3,888,451	67.87	69	2,366,245	39.48

Table 9-16 Total Departmental Expenditures, 2013

Classification	Police			Fire		
	No. of cities reporting	Mean ($)	Per capita ($)	No. of cities reporting	Mean ($)	Per capita ($)
Total	358	12,478,714	224.22	334	9,827,370	136.04
Population group						
Over 1,000,000	3	433,974,186	326.90	3	232,561,823	175.07
500,000-1,000,000	2	272,280,817	356.18	3	140,004,394	197.89
250,000-499,999	1	85,882,305	235.01	9	70,006,276	200.91
100,000-249,999	17	29,604,698	223.93	16	26,068,360	171.78
50,000-99,999	50	13,779,051	201.68	42	10,750,530	153.46
25,000-49,999	77	8,267,834	237.18	60	4,711,323	137.73
10,000-24,999	208	3,394,988	222.06	201	1,906,920	124.64
Geographic division						
New England	25	4,905,972	190.54	25	2,915,028	120.09
Mid-Atlantic	34	4,387,469	213.64	39	1,787,324	68.72
East North-Central	77	9,142,696	225.84	73	8,472,087	157.97
West North-Central	30	4,663,762	214.54	26	4,947,322	89.33
South Atlantic	69	9,097,800	258.11	61	7,902,710	174.63
East South-Central	18	5,785,690	199.70	23	4,452,444	163.81
West South-Central	44	32,415,601	205.11	46	20,554,163	129.62
Mountain	21	32,343,974	192.73	17	30,029,551	90.76
Pacific Coast	40	12,856,386	248.54	24	14,675,083	165.64

Directories

1

Directory Tables

Directory 1 in this section of the *Year Book* provides the names and websites of U.S. state municipal leagues; provincial and territorial associations and unions in Canada; state agencies for community affairs; provincial and territorial agencies for local affairs in Canada; U.S. municipal management associations; international municipal management associations; state associations of counties; and U.S. councils of governments recognized by ICMA. In all cases, where there is no website available, we have provided the name of the president/permanent officer/executive director and all contact information for that individual.

U.S. State Municipal Leagues

Directory Table 1–1 shows 49 state leagues of municipalities serving 49 states. (Hawaii does not have a league.) Information, which was obtained from the National League of Cities (nlc.org), includes league address and website. State municipal leagues provide a wide range of research, consulting, training, publications, and legislative representation services for their clients.

Provincial and Territorial Associations and Unions in Canada

Directory 1–2 shows the websites of the 16 associations and unions serving the 12 provinces and territories of Canada. Information was obtained from the Federation of Canadian Municipalities (fcm.org).

State Agencies for Community Affairs

Directory 1–3 shows the addresses and websites of 48 agencies for community affairs in the United States, as well as that for Puerto Rico. Information was obtained from the Council of State Community Development Agencies (coscda.org). These agencies of state governments offer a variety of research, financial information,

and coordination services for cities and other local governments.

Provincial and Territorial Agencies for Local Affairs in Canada

Directory 1–4 shows the addresses, phone numbers, fax numbers, and websites of the agencies for local affairs serving the 12 provinces and territories of Canada. Information was obtained from the Ontario Ministry of Municipal Affairs and Housing (mah.gov.on.ca).

U.S. Municipal Management Associations

Directory 1–5, with information obtained from ICMA files, shows the websites of municipal management associations serving 47 of the United States. (The states of Wyoming, Idaho, Montana, North Dakota, and South Dakota are served by the Great Open Spaces City Management Association; Idaho and South Dakota are also served by their own associations; and neither Hawaii nor Louisiana has an association.)

International Municipal Management Associations

Directory 1–6, with information obtained from ICMA files, shows the websites (where available) or contact information of municipal management associations serving Canada and 22 other countries.

U.S. State Associations of Counties

Directory 1–7 shows the websites for 53 county associations serving 47 states, as obtained from the National Association of Counties (naco.org). (Two associations serve the states of Arizona, South Dakota, Washington, and West Virginia; three associations serve the state of Illinois; and three states—Connecticut, Rhode Island, and Vermont—do not have associations.) Like their municipal league counterparts, these associations provide a wide range of research, training, consulting, publications, and legislative representation services.

U.S. Councils of Governments Recognized by ICMA

Directory 1–8, with information obtained from ICMA files, gives the websites for 96 councils of governments recognized by ICMA.

Other Local Government Directories

The names of municipal officials not reported in the *Year Book* are available in many states through directories published by state municipal leagues, state municipal management associations, and state associations of counties. Names and websites of these leagues and associations are shown in Directories 1–1, 1–5, and 1–7. In some states, the secretary of state, the state agency for community affairs (Directory 1–3), or another state agency publishes a directory that includes municipal and county officials. In addition, several directories with national coverage are published for health officers, welfare workers, housing and urban renewal officials, and other professional groups.

Directory 1-1 U.S. State Municipal Leagues

Shown below are the state municipal leagues of municipalities serving 49 states. For each league the directory provides the address and website so that readers can go directly to the site to find additional information.

Alabama
Alabama League of Municipalities
P.O. Box 1270
Montgomery 36102
alalm.org

Alaska
Alaska Municipal League
217 Second Street, Suite 200
Juneau 99801
akml.org

Arizona
League of Arizona Cities and Towns
1820 West Washington Street
Phoenix 85007
azleague.org

Arkansas
Arkansas Municipal League
301 West Second Street
Box 38
North Little Rock 72115
arml.org

California
League of California Cities
1400 K Street, Suite 400
Sacramento 95814
cacities.org

Colorado
Colorado Municipal League
1144 Sherman Street
Denver 80203
cml.org

Connecticut
Connecticut Conference of Municipalities
900 Chapel Street, 9th Floor
New Haven 06510-2807
ccm-ct.org

Delaware
Delaware League of Local Governments
P.O. Box 484
Dover 19903-0484
ipa.udel.edu/localgovt/dllg

Florida
Florida League of Cities
301 South Bronough Street, Suite 300
Tallahassee 32301
floridaleagueofcities.com

Georgia
Georgia Municipal Association
201 Pryor Street, S.W.
Atlanta 30303
www.gmanet.com/home

Idaho
Association of Idaho Cities
3100 South Vista Avenue, Suite 310
Boise 83705
idahocities.org

Illinois
Illinois Municipal League
500 East Capitol Avenue
Springfield 62701
iml.org

Indiana
Indiana Association of Cities and Towns
200 South Meridian Street, Suite 340
Indianapolis 46225
citiesandtowns.org

Iowa
Iowa League of Cities
500 S.W. 7th Street, Suite 101
Des Moines 50309-4111
iowaleague.org

Kansas
League of Kansas Municipalities
300 S.W. Eighth Avenue
Topeka 66603
lkm.org

Kentucky

Kentucky League of Cities
100 East Vine Street, Suite 800
Lexington 40507
klc.org

Louisiana

Louisiana Municipal Association
700 North 10th Street
Baton Rouge 70802
lamunis.org

Maine

Maine Municipal Association
60 Community Drive
Augusta 04330
memun.org

Maryland

Maryland Municipal League
1212 West Street
Annapolis 21401
mdmunicipal.org

Massachusetts

Massachusetts Municipal Association
One Winthrop Square
Boston 02110
mma.org

Michigan

Michigan Municipal League
1675 Green Road
Ann Arbor 48105
mml.org

Minnesota

League of Minnesota Cities
145 University Avenue West
St. Paul 55103-2044
lmnc.org

Mississippi

Mississippi Municipal League
600 East Amite Street, Suite 104
Jackson 39201
mmlonline.com

Missouri

Missouri Municipal League
1727 Southridge Drive
Jefferson City 65109
mocities.com

Montana

Montana League of Cities and Towns
208 North Montana Avenue, Suite 106
Helena 59601
mlct.com

Nebraska

League of Nebraska Municipalities
1335 L Street
Lincoln 68508
lonm.org

Nevada

Nevada League of Cities and Municipalities
310 South Curry Street
Carson City 89703
nvleague.org

New Hampshire

New Hampshire Local Government Center
25 Triangle Park Drive
Concord 03301
nhmunicipal.org

New Jersey

New Jersey State League of Municipalities
222 West State Street
Trenton 08608
njslom.com

New Mexico

New Mexico Municipal League
1229 Paseo de Peralta
Santa Fe 87501
nmml.org

New York

New York State Conference of Mayors and Municipal Officials
119 Washington Avenue
Albany 12210
nycom.org

North Carolina

North Carolina League of Municipalities
215 North Dawson Street
Raleigh 27603
nclm.org

North Dakota

North Dakota League of Cities
410 East Front Avenue
Bismarck 58504
ndlc.org

Ohio

Ohio Municipal League
175 South Third Street, Suite 510
Columbus 43215
omlohio.org

Oklahoma

Oklahoma Municipal League
201 N.E. 23rd Street
Oklahoma City 73105
oml.org

Oregon

League of Oregon Cities
1201 Court Street, N.E., Suite 200
Salem 97301
orcities.org

Pennsylvania

Pennsylvania League of Cities and Municipalities
414 North Second Street
Harrisburg 17101
plcm.org

Rhode Island

Rhode Island League of Cities and Towns
One State Street, Suite 502
Providence 02908
rileague.org

South Carolina

Municipal Association of South Carolina
1411 Gervais Street
Columbia 29211
masc.sc

South Dakota

South Dakota Municipal League
208 Island Drive
Fort Pierre 57532
sdmunicipalleague.org

Tennessee

Tennessee Municipal League
226 Capitol Boulevard, Suite 710
Nashville 37219
tml1.org

Texas

Texas Municipal League
1821 Rutherford Lane, Suite 400
Austin 78754
tml.org

Utah

Utah League of Cities and Towns
50 South 600 East, Suite 150
Salt Lake City 84102
ulct.org

Vermont

Vermont League of Cities and Towns
89 Main Street, Suite 4
Montpelier 05602-2948
vlct.org

Virginia

Virginia Municipal League
13 East Franklin Street
Richmond 23219
vml.org

Washington

Association of Washington Cities
1076 Franklin Street, S.E.
Olympia 98501
awcnet.org

West Virginia

West Virginia Municipal League
2020 Kanawha Boulevard
Charleston 25311
wvml.org

Wisconsin

League of Wisconsin Municipalities
122 West Washington Avenue, Suite 300
Madison 53703-2715
lwm-info.org

Wyoming

Wyoming Association of Municipalities
315 West 27th Street
Cheyenne 82001
wyomuni.org

Directory 1-2 Provincial and Territorial Associations and Unions in Canada

Shown below are the 16 associations and unions serving the provinces and territories of Canada. For each association, the directory provides the website so that readers can go directly to the site to find additional information.

Alberta

Alberta Association of Municipal Districts and Counties
aamdc.com

Alberta Urban Municipalities Association
munilink.net/live

British Columbia

Union of British Columbia Municipalities
ubcm.ca

Manitoba

Association of Manitoba Municipalities
amm.mb.ca

New Brunswick

Association Francophone des Municipalités du Nouveau-Brunswick
afmnb.org

Cities of New Brunswick Association
cnba-acnb.ca/en

Newfoundland and Labrador

Municipalities Newfoundland and Labrador
municipalitiesnl.ca

Northwest Territories

Northwest Territories Association of Communities
nwtac.com

Nova Scotia

Union of Nova Scotia Municipalities
unsm.ca

Ontario

Association of Municipalities of Ontario
amo.on.ca

Federation of Canadian Municipalities
fcm.ca

Prince Edward Island

Federation of Prince Edward Island Municipalities
fpeim.ca

Québec

Union des Municipalités du Québec
umq.qc.ca

Saskatchewan

Saskatchewan Association of Rural Municipalities
sarm.ca

Saskatchewan Urban Municipalities Association
suma.org

Yukon

Association of Yukon Communities
ayc-yk.ca

Directory 1-3 State Agencies for Community Affairs

Shown below are the agencies for community affairs for 48 states and Puerto Rico. For each agency the directory provides the name, address, and website so that readers can go directly to the site to find additional information.

Alabama

Department of Economic and Community Affairs
401 Adams Avenue
Montgomery 36104
adeca.alabama.gov

Alaska

Department of Commerce, Community and Economic Development
P.O. Box 110800
Juneau 99811-0800
dced.state.ak.us

Arizona

Arizona Commerce Authority
333 North Central Avenue, Suite 1900
Phoenix 85004
azcommerce.com

Arkansas

Economic Development Commission
900 West Capitol Avenue
Little Rock 72201
arkansasedc.com

California

Department of Housing and Community Development
2020 West El Camino Avenue
Sacramento 95833
hcd.ca.gov

Colorado

Department of Local Affairs
1313 Sherman Street, Suite 518
Denver 80203
dola.state.co.us

Connecticut

Department of Economic and Community Development
505 Hudson Street
Hartford 06106-7106
ct.gov/ecd/site/default.asp

Delaware

State Housing Authority
18 The Green
Dover 19901
destatehousing.com

Florida

Department of Economic Opportunity
107 East Madison Street
Caldwell Building
Tallahassee 32399-4120
dca.state.fl.us

Georgia

Department of Community Affairs
60 Executive Park South, N.E.
Atlanta 30329
dca.state.ga.us

Idaho

Department of Commerce
700 West State Street
Boise 83720-0093
commerce.idaho.gov

Illinois

Department of Commerce and Economic Opportunity
500 East Monroe
Springfield 62701
commerce.state.il.us/dceo

Indiana

Housing and Community Development Authority
30 South Meridian Street, Suite 1000
Indianapolis 46204
in.gov/ihfa

Iowa

Economic Development Authority
200 East Grand Avenue Des Moines 50309
iowaeconomicdevelopment.com

Kansas

Department of Commerce
Division of Community Development
1000 S.W. Jackson Street, Suite 100
Topeka 66612
kansascommerce.com

Kentucky

Department for Local Government
1024 Capital Center Drive, Suite 340
Frankfort 40601
dlg.ky.gov

Louisiana

Office of Community Development
Division of Administration
1201 North Third Street
Claiborne Building, Suite 7-210
Baton Rouge 70802
doa.louisiana.gov

Maine

Department of Economic and Community Development
59 State House Station
Augusta 04333-0059
maine.gov/decd

Maryland

Department of Housing and Community Development
100 Community Place
Crownsville 21032
dhcd.state.md.us

Massachusetts

Department of Housing and Community Development
100 Cambridge Street, Suite 300
Boston 02114
state.ma.us/dhcd/dhcd.htm

Michigan

Economic Development Corporation
300 North Washington Square
Lansing 48913
medc.michigan.org

Minnesota

Department of Employment and Economic Development
First National Bank Building
332 Minnesota Street, Suite E-200
St. Paul 55101-1351
mn.gov/deed

Mississippi

Mississippi Development Authority
501 North West Street
Jackson 39201
Mississippi.org

Missouri

Department of Economic Development
301 West High Street
P.O. Box 1157
Jefferson City 65102
ded.mo.gov

Montana

Department of Commerce
Local Government Assistance Division
301 South Park Avenue
P.O. Box 200501
Helena 59620-0501
commerce.mt.gov

Nebraska

Department of Economic Development
301 Centennial Mall South
P.O. Box 94666
Lincoln 68509-4666
neded.org

Nevada

Commission on Economic Development
808 West Nye Lane
Carson City 89703
diversifynevada.com

New Hampshire

Office of Energy and Planning
Johnson Hall, 3rd Floor
107 Pleasant Street
Concord 03301
nh.gov/oep

New Jersey

Department of Community Affairs
101 South Broad Street
P.O. Box 800
Trenton 08625-0800
state.nj.us/dca

New Mexico

Department of Finance and Administration
Local Government Division
407 Galisteo Street
Santa Fe, 87501
local.nmdfa.state.nm.us

New York

New York State Division of Homes and Community Renewal
Hampton Plaza, 38-40 State Street
Albany 12207
nysdhcr.gov

North Carolina

Department of Commerce
4302 Mail Service Center
Raleigh 27699-4302
nccommerce.com/en

North Dakota

Department of Commerce
Division of Community Services
1600 East Century Avenue, Suite 2
P.O. Box 2057
Bismarck 58503-2057
state.nd.us

Ohio

Department of Development
77 South High Street
Columbus 43216-1001
odod.state.oh.us

Oklahoma

Department of Commerce
900 North Stiles Avenue
Oklahoma City 73104
okcommerce.gov

Oregon

Business Oregon
775 Summer Street, N.E., Suite 200
Salem 97301-1280
oregon4biz.com

Pennsylvania

Department of Community and Economic Development
Commonwealth Keystone Building
400 North Street, 4th Floor
Harrisburg 17120-0225
newpa.com

Puerto Rico

Office of the Commissioner of Municipal Affairs
P.O. Box 70167
San Juan 00936-8167
ocam.gobierno.pr

Rhode Island

Rhode Island Housing Resources Commission
One Capitol Hill, 3rd Floor
Providence 02903
hrc.ri.gov

South Carolina

Department of Commerce
1201 Main Street, Suite 1600
Columbia 29201-3200
sccommerce.com

South Dakota

Department of Tourism and State Development
711 East Wells Avenue
Pierre 57501-3369
tsd.sd.gov/index.asp

Tennessee

Housing Development Agency
404 James Robertson Parkway, Suite 1200
Nashville 37243-0900
state.tn.us/thda

Texas

Department of Housing and Community Affairs
221 East 11th Street
Austin 78701-2401
tdhca.state.tx.us

Utah

Department of Heritage and Arts
Rio Grande Building
300 South Rio Grande Street
Salt Lake City 84101
heritage.utah.gov

Governor's Office of Economic Development
60 East South Temple, 3rd Floor
Salt Lake City 84111
goed.utah.gov

Vermont

Vermont Department of Housing and Community Affairs
National Life Drive, 6th Floor
One National Life Drive
Montpelier 05620
dhca.state.vt.us/

Virginia

Department of Housing and Community Development
Main Street Centre
600 East Main Street, Suite 300
Richmond 23219
dhcd.virginia.gov

Washington

Department of Commerce
1011 Plum Street S.E.
P.O. Box 42525
Olympia 98504-2525
cted.wa.gov

West Virginia

Department of Commerce
Capitol Complex
Building 6, Room 525
1900 Kanawha Boulevard East
Charleston 25305-0311
wvcommerce.org

Wisconsin

Economic Development Corporation
201 West Washington Avenue
Madison 53703
wedc.org

Directory 1-4 Provincial and Territorial Agencies for Local Affairs in Canada

Shown below are the agencies for local affairs serving the 12 provinces and territories of Canada. For each agency the directory provides the address and website for the ministry so that readers can go directly to the site to find additional information.

Alberta

Alberta Municipal Affairs
Communications Branch
Commerce Place, 18th Floor
10155-102 Street
Edmonton T5J 4L4
municipalaffairs.gov.ab.ca

British Columbia

Ministry of Community, Sport and Cultural Development
P.O. Box 9490
Station Provincial Government
Victoria V8W 9N7
gov.bc.ca/cserv/index.html

Manitoba

Manitoba Aboriginal and Northern Affairs
344-450 Broadway
Winnipeg R3C 0V8
gov.mb.ca/ana

New Brunswick

Aboriginal Affairs Secretariat
Kings Place
P.O. Box 6000
Fredericton E3B 5H1
www2.gnb.ca

Newfoundland and Labrador

Department of Municipal Affairs
Confederation Building, 4th Floor
(West Block)
P.O. Box 8700
St. John's A1B 4J6
ma.gov.nl.ca/ma

Northwest Territories

Department of Education, Culture and Employment
P.O. Box 1320
Yellowknife X1A 2L9
ece.gov.nt.ca

Nova Scotia

Service Nova Scotia and Municipal Relations
P.O. Box 2734
Halifax B3J 3K5
gov.ns.ca/snsmr

Ontario

Ministry of Municipal Affairs and Housing
777 Bay Street, 17th Floor
Toronto M5G 2E5
mah.gov.on.ca

Prince Edward Island

Department of Finance, Energy, and Municipal Affairs
Shaw Building, Second Floor South
95 Rochford Street
P.O. Box 2000
Charlottetown C1A 7N8
gov.pe.ca/finance

Québec

**Affaires Municipales, Régions et Occupation du territoire
(Ministry of Municipal Affairs, Regions and Land Occupancy)**
10, rue Pierre-Olivier-Chauveau
Québec G1R 4J3
mamrot.gouv.qc.ca

Saskatchewan

Public Service Commission
2350 Albert Street
Regina S4P 4A6
psc.gov.sk.ca

Yukon

Department of Community Services
Government of Yukon
Box 2703
Whitehorse Y1A 2C6
community.gov.yk.ca

Directory 1-5   U.S. Municipal Management Associations

Shown below are the names of the 47 municipal management associations in the United States. For each association the directory provides the website so that readers can go directly to the site to find additional information. Where there is no website available, we have provided the name, address, and all contact information for the association president (current as of January 6, 2014).

Alabama

Alabama City/County Management Association
accma-online.org

Alaska

Alaska Municipal Management Association
alaskamanagers.org

Arizona

Arizona City/County Management Association
azmanagement.org

Arkansas

Arkansas City Management Association
David F. Watkins (thru 4/15/2014)
City Manager
City of Hot Springs
134 Cataline Circle, Apt. G
Hot Springs 71913-8235
wareagle526@yahoo.com

Arkansas Municipal League
arml.org/resources.html

California

City Managers Department, League of California Cities
cacities.org

Cal-ICMA
icma.org/en/ca/home

Colorado

Colorado City and County Management Association
coloradoccma.org

Connecticut

Connecticut Town and City Management Association
cttcma.govoffice3.com

Delaware

City Management Association of Delaware
Teresa A. Tieman
City Manager
City of Harrington
106 Dorman Street
Harrington 19952-1052
ttieman@cityofharrington.com

Florida

Florida City and County Management Association
fccma.org

Georgia

Georgia City-County Management Association
gccma.com

Idaho

Idaho City/County Management Association
See Wyoming

Illinois

Illinois City/County Management Association
ilcma.org

Indiana

Indiana Association of Cities and Towns
citiesandtowns.org

Iowa

Iowa City/County Management Association
iacma.net

Kansas

Kansas Association of City/County Management
kacm.us

Kentucky

Kentucky City/County Management Association kccma.org/

Maine

Maine Town and City Management Association
mtcma.org

Maryland

Maryland City County Management Association
icma.org/en/md/home

Massachusetts

Massachusetts Municipal Management Association
massmanagers.org

Michigan

Michigan Local Government Management Association
mlgma.org

Minnesota

Minnesota City/County Management Association
mncma.org

Missouri

Missouri City/County Management Association
momanagers.org

Montana

See Wyoming

Nebraska

Nebraska City/County Management Association
nebraskacma.org

Nevada

Local Government Managers Association of Nevada
nevadalogman.org

New Hampshire

New Hampshire Municipal Management Association
nhmunicipal.org

New Jersey

New Jersey Municipal Management Association
njmma.org

New Mexico

New Mexico City Management Association
nmml.org/subsections/city-managers

New York

New York State City/County Management Association
nyscma.govoffice.com

North Carolina

North Carolina City and County Management Association
ncmanagers.org

North Dakota

See Wyoming

Ohio

Ohio City/County Management Association
ocmaohio.org

Oklahoma

City Management Association of Oklahoma
cmao-ok.org

Oregon

Oregon City/County Management Association
occma.org

Pennsylvania

Association for Pennsylvania Municipal Management
apmm.net

Rhode Island

Rhode Island City and Town Management Association
Michael C. Wood (thru 7/2014)
Town Manager
Town of Burrillville
105 Harrisville Main Street
Harrisville 02830-1420
mcwood@burrillville.org

South Carolina

South Carolina City and County Management Association
icma.org/en/sc/home

South Dakota

South Dakota City Management Association
sdmunicipalleague.org (Go to "Affiliate Organizations" and then to "City Management")

Tennessee

Tennessee City Management Association
tncma.org

Texas

Texas City Management Association
tcma.org

Utah

Utah City Management Association
ucma-utah.org

Vermont

Vermont Town and City Management Association
Brian M. Palaia (As of 5/2014)
Town Manager
Town of Milton
43 Bombardier Road
Milton 05468
bpalaia@town.milton.vt.us

Virginia

Virginia Local Government Management Association
icma.org/en/va/home

Washington

Washington City/County Management Association
wccma.org

West Virginia

West Virginia City Management Association
wvmanagers.org

Wisconsin

Wisconsin City/County Management Association
wcma-wi.org

Wyoming, Idaho, Montana, North Dakota, and South Dakota

Great Open Spaces City Management Association
icma.org/en/go/home

Directory 1-6 International Municipal Management Associations

Shown below are the names of 25 international municipal management associations. For each association the directory provides the website so that readers can go directly to the site to find additional information. Where there is no website available, we have provided the name, address, and all contact information for the president of the association (current as of January 6, 2014).

Australia
Local Government Managers Australia (LGMA)
lgma.org.au

Canada
Canadian Association of Municipal Administrators (CAMA)
camacam.ca

Denmark
National Association of Chief Executives in Danish Municipalities (KOMDIR)
komdir.dk

Georgia
Municipal Service Providers' Association (Georgia)
mspa.ge

Hungary
Small Municipalities Association of National Interest
kisvarosok.hu

India
City Managers' Association, Gujarat
cmag-india.com

City Managers' Association, Karnataka (CMAK)
cmakarnataka.com

City Managers' Association, Orissa
cmao.nic.in

Indonesia
All-Indonesia Association of City Government (APEKSI)
apeksi.or.id

Ireland
County and City Managers' Association
lgcsb.ie/en/CCMA

Israel
Union of Local Authorities in Israel (ULAI)
masham.org.il/English

Mexico
ICMA México-Latinoamérica
icma.org/en/international/Page/100260/ICMA_Latinoamrica

Nepal
Municipal Association of Nepal (MuAN)
muannepal.org.np

Netherlands
Dutch City Managers Association
gemeentesecretaris.nl

New Zealand
New Zealand Society of Local Government Managers
solgm.org.nz

Norway
Norwegian Forum of Municipal Executives
Oystein Sivertsen, President
477-785-0100

Russia
Russian National Congress of Municipalities
www.rncm.ru (no English version)

Slovakia
Slovak City Managers' Association
apums.sk

South Africa
Institute for Local Government Management of South Africa
ilgm.co.za

South Korea
Korean Urban Management Association
kruma.org

Spain
L'Union des Dirigeants Territoriaux de l'Europe (U.Di.T.E.)
udite.eu

Sri Lanka
Federation of Sri Lankan Local Government Authorities (FSLGA)
fslga.wordpress.com

Sweden
Association of Swedish City Managers
Anna Sandborgh, Chair
Karlstads kommun
Kommunledningskontoret
651 84 Karlstad
anna.sandborgh@karlstad.se
46-5-429-5102

United Kingdom
Society of Local Authority Chief Executives (SOLACE)
solace.org.uk

Viet Nam
Association of Cities of Viet Nam
acvn.vn

Directory 1-7   U.S. State Associations of Counties

Shown below are the names of the 53 state associations of counties in the United States. For each association the directory provides the address and website so that readers can go directly to the site to find additional information. Where there is no website available, we have provided the name and phone number for the executive director (current as of January 6, 2014).

Alabama

Association of County Commissions of Alabama
100 North Jackson Street
Montgomery 36104
acca-online.org

Alaska

Alaska Municipal League
217 Second Street, Suite 200
Juneau 99801
akml.org

Arizona

Arizona Association of Counties
1910 West Jefferson, Suite 1
Phoenix 85009
azcounties.org

County Supervisors Association of Arizona
1905 West Washington Street, Suite 100
Phoenix 85009
countysupervisors.org

Arkansas

Association of Arkansas Counties
1415 West Third Street
Little Rock 72201
arcounties.org

California

California State Association of Counties
1100 K Street, Suite 101
Sacramento 95814
csac.counties.org

Colorado

Colorado Counties, Inc.
800 Grant Street, Suite 500
Denver 80203
ccionline.org

Delaware

Delaware Association of Counties
Richard Cecil, Executive Director
12 North Washington Avenue
Lewes 19958-1806
302-645-0432 (phone)
302-645-2232 (fax)
dick_cecil@yahoo.com

Florida

Florida Association of Counties
100 South Monroe Street
Tallahassee 32301
fl-counties.com

Georgia

Association County Commissioners of Georgia
50 Hurt Plaza, Suite 1000
Atlanta 30303
accg.org

Hawaii

Hawaii State Association of Counties
4396 Rice Street, Suite 206
Lihue 96766
mauicounty.gov/Blog.aspx?tag=
Hawaii%20State%20Association%20
of%20Counties

Idaho

Idaho Association of Counties
700 West Washington
P.O. Box 1623
Boise 83701
idcounties.org

Illinois

Illinois Association of County Board Members
413 West Monroe Street, 2nd Floor
Springfield 62704
ilcounty.org

Metro Counties of Illinois
Dwight Magalis, Executive Director
1303 Brandywine Road
Libertyville 60048-3000
847-816-0889 (phone)
847-247-9915 (fax)
magalisike@msn.com

United Counties Council of Illinois
217 East Monroe, Suite 101
Springfield 62701-1743
UCCI@unitedcounties.com

Indiana

Association of Indiana Counties
101 West Ohio Street, Suite 1575
Indianapolis 46204
indianacounties.org

Iowa

Iowa State Association of Counties
5500 Westown Parkway, Suite 190
West Des Moines 50266
iowacounties.org

Kansas

Kansas Association of Counties
300 S.W. Eighth Avenue, 3rd Floor
Topeka 66603
kansascounties.org

Kentucky

Kentucky Association of Counties
400 Englewood Drive
Frankfort 40601
kaco.org

Louisiana

Police Jury Association of Louisiana
707 North Seventh Street
Baton Rouge 70802
lpgov.org

Maine

**Maine County Commissioners
Association**
4 Gabriel Drive
Augusta 04330
mainecounties.org

Maryland

Maryland Association of Counties
169 Conduit Street
Annapolis 21401
mdcounties.org

Massachusetts

**Massachusetts Association of County
Commissioners**
William P. O'Donnell, Executive Director
614 High Street
Dedham 02027-0310
781-461-6105 (phone)
781-326-6480 (fax)

Michigan

Michigan Association of Counties
935 North Washington Avenue
Lansing 48906
micounties.org

Minnesota

Association of Minnesota Counties
125 Charles Avenue
St. Paul 55103-2108
mncounties.org

Mississippi

Mississippi Association of Supervisors
793 North President Street
Jackson 39202
masnetwork.org

Missouri

Missouri Association of Counties
516 East Capitol Avenue
P.O. Box 234
Jefferson City 65102-0234
mocounties.com

Montana

Montana Association of Counties
2715 Skyway Drive
Helena 59602-1213
maco.cog.mt.us

Nebraska

**Nebraska Association of County
Officials**
625 South 14th Street
Lincoln 68508
nacone.org

Nevada

Nevada Association of Counties
304 South Minnesota Street
Carson City 89703
nvnaco.org

New Hampshire

**New Hampshire Association of
Counties**
Bow Brook Place
46 Donovan Street, Suite 2
Concord 03301-2624
nhcounties.org

New Jersey

New Jersey Association of Counties
150 West State Street
Trenton 08608
njac.org

New Mexico

New Mexico Association of Counties
444 Galisteo Street
Santa Fe 87501
nmcounties.org

New York

**New York State Association of
Counties**
540 Broadway, 5th Floor
Albany 12207
nysac.org

North Carolina

**North Carolina Association of County
Commissioners**
215 North Dawson Street
Raleigh 27603
ncacc.org

North Dakota

North Dakota Association of Counties
1661 Capitol Way
P.O. Box 877
Bismarck 58502-0877
ndaco.org

Ohio

**County Commissioners Association
of Ohio**
209 East State Street
Columbus 43215-4309
ccao.org

Oklahoma

**Association of County Commissioners
of Oklahoma City**
429 N.E. 50th Street
Oklahoma City 73105
okacco.com

Oregon

Association of Oregon Counties
1201 Court Street NE, Suite 300
Salem 97301
aocweb.org

Pennsylvania

**County Commissioners Association of
Pennsylvania**
P.O. Box 60769
Harrisburg 17106-0769
pacounties.org

South Carolina

**South Carolina Association of
Counties**
1919 Thurmond Mall
Columbia 29202
sccounties.org

South Dakota

**South Dakota Association of County
Officials**
211 East Prospect Avenue
Pierre 57501
sdcounties.org

**South Dakota Association of County
Commissioners**
211 East Prospect Avenue
Pierre 57501
sdcc.govoffice2.com

Tennessee

**Tennessee County Services
Association**
226 Capitol Boulevard, Suite 700
Nashville 37219-1896
tncounties.org

Texas

Texas Association of Counties
1210 San Antonio Street
Austin 78701
county.org

Utah

Utah Association of Counties
5397 South Vine Street
Murray 84107
uacnet.org

Virginia

Virginia Association of Counties
1207 East Main Street, Suite 300
Richmond 23219-3627
vaco.org

Washington

Washington Association of County Officials
206 Tenth Avenue, S.E.
Olympia 98501
wacounties.org/waco

Washington State Association of Counties
206 Tenth Avenue, S.E.
Olympia 98501
wacounties.org/wsac

West Virginia

County Commissioners' Association of West Virginia
2309 Washington Street, East
Charleston 25311
cawv.org

West Virginia Association of Counties
2211 Washington Street East
Charleston 25311-2118
wvcounties.org

Wisconsin

Wisconsin Counties Association
22 East Mifflin Street, Suite 900
Madison 53703
wicounties.org

Wyoming

Wyoming County Commissioners Association
P.O. Box 86
Cheyenne 82003
wyo-wcca.org

Directory 1-8 U.S. Councils of Governments Recognized by ICMA

Shown below are the names and websites of the 96 U.S. councils of government recognized by ICMA state associations of counties in the United States. Where there is no website available, we have provided the phone number for the council office.

ALABAMA-4

Central Alabama Regional Planning and Development Commission
carpdc.com

East Alabama Regional Planning & Development Commission
earpdc.org

Regional Planning Commission of Greater Birmingham
rpcgb.org

South Central Alabama Development Commission
scadc.net

ARIZONA-2

Maricopa Association of Governments
azmag.gov

Pima Association of Governments
pagnet.org

ARKANSAS-3

Metroplan
metroplan.org

Northwest Arkansas Regional Planning Commission
nwarpc.org

White River Planning & Development District
wrpdd.org

CALIFORNIA-9

Association of Bay Area Governments
abag.ca.gov

Fresno Council of Governments
fresnocog.org

Sacramento Area Council of Governments
sacog.org

San Bernardino Associated Governments
sanbag.ca.gov

San Diego Association of Governments
sandag.org

Santa Barbara County Association of Governments
sbcag.org

Southern California Association of Governments
scag.ca.gov

Stanislaus Council of Governments
stancog.org

Western Riverside Council of Governments
wrcog.cog.ca.us

COLORADO-1

Denver Regional Council of Governments
drcog.org

DISTRICT OF COLUMBIA-1

Metropolitan Washington Council of Governments
mwcog.org

FLORIDA-2

Solid Waste Authority of Palm Beach County
swa.org

Tampa Bay Regional Planning Council
tbrpc.org

GEORGIA-3

Atlanta Regional Commission
atlantaregional.com

Middle Georgia Regional Commission
middlegeorgiarc.org

Southern Georgia Regional Commission
sgrdc.com

IDAHO-1

Panhandle Area Council
pacni.org

ILLINOIS-9

Bi-State Regional Commission
bistateonline.org

Champaign County Regional Planning Commission
ccrpc.org

DuPage Mayors and Managers Conference
dmmc-cog.org

Lake County Municipal League
lakecountyleague.org

North Central Illinois Council of Governments
ncicg.org

Northwest Municipal Conference
nwmc-cog.org

South Central Illinois Regional Planning and Development Commission
scirpdc.com

Southwestern Illinois Metropolitan and Regional Planning Commission
618-344-4250

Tri-County Regional Planning Commission
tricountyrpc.org

IOWA-1

Midas Council of Governments
midascog.net

KENTUCKY-4

Barren River Area Development District
bradd.org

Big Sandy Area Development District
bigsandy.org

Lincoln Trail Area Development District
ltadd.org

Northern Kentucky Area Development District
nkadd.org

MARYLAND-2

Baltimore Metropolitan Council
baltometro.org

Tri-County Council For Southern Maryland
tccsmd.org

MICHIGAN-1

Southeast Michigan Council of Governments
semcog.org

MISSISSIPPI-1

Central Mississippi Planning & Development District
cmpdd.org

MISSOURI-3

East-West Gateway Council of Governments
ewgateway.org

Mid-America Regional Council
marc.org

South Central Ozark Council of Governments
scocog.org

NEW MEXICO-2

Mid-Region Council of Governments
mrcog-nm.gov

Southwest New Mexico Council of Governments
swnmcog.org

NEW YORK-1

Capital District Regional Planning Commission
cdrpc.org

NORTH CAROLINA-5

Centralina Council of Governments
centralina.org

Lumber River Council of Governments
lumberrivercog.org

Piedmont Triad Council of Governments
ptcog.org

Upper Coastal Plain Council of Governments
ucpcog.org

Eastern Carolina Council of Governments
eccog.org

OHIO-4

Miami Valley Regional Planning Commission
mvrpc.org

Ohio-Kentucky-Indiana Regional Council of Governments
oki.org

Ohio Mid-Eastern Governments Association
omegadistrict.org

Toledo Metropolitan Area Council of Governments
tmacog.org

OKLAHOMA-2

Association of Central Oklahoma Governments
acogok.org

Central Oklahoma Economic Development District
coedd.org

OREGON-4

Lane Council of Governments
lcog.org

Mid-Columbia Economic Development District
mcedd.org

Mid-Willamette Valley Council of Governments
mwvcog.org

Oregon Cascades West Council of Governments
ocwcog.org

SOUTH CAROLINA-3

Central Midlands Council of Governments
centralmidlands.org

South Carolina Appalachian Council of Governments
scacog.org

Upper Savannah Council of Governments
uppersavannah.com

SOUTH DAKOTA-2

Northeast Council of Governments
necog.org

Planning and Development District III
districtiii.org

TEXAS-15

Alamo Area Council of Governments
aacog.dst.tx.us

Ark-Tex Council of Governments
atcog.org

Capital Area Council of Governments
capcog.org

Central Texas Council of Governments
ctcog.org

Coastal Bend Council of Governments
cbcog98.org

Concho Valley Council of Governments
cvcog.org

Deep East Texas Council of Governments
detcog.org

Heart of Texas Council of Governments
hotcog.org

Houston-Galveston Area Council
h-gac.com

Nortex Regional Planning Commission
nortexrpc.org

North Central Texas Council of Governments
nctcog.org

Panhandle Regional Planning Commission
theprpc.org

South Plains Association of Governments
spag.org

Texoma Council of Governments
texoma.cog.tx.us

West Central Texas Council of Governments
wctcog.org

UTAH-1

Five County Association of Governments
fcaog.state.ut.us

VIRGINIA-5

Crater Planning District Commission
craterpdc.org

Hampton Roads Planning District Commission
hrpdc.org

Northern Neck Planning District Commission
nnpdc.org

Northern Virginia Regional Commission
novaregion.org

West Piedmont Planning District Commission
wppdc.org

WASHINGTON-1

Benton-Franklin Council of Governments
bfcog.us

WEST VIRGINIA-3

Belomar Regional Council
belomar.org

Mid-Ohio Valley Regional Council
movrc.org

Region One Planning & Development Council
regiononepdc.org

WISCONSIN-1

East Central Wisconsin Regional Planning Commission
eastcentralrpc.org

2

Professional, Special Assistance, and Educational Organizations Serving Local and State Governments

This article briefly describes 79 organizations that provide services of particular importance to cities, counties, and other local and state governments. Most of the organizations are membership groups for school administrators, health officers, city planners, city managers, public works directors, city attorneys, and other administrators who are appointed rather than elected. Several are general service and representational organizations for states, cities, counties, and administrators and citizens. Some organizations provide distinctive research, technological, consulting, and educational programs on a cost-of-service basis and have been established to meet specific needs of state and local governments. The others support educational activities and conduct research in urban affairs or government administration, thereby indirectly strengthening professionalism in government administration.

The assistance available through the secretariats of these national organizations provides an excellent method of obtaining expert advice and actual information on specific problems. The information secured in this way enables local and state officials to improve administrative practices, organization, and methods and thus improve the quality of services rendered. Many of these organizations also are active in raising the professional standards of their members through in-service training, special conferences and seminars, and other kinds of professional development.

Research on current problems is a continuing activity of many of these groups, and all issue a variety of publications ranging from newsletters and occasional bulletins to diversified books, monographs, research papers, conference proceedings, and regular and special reports.

These organizations provide many of the services that in other countries would be the responsibility of the national government. They arrange annual conferences, answer inquiries, provide in-service training and other kinds of professional development, provide placement services for members, and develop service and cost standards for various activities. Most of the organizations listed have individual memberships, and several also have agency or institutional memberships. Some of these organizations have service memberships that may be based on the population of the jurisdiction, the annual revenue of the jurisdiction or agency, or other criteria that roughly measure the costs of providing service. In addition to these kinds of membership fees, some of the organizations provide specialized consulting, training, and information services both by annual subscription and by charges for specific projects.

Listing of Organizations

Airports Council International–North America (ACI-NA)

1615 L Street N.W., Suite 300
Washington, D.C. 20006
202-293-8500; fax: 202-331-1362

Website: aci-na.org

President/CEO: Kevin M. Burke

Major publications: *Airport Highlights;* studies, surveys, reports

Purpose: To advocate policies and provide services that enhance the ability of airports to serve their passengers, customers, and communities. ACI is recognized as the authoritative voice of airports worldwide. ACI-NA presents the unique views and recommendations of airport management to federal, state, provincial, and local governments, industry, the media and the general public. As the "Voice of Airports®" ACI-NA (1) promotes cooperation with all elements of the commercial civil aviation industry; (2) exchanges ideas, information, and experiences on common airport issues; (3) identifies, interprets, and disseminates information to its members on current industry trends and practices; and (4) creates forums of common interest, builds professional relationships, and interprets key airport policy and business issues to the ACI-NA membership. Established 1948.

American Association of Airport Executives (AAAE)

601 Madison Street, Suite 400
Alexandria, Virginia 22314
703-824-0500; fax: 703-820-1395

Website: aaae.org

President: Charles M. Barclay

Major publications: *AAAE This Week; AAAE Security SmartBrief; Airport Report; Airport Magazine; Airport Report Express*

Purpose: To assist airport managers in performing their complex and diverse responsibilities through an airport management reference library; a consulting service; publications containing technical, administrative, legal, and operational information; an electronic bulletin board system; a professional accreditation program for airport executives; and Aviation News and Training Network, a private satellite broadcast network for airport employee training and news. AAAE is the world's largest professional organization for airport executives, representing thousands of airport management personnel at public-use commercial and general aviation airports. Its members represent some 850 airports and hundreds of companies and organizations that support airports. AAAE serves its membership through results-oriented representation in Washington, D.C. and delivers a wide range of industry services and professional development opportunities, including training, meetings and conferences, and a highly respected accreditation program. Established 1928.

American Association of Port Authorities (AAPA)

1010 Duke Street
Alexandria, Virginia 22314-3589
703-684-5700; fax: 703-684-6321

E-mail: info@aapa-ports.org

Website: aapa-ports.org

President: Kurt J. Nagle

Major publications: *Alert Newsletter; AAPA Directory-Seaports of the Americas; Seaport Magazine*

Purpose: To promote the common interests of the port community and provide leadership on trade, transportation, environmental, and other issues related to port development and operations. As the alliance of ports of the Western Hemisphere, AAPA furthers public understanding of the essential role fulfilled by ports within the global transportation system. It also serves as a resource to help members accomplish their professional responsibilities. Established 1912.

American Association of School Administrators (AASA)

1615 Duke Street
Alexandria, Virginia 22314
703-528-0700; fax: 703-841-1543

Website: aasa.org

Executive director: Daniel A. Domenech

Major publications: *The School Administrator;* Critical Issues Series

Purpose: To develop qualified educational leaders and support excellence in educational administration; to initiate and support laws, policies, research, and practices that will improve education; to promote programs and activities that focus on leadership for learning and excellence in education; and to cultivate a climate in which quality education can thrive. Established 1865.

American College of Healthcare Executives (ACHE)

One North Franklin Street, Suite 1700
Chicago, Illinois 60606-3529
312-424-2800; fax: 312-424-0023

Website: ache.org

President/CEO: Deborah J. Bowen, FACHE, CAE

Major publications: *Journal of Healthcare Management; Healthcare Executive; Frontiers of Health Services Management;* miscellaneous studies and task force, committee, and seminar reports

Purpose: To be the premier professional society for health care executives who are dedicated to improving health care delivery and to advancing health care management excellence. Established 1933.

American Institute of Architects (AIA)

1735 New York Avenue, N.W.
Washington, D.C. 20006
202-626-7300; fax: 202-626-7547
800-242-3837

Website: aia.org

President: Helene Combs Dreiling, FAIA

Major publication: *AIArchitect*

Purpose: To organize and unite in fellowship the members of the architectural profession; to promote the aesthetic, scientific, and practical efficiency of the profession; to advance the science and art of planning and building by advancing the standards of architectural education, training, and practice; to coordinate the efforts of the building industry and the profession of architecture to ensure the advancement of living standards for people through improved environment; and to make the profession of architecture one of ever-increasing service to society. Established 1857.

American Library Association (ALA)

50 East Huron Street
Chicago, Illinois 60611
312-944-6780; fax: 312-440-9374
800-545-2433
Also at 1615 New Hampshire Avenue, N.W.
Washington, D.C. 20009-2520
202-628-8410; fax: 202-628-8419
800-941-8478

Website: www.ala.org

Executive director: Keith Michael Fiels

Major publications: *American Libraries; Booklist; Book Links; Smart Libraries Newsletter; Library Technology Reports;* Guide to Reference (a subscription database); and the ALA TechSource and RDA [Research Description and Access] Toolkit websites

Purpose: To assist libraries and librarians in promoting and improving library service and librarianship. Established 1876.

American Planning Association (APA) and its professional institute, the American Institute of Certified Planners (AICP)

1030 15th Street, N.W., Suite 750 West
Washington, D.C. 20005-1503
202-872-0611; fax: 202-872-0643
Also at 205 North Michigan Avenue, Suite 1200
Chicago, Illinois 60601
312-431-9100; fax: 312-786-6700

Website: planning.org

Executive director/CEO: W. Paul Farmer, FAICP

Major publications: *Journal of the American Planning Association; Planning; Planning and Environmental Law; Zoning Practice; Practicing Planner; APA Interact;* Planning Advisory Service (PAS) Reports; Planners Press books

Purpose: To encourage planning that will meet the needs of people and society more effectively. APA is a nonprofit public interest and research organization representing around 40,000 practicing planners, officials, and citizens involved with urban and rural planning issues. Sixty-five percent of its members work for state and local government agencies and are involved, on a day-to-day basis, in formulating planning policies and preparing land use regulations. AICP is APA's professional institute, providing recognized leadership nationwide in the certification of professional planners, ethics, professional development, planning education, and the standards of planning practice. APA resulted from a 1978 consolidation of the American Institute of Planners, founded in 1917, and the American Society of Planning Officials, established in 1934.

American Public Gas Association (APGA)

201 Massachusetts Avenue, N.E., Suite C-4
Washington, D.C. 20002
202-464-2742; fax: 202-464-0246

E-mail: bkalisch@apga.org

Website: apga.org

President/CEO: Bert Kalisch

Major publications: *Public Gas News* (bi-weekly newsletter); *Publicly Owned Natural Gas System Directory* (annual); *The Source* (quarterly magazine)

Purpose: To be an advocate for publicly owned natural gas distribution systems, and effectively educate and communicate with members to promote safety, awareness, performance, and competitiveness. Established 1961.

American Public Health Association (APHA)

800 I Street, N.W.
Washington, D.C. 20001-3710
202-777-2742; fax: 202-777-2534

Website: apha.org

Executive director: Georges Benjamin, MD

Major publications: *American Journal of Public Health; The Nation's Health; Control of Communicable Diseases Manual; Public Health Newswire*

Purpose: To strengthen the profession of public health, share the latest public health research and information, promote best practices, and advocate for public health issues and policies grounded in research. Established 1872.

American Public Human Services Association (APHSA)

1133 19th Street, N.W., Suite 400
Washington, D.C. 20036
202-682-0100; fax: 202-289-6555

Website: aphsa.org

Executive director: Tracy Wareing

Major publications: *Policy and Practice* magazine; *This Week in Health; This Week in Washington*

Purpose: To pursue excellence in health and human services by supporting state and local agencies, informing policy makers, and working with its partners to drive innovative, integrated, and efficient solutions in policy and practice. Through its initiative *Pathways: The Opportunities Ahead for Human Services,* the overarching frame by which it is advancing a national agenda, APHSA aims to help its members and the health and human services field at large attain gainful employment and independence; realize stronger and healthier families, adults, and communities; and achieve the sustained well-being of children and youth. Established 1930.

American Public Power Association (APPA)

1875 Connecticut Avenue, N.W., Suite 1200
Washington, D.C. 20009
202-467-2900; fax: 202-467-2910

Website: publicpower.org

President/CEO: Mark Crisson

Major publications: *Public Power* (magazine); *Public Power Weekly* (newsletter); *Public Power Daily*

Purpose: To promote the efficiency and benefits of publicly owned electric systems; to achieve cooperation among public systems; to protect the interests of publicly owned utilities; and to provide service in the fields of management and operation, energy conservation, consumer services, public relations, engineering, design, construction, research, and accounting practice. APPA represents more than 2,000 community-owned electric utilities and provides services in the areas of government relations, engineering and operations, accounting and finance, energy research and development, management, customer relations, and public communications. The association represents public power interests before Congress, federal agencies, and the courts; provides educational programs and energy planning services in technical and management areas; and collects, analyzes, and disseminates information on public power and the electric utility industry. APPA publishes a weekly newsletter, a magazine, and many specialized publications; funds energy research and development projects; recognizes utilities and individuals for excellence in management and operations; and serves as a resource for federal, state, and local policy makers and officials, news reporters, public interest and other organizations, and the general public on public power and energy issues. Established 1940.

American Public Transportation Association (APTA)

1666 K Street, N.W., Suite 1100
Washington, D.C. 20006
202-496-4800; fax: 202-496-4324

Website: apta.com

President: Michael Melaniphy

Major publications: *Passenger Transport; Public Transportation Fact Book*

Purpose: To represent the operators of and suppliers to public transit; to provide a medium for discussion, exchange of experiences, and comparative study of industry affairs; and to research and investigate methods to improve public transit. The association also assists public transit entities with special issues, and collects and makes available public transit-related data and information. Established 1882.

American Public Works Association (APWA)

2345 Grand Boulevard, Suite 700
Kansas City, Missouri 64108-2625
816-472-6100; fax: 816-472-1610
Also at 1275 K Street, N.W., Suite 750
Washington, D.C. 20005-4083
202-408-9541; fax: 202-408-9542

Website: apwa.net

Executive director: Peter B. King

Major publications: *APWA Reporter* (12 issues); research reports, technical publications, and manuals

Purpose: To develop and support the people, agencies, and organizations that plan, build, maintain, and improve our communities. Established 1894.

American Society for Public Administration (ASPA)

1301 Pennsylvania Avenue, N.W., Suite 700
Washington, D.C. 20004
202-393-7878; fax: 202-638-4952

Website: aspanet.org

Executive director: William Shields

Major publications: *Public Administration Review; PA Times; Public Integrity; GovManagement Daily*

Purpose: To improve the management of public service at all levels of government; to advocate on behalf of public service; to advance the science, processes, and art of public administration; and to disseminate information and facilitate the exchange of knowledge among persons interested in the practice or teaching of public administration. Established 1939.

American Water Works Association (AWWA)

6666 West Quincy Avenue
Denver, Colorado 80235
303-794-7711; fax: 303-347-0804

Website: awwa.org

Executive director: David B. LaFrance

Major publications: *AWWA Journal; MainStream; OpFlow; AWWA Standards; Manuals of Water Supply Practices*

Purpose: To promote public health and welfare in the provision of drinking water of unquestionable and sufficient quality. Founded 1881.

Association of Public-Safety Communications Officials—International, Inc.

351 North Williamson Boulevard
Daytona Beach, Florida 32114-1112
386-322-2500; fax: 386-322-2501
Also at 1426 Prince Street
Alexandria, Virginia 22314-2815
571-312-4400; fax: 386-322-2501

Website: apcointl.org

Eexecutive director: Derek Poarch

Major publications: *APCO BULLETIN; The Journal of Public Safety Communications; Public Safety Operating Procedures Manual;* APCO training courses

Purpose: To promote the development and progress of public safety telecommunications through research, planning, and training; to promote cooperation among public safety agencies; to perform frequency coordination for radio services administered by the Federal Communications Commission; and to act as a liaison with federal regulatory bodies. Established 1935.

Association of Public Treasurers of the United States and Canada (APTUSC)

2851 South Parker Road, Suite 560
Aurora, Colorado 80014
720-248-2771; fax: 303-755-7363

Website: aptusc.org

Executive director: Nicole Singleton

Major publications: *Cash Flow Forecasting Guide; Cash Handling Training Manual; Debt Policy Handbook; Disaster Preparedness Guide; Guide to Internal Controls; Revenue Collections Manual; Stop That Fraud Handbook*

Purpose: To enhance local treasury management by providing educational training, technical assistance, legislative services, and a forum for treasurers to exchange ideas and develop policy papers and positions. Established 1965.

Canadian Association of Municipal Administrators (CAMA)

P.O. Box 128, Station A
Fredericton, New Brunswick E3B 4Y2
866-771-2262; fax: 506-460-2134

Website: camacam.ca

Executive director: Jennifer Goodine

Purpose: To achieve greater communication and cooperation among municipal managers across Canada, and to focus the talents of its members on the preservation and advancement of municipal government by enhancing the quality of municipal management in Canada. Established 1972.

Center for State and Local Government Excellence (SLGE)

777 North Capitol Street, N.E., Suite 500
Washington, D.C. 20002-4201
202-682-6100; fax: 202-962-3604

Website: slge.org

President and CEO: Elizabeth Kellar

Recent research reports: *The Funding of State and Local Pensions: 2012-2016, The Evolving Role of Defined Contribution Plans in the Public Sector, State and Local Pensions: An Overview of Funding Issues and Challenges, Locally-Administered Pension Plans: 2007-2011, Local Health Department Workforce Recruitment and Retention, State and Local Government Workforce: 2013 Trends,* and case studies on public sector pensions and retiree health, wellness and chronic care management programs, and other health care reform issues.

Purpose: To help state and local governments become knowledgeable and competitive employers so that they can attract and retain talented, committed, and well-prepared individuals to public service. Research areas include workforce analyses and implications of changing demographics, competitive employment practices, compensation analyses, state and local government retirement plans, active and retiree health care benefits, and financial wellness and retirement planning. Public Plans Database, developed in partnership with the Center for Retirement Research at Boston College, provides comprehensive financial, governance, and plan design information for more than 120 state and local defined benefit plans. Established 2006.

Council of State Community Development Agencies (COSCDA)

1825 K Street, Suite 515
Washington, D.C. 20006
202-293-5820; fax: 202-293-2820

Website: coscda.org

Executive director: Dianne Taylor

Major publications: *The National Line; StateLine; Member Update; Annual Report*

Purpose: To promote the value and importance of state involvement in community development, economic development, affordable housing, and homelessness programs. For over 30 years, COSCDA has positioned itself as the premier national association charged with advocating and enhancing the leadership role of states in these issue areas, which it accomplishes through information sharing and a variety of technical assistance programs. COSCDA seeks to support, facilitate, and communicate states' priorities to its membership, as well as to elected and appointed officials and to state and federal policy makers. Its Training Academy offers basic and advanced courses on community development block grants and an introductory course on housing programs. COSCDA also holds an annual training conference in the fall and a program managers' conference in the spring. Established 1974.

Council of State Governments (CSG)

2760 Research Park Drive
Lexington, Kentucky 40578
859-244-8000; fax: 859-244-8001

Website: csg.org

Executive director/CEO: David Adkins

Major publications: *Book of the States; Capitol Ideas* magazine; *CSG State Directories*

Purpose: To prepare states for the future by interpreting changing national and international trends and conditions; to promote the sovereignty of the states and their role in the American federal system; to advocate multistate problem solving and partnerships; and to build leadership skills to improve decision making. CSG is a multibranch and regionally focused association of the states, U.S. territories, and commonwealths. Established 1933.

Federation of Canadian Municipalities (FCM)

24 Clarence Street
Ottawa, Ontario K1N 5P3
613-241-5221; fax: 613-241-7440

E-mail: ceo@fcm.ca

Website: fcm.ca

CEO: Brock Carlton

Resources: Case studies, multimedia presentations, reports, guides, and templates for legal documents.

Purpose: To represent the interests of all municipalities on policy and program matters within federal jurisdictions. Policy and program priorities are determined by FCM's board of directors, standing committees, and task forces. Issues include payments in lieu of taxes, goods and service taxes, economic development, municipal infrastructure, environment, transportation, community safety and crime prevention, quality-of-life social indicators, housing, race relations, and international trade and aid. FCM members include Canada's largest cities, small urban and rural communities, and the 18 major provincial and territorial municipal associations, which together represent more than 20 million Canadians. Established 1937.

GMIS International (GMIS)

P.O. Box 27923
Austin, Texas 78755
877-963-4647; fax: 512-857-7711

Website: gmis.org

Executive director: Paul Ruth

Purpose: To provide a forum for the exchange of ideas, information, and techniques; and to foster enhancements in hardware, software, and communication developments as they relate to government activities. State and local government agencies are members represented by their top computer or information technology professionals. The GMIS Annual Educational Conference promotes sharing of ideas and the latest technology. GMIS sponsors an annual "Professional of the Year" program, publishes a newsletter, and provides organizational support to 19 state chapters. State chapters enable member agencies within a geographical area to develop close relationships and to foster the spirit and intent of GMIS through cooperation, assistance, and mutual support. GMIS is affiliated with KommITS, a sister organization of local governments in Sweden; SOCITM in the United Kingdom; ALGIM in New Zealand; VIAG in The Netherlands; MISA/ASIM in Ontario, Canada; LOLA-International (Linked Organisation of Local Authority ICT Societies); and V-ICT-OR in Belgium. Established 1971.

Government Finance Officers Association (GFOA)

203 North LaSalle Street, Suite 2700
Chicago, Illinois 60601-1210
312-977-9700; fax: 312-977-4806
Also at 1301 Pennsylvania Avenue, N.W., Suite 309
Washington, D.C. 20004
202-393-8020; fax: 202-393-0780

Website: gfoa.org

Executive director/CEO: Jeffrey L. Esser

Major publications: GFOA *Newsletter; Government Finance Review Magazine; Public Investor; GAAFR Review; Pension & Benefits Update; Governmental Accounting, Auditing, and Financial Reporting; Investing Public Funds; Elected Official's Series*

Purpose: To enhance and promote the professional management of governmental financial resources by identifying, developing, and advancing fiscal strategies, policies, and practices for the public benefit. Established 1906.

Governmental Accounting Standards Board (GASB)

401 Merritt 7
P.O. Box 5116
Norwalk, Connecticut 06856-5116
203-847-0700; fax: 203-849-9714

Website: gasb.org

Director of research and technical activities: David R. Bean

Major publications: Governmental Accounting Standards Series; Codification of Standards; implementation guides; Suggested Guidelines for Voluntary Reporting; exposure drafts; Preliminary Views documents; *The GASB Report* (monthly newsletter); plain-language user guides

Purpose: To establish and improve standards of financial accounting and reporting for state and local governmental entities. GASB standards guide the preparation of those entities' external financial reports so that users of the reports can obtain the state and local government financial information needed to make economic, social, and political decisions. Interested parties are encouraged to read and comment on discussion documents of proposed standards, which can be downloaded free of charge from the GASB website. Final standards, guides to implementing standards and using government financial reports, and subscriptions to GASB's publications can be ordered through the website as well. GASB's website also provides up-to-date information about current projects, forms for submitting technical questions and signing up for e-mail news alerts, a section devoted to financial report users, and a link to its Performance Measurement for Government website. GASB is overseen by the Financial Accounting Foundation's Board of Trustees. Established 1984.

Governmental Research Association (GRA)

P.O. Box 292300
402 Samford Hall
Samford University
Birmingham, Alabama 35229
585-327-7054

Website: graonline.org

President: Kent Garder

Major publications: *Directory of Organizations and Individuals Professionally Engaged in Governmental Research and Related Activities* (annual); *GRA Reporter* (quarterly)

Purpose: To promote and coordinate the activities of governmental research agencies; to encourage the development of effective organization and methods for the administration and operation of government; to encourage the development of common standards for the appraisal of results; to facilitate the exchange of ideas and experiences; and to serve as a clearinghouse. Established 1914.

ICMA

777 North Capitol Street, N.E., Suite 500
Washington, D.C. 20002-4201
202-289-4262; fax: 202-962-3500

Website: icma.org

Executive director: Robert J. O'Neill Jr.

Major publications: *A Budgeting Guide for Local Government* (3rd ed.); *Effective Supervisory Practices* (5th ed.); *Effective Supervisory Skill Building; Statistics for Public Administration: Practical Uses for Better Decision Making* (2nd ed.); *Economic Development: Strategies for State and Local Practice* (2nd ed.); *Capital Budgeting and Finance: A Guide for Local Governments* (2nd ed.); *Human Resource Management in Local Government: An Essential Guide* (3rd ed.); *Homeland Security: Best Practices for Local Government; Managing Local Government: Cases in Effectiveness; Leading Your Community: A Guide for Local Elected Leaders;* "Green" Books, *The Municipal Year Book, Public Management (PM)* magazine, *InFocus* (formerly *IQ Reports*), *ICMA Newsletter;* self-study courses, training packages

Purpose: To create excellence in local governance by developing and advocating professional management of local government worldwide. ICMA provides member support; publications, data, and information; peer and results-oriented assistance; and training and professional development to more than 9,000 city, town, and county experts and other individuals throughout the world. The management decisions made by ICMA's members affect 185 million individuals living in thousands of communities, from small villages and towns to large metropolitan areas. Established 1914.

ICMA Retirement Corporation (ICMA-RC)

777 North Capitol Street, N.E., Suite 600
Washington, D.C. 20002
202-962-4600; fax: 202-962-4601
800-669-7400

Website: www.icmarc.org

President/CEO: Joan McCallen

Purpose: To provide retirement plans and related services for more than 920,000 public employees in over 9,000 retirement plans. An independent financial services corporation focused on the retirement savings needs of the public sector, ICMA-RC is dedicated to helping build retirement security for public employees by providing investment tools, financial education, and other retirement-related services. The corporation also works to ease the administrative responsibility of local, city, and state governments that offer these benefits to their employees. Established 1972.

Institute of Internal Auditors, Inc. (The IIA)

247 Maitland Avenue
Altamonte Springs, Florida 32701-4201
407-937-1111; fax: 407-937-1101

Website: theiia.org

Chairman of the Board: Paul J. Sobel, CIA, CRMA

Major publications: *Internal Auditor;* (quarterly corporate governance newsletter); *Sawyer's Guide for Internal Auditors, 6th ed.*

Purpose: To provide comprehensive professional development and standards for the practice of internal auditing; and to research, disseminate, and promote education in internal auditing and internal control. The IIA offers the Certified Government Auditing Professional (CGAP) to distinguish leaders in public sector auditing. In addition to offering quality assessment services, The IIA performs custom on-site seminars for government auditors and offers educational products that address issues pertaining to government auditing. An international professional association with global headquarters in Altamonte Springs, Florida, The IIA has more than 140,000 members in internal auditing, governance, internal control, information technology audit, education, and security. With representation from more than 165 countries, The IIA is the internal audit profession's global voice, recognized authority, acknowledged leader, chief advocate, and principal educator worldwide. Established 1941.

Institute for Public Administration (IPA)

180 Graham Hall
University of Delaware
Newark, Delaware 19716-7380
302-831-8971; fax: 302-831-3488

Website: ipa.udel.edu

Director: Jerome R. Lewis

Major publications: IPA Reports, available at dspace.udel.edu:8080/dspace/handle/19716/7

Purpose: To address the policy, planning, and management needs of its partners through the integration of applied research, professional development, and the education of tomorrow's leaders. IPA provides direct staff assistance, research, policy analysis, training, and forums while contributing to the scholarly body of knowledge in public administration. Established 1973.

Institute of Transportation Engineers (ITE)

1627 Eye Street, N.W., Suite 600
Washington, D.C. 20006
202-785-0060; fax: 202-785-0609

Website: ite.org

Executive director: Thomas W. Brahms

Major publications: *Trip Generation, Parking Generation; Innovative Bicycle Treatments; Transportation and Land Use Development; Traffic Engineering Handbook; Transportation Planning Handbook; Manual of Transportation Engineering Studies; Designing Walkable Urban Thoroughfares; Urban Street Geometric Design Handbook; Traffic Safety Toolbox, A Primer on Traffic Safety; Manual of Uniform Traffic Control Devices, 2009; Traffic Control Devices Handbook; ITE Journal*

Purpose: To promote professional development in the field through education, research, development of public awareness, and exchange of information. Established 1930.

International Association of Assessing Officers (IAAO)

314 West 10th Street
Kansas City, Missouri 64105
816-701-8100; fax: 816-701-8149

Website: iaao.org

Executive director: Lisa J. Daniels

Major publications: *Journal of Property Tax Assessment & Administration* (quarterly); *Fair & Equitable* (monthly magazine); Technical Standards (iaao.org/sitePages.cfm?Page=219); *Fundamentals of Mass Appraisal* (2011); *Property Assessment Valuation* (3rd ed., 2010); *Fundamentals of Tax Policy* (2008); *Fundamentals of Industrial Valuation* (2007)

Purpose: To promote innovation and excellence in property appraisal, assessment administration, and property tax policy through professional development, education, research, and technical assistance. A nonprofit educational and research association, IAAO is a professional membership organization of government assessment officials and others interested in the administration of the property tax. Its members—more than 7,300 worldwide from governmental, business, and academic communities—subscribe to a Code of Ethics and Standards of Professional Conduct and to the Uniform Standards of Professional Appraisal Practice. Established 1934.

International Association of Chiefs of Police (IACP)

44 Canal Center Plaza, Suite 200
Alexandria, Virginia 22314
703-836-6767; fax: 703-836-4543
800-THE IACP

Website: theiacp.org

Executive director: Bart Johnson

Major publications: *Police Chief; Training Keys*

Purpose: To advance the art of police science through the development and dissemination of improved administrative, technical, and operational practices, and to promote the use of such practices in police work. Fosters police cooperation through the exchange of information among police administrators, and encourages all police officers to adhere to high standards of performance and conduct. Established 1893.

International Association of Fire Chiefs (IAFC)

4025 Fair Ridge Drive, Suite 300
Fairfax, Virginia 22033-2868
703-273-0911; fax: 703-273-9363

Website: iafc.org

Executive director/CEO: Mark W. Light, CAE

Major publication: *On Scene* (twice-monthly newsletter)

Purpose: To lead, educate, and serve the fire service. To enhance the professionalism and capabilities of career and volunteer fire chiefs, chief fire officers, company officers, and managers of emergency service organizations throughout the international community through vision, services, information, education, and representation. Established 1873.

International Association of Venue Managers (IAVM)

635 Fritz Drive, Suite 100
Coppell, Texas 75019-4442
972-906-7441; fax: 972-906-7418

Website: iavm.org

President/CEO: Vicki Hawarden, CMP

Major publications: *Facility Manager; IAVM Guide to Members and Services; IAVM E-Newsletter*

Purpose: To educate, advocate for, and inspire public assembly venue professionals worldwide. Established 1925.

International Code Council

500 New Jersey Avenue, N.W., 6th Floor
Washington, D.C. 20001-2070
888-422-7233; fax: 202-783-2348

Website: iccsafe.org

CEO: Dominic Sims

Major publication: *The International Codes*

Purpose: To build safety and fire prevention by developing the codes used to construct residential and commercial buildings, including homes and schools. Most U.S. cities, counties, and states that adopt codes choose the international codes developed by the ICC, a membership association. Established 1994.

International Economic Development Council (IEDC)

734 15th Street, N.W., Suite 900
Washington, D.C. 20005
202-223-7800; fax: 202-223-4745

Website: iedconline.org

President/CEO: Jeffrey A. Finkle, CEcD

Major publications: *Economic Development Journal; Economic Development Now; Economic Development America; Federal Directory; Federal Review; Budget Overview*

Purpose: To help economic development professionals improve the quality of life in their communities. With more than 4,000 members, IEDC represents all levels of government, academia, and private industry, providing a broad range of member services that includes research, advisory services, conferences, professional certification, professional development, publications, and legislative tracking. Established 2001.

International Institute of Municipal Clerks (IIMC)

8331 Utica Avenue, Suite 200
Rancho Cucamonga, California 91730
909-944-4162; fax: 909-944-8545
800-251-1639

Website: iimc.com

Executive director: Chris Shalby

Major publications: *IIMC News Digest; The Language of Local Government; Meeting Administration Handbook; Parliamentary Procedures in Local Government; Role Call: Strategy for a Professional Clerk;* "Partners in Democracy" video, case study packets, technical bulletins

Purpose: To promote continuing education and certification through university- and college-based institutes, and provide networking solutions, services, and benefits to its members worldwide. Established 1947.

International Municipal Lawyers Association (IMLA)

7910 Woodmont Avenue, Suite 1440
Bethesda, Maryland 20814
202-466-5424; fax: 202-785-0152

E-mail: info@imla.org

Website: imla.org

General counsel/executive director: Chuck Thompson

Major publications: *The IMLA Model Ordinance Service; Municipal Lawyer*

Purpose: To provide continuing legal education events, publications, research, legal advocacy assistance, and excellent networking opportunities for the local government legal community. IMLA is a membership organization of U.S. and Canadian city and county attorneys. Established 1935.

International Public Management Association for Human Resources (IPMA-HR)

1617 Duke Street
Alexandria, Virginia 22314
703-549-7100; fax: 703-684-0948

Website: ipma-hr.org

Executive director: Neil E. Reichenberg

Major publications: *Public Personnel Management; HR Bulletin; IPMA-HR News*

Purpose: To improve service to the public by promoting quality human resource management in the public sector. Established 1906.

League of Women Voters of the United States (LWVUS)

1730 M Street, N.W., Suite 1000
Washington, D.C. 20036-4508
202-429-1965; fax: 202-429-0854

Website: lwv.org

Executive director: Nancy Tate

Major publications: *High School Voter Registration Training Manual; Debate Watching 101;* "From Theory to Practice: A Grassroots Education Campaign" *Shares Lessons Learned by Leagues in Kansas and South Carolina;* voters' reference guides and brochures in English and Spanish

Purpose: To encourage informed and active participation in government and to influence public policy through education and advocacy. The league's current advocacy priorities are health care reform, climate change, election reform, a fair judiciary, immigration, openness in government, redistricting reform, campaign finance, lobbying, and election reform. The League of Women Voters Education Fund, a separate but complementary organization, provides research and education services to the public to encourage and enable citizen participation in government. Current public education programs include voter outreach and education, the Vote 411.org website, election reform, judicial independence, and international forms and exchange activities. The league is a nonpartisan political organization. Established 1920.

National Animal Control Association (NACA)

101 North Church Street
Olathe, Kansas 66061
913-768-1319; fax: 913-768-1378

Website: nacanet.org

President: Todd Stosuy

Major publications: *The NACA News; The NACA Training Guide*

Purpose: To provide training for animal control personnel; consultation and guidance for local governments on animal control ordinances, animal shelter design, budget and program planning, and staff training; and public education. Established 1978.

National Association of Counties (NACo)

25 Massachusetts Avenue, N.W., Suite 500
Washington, D.C. 20001-1431
202-393-6226; fax: 202-393-2630

Website: naco.org

Executive director: Matthew D. Chase

Major publications: *County News; NACo e-News*

Purpose: To provide essential services to the nation's 3,069 counties. The only national organization that represents county governments in the United States, NACo advances issues with a unified voice before the federal government; improves the public's understanding of county government, assists counties in finding and sharing innovative solutions through education and research, and provides value-added services to save counties and taxpayers money. Established 1935.

National Association of County and City Health Officials (NACCHO)

1100 17th Street, N.W., 7th Floor
Washington, D.C. 20036
202-783-5550; fax: 202-783-1583

Website: naccho.org

Executive director: Robert M. Pestronk, MPH

Major publications: *National Profile of Local Health Departments* (annual); *Public Health Dispatch* (newsletter); *NACCHO Exchange* (quarterly); research briefs and videos

Purpose: To support efforts that protect and improve the health of all people and all communities by promoting national policy, developing resources and programs, seeking health equity, and supporting effective local public health practice and systems. Established 1960s.

National Association for County Community and Economic Development (NACCED)

2025 M Street, N.W., Suite 800
Washington, D.C. 20036-3309
202-367-1149; fax: 202-367-2149

Website: nacced.org

Executive director: John Murphy

Purpose: To help develop the technical capacity of county agencies in administering community development, economic development, and affordable housing programs. Created as an affiliate of the National Association of Counties (NACo), NACCED is a nonprofit national organization that also serves as a voice within NACo to articulate the needs, concerns, and interests of county agencies. Established 1978.

National Association of Development Organizations (NADO)

400 North Capitol Street, N.W., Suite 390
Washington, D.C. 20001
202-624-7806; fax: 202-624-8813

Website: nado.org

Executive director: Joe McKinney

Major publications: *EDFS Reporter; NADO News; Regional Development Digest*

Purpose: To provide training, information, and representation for regional development organizations serving small metropolitan and rural America. Building on nearly four decades of experience, the association offers its members exclusive access to a variety of services and benefits—all of which are crafted to enhance the activities, programs, and prospects of regional development organizations. Established 1970s.

National Association of Housing and Redevelopment Officials (NAHRO)

630 Eye Street, N.W.
Washington, D.C. 20001
202-289-3500; fax: 202-289-8181
877-866-2476

Website: nahro.org

CEO: Saul N. Ramirez

Major publications: *Journal of Housing and Community Development; NAHRO Monitor; Directory of Local Agencies; The NAHRO Public Relations Handbook; Commissioners Handbook*

Purpose: To help create a nation in which all people, especially those of low and moderate income, have decent, safe, affordable housing and economic opportunity in viable, sustainable communities. To this end, NAHRO (1) ensures that housing and community development professionals have the leadership skills, education, information, and tools to serve communities in a rapidly changing environment; (2) advocates for adequate funding levels and responsible public policies that address the needs of the people served, are financially and programmatically viable for our industry, are flexible, reduce regulatory burdens, and promote local decision making; and (3) fosters the highest standards of ethical behavior, service, and accountability to ensure public trust. A professional membership organization comprising about 23,000 housing and community development agencies and officials throughout the United States who administer a variety of affordable housing and community development programs at the local level, NAHRO enhances the professional development and effectiveness of its members and the industry through its comprehensive professional development curriculum, including certifications, conferences, and publications. Established 1933.

National Association of Regional Councils (NARC)

777 North Capitol Street, N.E., Suite 305
Washington, D.C. 20002
202-986-1032; fax: 202-986-1038

Website: narc.org

Executive director: Fred Abousleman

Major publications: *Transportation Thursdays; eRegions;* reports and presentations

Purpose: To promote regional approaches and collaboration in addressing diverse development challenges. A nonprofit membership organization, NARC has represented the interests of its members and has advanced regional cooperation through effective interaction and advocacy with Congress, federal officials, and other related agencies and interest groups for more than 40 years. Its member organizations are composed of multiple local government units, such as regional councils and metropolitan planning organizations, that work together to serve American communities, large and small, urban and rural. Among the issues it addresses are transportation, homeland security and regional preparedness, economic and community development, the environment, and a variety of community concerns of interest to member organizations. NARC provides its members with valuable information and research on key national policy issues, federal policy developments, and best practices; in addition, it conducts enriching training sessions, conferences, and workshops. Established 1967.

National Association of Schools of Public Affairs and Administration (NASPAA)

1029 Vermont Avenue, N.W., Suite 1100
Washington, D.C. 20005
202-628-8965; fax: 202-626-4978

E-mail: naspaa@naspaa.org

Websites: naspaa.org; globalmpa.org; and publicservicecareers.org

Executive director: Laurel McFarland

Major publications: *Journal of Public Affairs Education (J-PAE); Newsletter; MPA Accreditation Standards; MPA/MPP Brochure;* peer review and accreditation documents

Purpose: To serve as a national and international center for information about programs and developments in the area of public affairs and administration; to foster goals and standards of educational excellence; to represent members' concerns and interests in the formulation and support of national, state, and local policies for public affairs education and research; and to serve as a specialized accrediting agency for MPA/MPP degrees. Established 1970.

National Association of State Chief Information Officers (NASCIO)

c/o AMR Management Services
201 East Main Street, Suite 1405
Lexington, Kentucky 40507
859-514-9153; fax: 859-514-9166

Website: nascio.org

Executive director: Doug Robinson

Major publications: *State CIO Top Ten Policy and Technology Priorities for 2014; 2013 Best Practices in the Use of Information Technology in State Government; The 2013 State CIO Survey The Enterprise Imperative: Leading Through Governance, Portfolio Management, and Collaboration; State Cyber Security Resource Guide: Awareness, Education, and Training Initiatives; State Governments at Risk: A Call for Collaboration and Compliance; Capitals in the Clouds-The Case for Cloud Computing in State Government, Parts I–IV; CIO Leadership for State Governments: Emerging Trends and Practices; On the Fence: IT Implications of the Health Benefit Exchanges; State IT Workforce: Under Pressure; Friends, Followers, and Feeds: A National Survey of Social Media Use in State Government; The Heart of the Matter: A Core Services Taxonomy for State IT Security Programs; NASCIO Connections* (newsletter)

Purpose: To be the premier network and resource for state chief information officers (CIOs) and a leading advocate for information technology (IT) policy at all levels of government. NASCIO represents state CIOs and IT executives from the states, territories, and the District of Columbia. Its primary state government members are senior officials who have executive-level and state-wide responsibility for IT leadership. State officials involved in agency-level IT management may participate as state members; representatives from other public sector and nonprofit organizations may participate as associate members. Private sector firms may join as corporate members and participate in the Corporate Leadership Council. Established 1969.

National Association of Towns and Townships (NATaT)

1130 Connecticut Avenue, N.W., Suite 300
Washington, D.C. 20036
202-454-3950; fax: 202-331-1598

Website: natat.org

Federal director: Jennifer Imo

Major publication: *Washington Report*

Purpose: To strengthen the effectiveness of town and township government by educating lawmakers and public policy officials about how small-town governments operate and by advocating policies on their behalf in Washington, D.C. Established 1976.

National Career Development Association (NCDA)

305 North Beech Circle
Broken Arrow, Oklahoma 74012
918-663-7060; fax: 918-663-7058

Website: ncda.org

Executive director: Deneen Pennington

Major publications: *A Counselor's Guide to Career Assessments; The Internet: A Tool for Career Planning; Career Developments* magazine; *Career Development Quarterly Journal; Career Convergence* webmagazine

Purpose: To promote career development of all people throughout the lifespan. A division of the American Counseling Association, NCDA provides services to the public and to professionals involved with or interested in career development; services include professional development activities, publications, research, public information, professional standards, advocacy, and recognition for achievement and service. Established 1913.

National Civic League (NCL)

1889 York Street
Denver, Colorado 80206
303-571-4343; fax: 888-314-6053

E-mail: ncl@ncl.org

Website: ncl.org

Blog: allamericacityaward.com

President: Gloria Rubio-Cortés

Major publications: *The Community Visioning and Strategic Planning Handbook; Model County Charter; National Civic Review; 8th Edition of the Model City Charter; New Civic Index; The Guide for Charter Commission*

Purpose: To strengthen democracy by increasing the capacity of our nation's people to fully participate in and build healthy and prosperous communities across America. NCL facilitates community-wide strategic planning in fiscal sustainability and comprehensive plans. Good at the science of local government and the art of public engagement, NCL leads and celebrates the progress that can be achieved when people work together. NCL is the home of the All-America City Award, now in its 64th year. Established 1894.

National Community Development Association (NCDA)

522 21st Street, N.W., #120
Washington, D.C. 20006
202-293-7587; fax: 202-887-5546

Website: ncdaonline.org

Executive director: Cardell Cooper

Purpose: To serve as a national clearinghouse of ideas for local government officials and federal policy makers on pertinent national issues affecting America's communities. NCDA is a national nonprofit organization comprising more than 550 local governments across the country that administer federally supported community and economic development, housing, and human service programs, including those of the U.S. Department of Housing and Urban Development (HUD), the Community Development Block Grant program, and HOME Investment Partnerships. NCDA provides timely, direct information and technical support to its members in their efforts to secure effective and responsive housing and community development programs. Established 1968.

National Conference of State Legislatures (NCSL)

7700 East First Place
Denver, Colorado 80230
303-364-7700; fax: 303-364-7800
Also at 444 North Capitol Street, N.W., Suite 515
Washington, D.C. 20001-1201
202-624-5400; fax: 202-737-1069

Website: ncsl.org

Executive director: William T. Pound

Major Resources: *All Access, StateConnect, Mason's Manual, Federal Update, State Legislatures*

Purpose: To improve the quality and effectiveness of state legislatures; to ensure that states have a strong, cohesive voice in the federal decision-making process; and to foster interstate communication and cooperation. A bipartisan organization that serves the legislators and staffs of the nation's states, commonwealths, and territories, NCSL provides research, technical assistance, and opportunities for policy makers to exchange ideas on the most pressing state issues. Established 1975.

National Environmental Health Association (NEHA)

720 South Colorado Boulevard, Suite 1000-N
Denver, Colorado 80246
303-756-9090; fax: 303-691-9490

E-mail: staff@neha.org

Website: neha.org

Executive director: Nelson E. Fabian

Major publications: *2009 H1N1 Pandemic Influenza Planning Manual; Microbial Safety of Fresh Produce; Planet Water: Investing in the World's Most Valuable Resource; Environmental Toxicants: Human Exposures and Their Health Effects; Resolving Messy Policy Problems; Journal of Environmental Health*

Purpose: To advance the professional in the environmental field through education, professional meetings, and the dissemination of information. NEHA also publishes information relating to environmental health and protection and promotes professionalism in the field. Established 1937.

National Fire Protection Association (NFPA)

One Batterymarch Park
Quincy, Massachusetts 02169-7471
617-770-3000; fax: 617-770-0700

Website: nfpa.org

President/CEO: James M. Shannon

Major publications: *NFPA Journal; National Electrical Code®; National Fire Codes®; Life Safety Code®; Fire Technology; Risk Watch®; Learn Not to Burn® Curriculum;* and textbooks, manuals, training packages, detailed analyses of important fires, and fire officers guides

Purpose: To reduce the worldwide burden of fire and other hazards on the quality of life by providing and advocating scientifically based consensus codes and standards, research, training, and education. Established 1896.

National Governors Association (NGA)

Hall of the States
444 North Capitol Street, N.E., Suite 267
Washington, D.C. 20001-1512
202-624-5300; fax: 202-624-5313

Website: nga.org

Executive director: Dan Crippen

Major publications: *The Fiscal Survey of States; Policy Positions;* reports on a wide range of state issues

Purpose: To act as a liaison between the states and the federal government, and to serve as a clearinghouse for information and ideas on state and national issues. Established 1908.

National Housing Conference (NHC)

1900 M Street, N.W., Suite 200
Washington, D.C. 20036
202-466-2121; fax: 202-466-2122

Website: nhc.org

Interim president/CEO: Chris Estes

Major publications: *Losing Ground: The Struggle of Moderate-Income Households to Afford the Rising Costs of Housing and Transportation; NHC at Work; NHC Affordable Housing Policy Review; Washington Wire*

Purpose: To promote better communities and affordable housing for Americans through education and advocacy. Established 1931.

National League of Cities (NLC)

1301 Pennsylvania Avenue, N.W., Suite 550
Washington, D.C. 20004-1763
202-626-3000; fax: 202-626-3043

Website: nlc.org

Executive director: Clarence Anthony

Major publications: *Nation's Cities Weekly,* guide books, directories, and research reports

Purpose: To strengthen and promote cities as centers of opportunity, leadership, and governance; to serve as an advocate for its members in Washington in the legislative, administrative, and judicial processes that affect them; to offer training, technical assistance, and information to local government and state league officials to help them improve the quality of local government; and to research and analyze policy issues of importance to cities and towns in America. Established 1924.

National Public Employer Labor Relations Association (NPELRA)

1012 South Coast Highway, Suite M
Oceanside, California 92054
760-433-1686; fax: 760-433-1687
E-mail: info@npelra.org

Website: npelra.org

Executive director: Michael T. Kolb

Purpose: To provide its members with high-quality, progressive labor relations professional development that balances the needs of management, employees, and the public. The premier organization for public sector labor relations and human resource professionals, NPELRA is a network of state and regional affiliates. Its more than 3,000 members around the country represent public employers in a wide range of areas, from employee-management contract negotiations to arbitration under grievance and arbitration procedures. NPELRA also works to promote the interests of public sector management in the judicial and legislative arenas, and to provide opportunities for networking among members by establishing state and regional organizations throughout the country. The governmental agencies represented in NPELRA employ more than 4 million workers in federal, state, and local government.

National Recreation and Park Association (NRPA)

22377 Belmont Ridge Road
Ashburn, Virginia 20148
800-858-0784; fax: 703-858-0794

Website: nrpa.org

CEO: Barbara Tulipane

Major publication: *Parks & Recreation Magazine*

Purpose: To advance parks, recreation, and environmental conservation efforts that enhance the quality of life for all people. Established 1965.

National School Boards Association (NSBA)

1680 Duke Street
Alexandria, Virginia 22314-3493
703-838-6722; fax: 703-683-7590

Website: nsba.org

Executive director: Thomas Gentzel

Major publications: *American School Board Journal;* ASBK.com; *Inquiry and Analysis; Leadership Insider*

Purpose: To work with and through all our state associations to advocate for excellence and equity in public education through school board leadership. Established 1940.

NIGP: The Institute for Public Procurement

151 Spring Street
Herndon, Virginia 20170-5223
703-736-8900; fax: 703-736-2818
800-FOR NIGP (800-367-6447)

Website: nigp.org

CEO: Rick Grimm, CPPO, CPPB

Major publications: *GoPro: Government Procurement* magazine, a bimonthly publication distributed to NIGP members and procurement professionals; NIGP *Sector Spotlight* edition of *BuyWeekly*, published electronically at the beginning of the month to NIGP members with procurement-related news briefs that affect the procurement community; NIGP's *BuyWeekly*, electronic newsletter, distributed midmonth, a quick overview of current highlights in the profession

Purpose: To develop, support, and promote the public procurement profession through premier educational and research programs, professional support, technical services, and advocacy initiatives that have benefited members and constituents since 1944. With over 20,000 professionals from more than 2,500 local, state, provincial, and federal government contracting agencies across the United States, Canada, and countries outside of North America, NIGP is international in its reach. Its goal is recognition and esteem for the government procurement profession and its dedicated practitioners. NIGP led the way in developing Values and Guiding Principles of Public Procurement. Its Learning Central offers traditional face-to-face courses, independent and interactive online courses, and webinars that address current industry issues and trends affecting how governments do business; all NIGP education experiences qualify toward achieving certification from the Universal Public Procurement Certification Council (UPPCC). NIGP hosts an annual Forum and Products Exposition, the largest gathering of public procurement officials in North America. Spikes Cavell and NIGP brings a proven spend analysis solution to the U.S. public sector. The NIGP Observatory is a spend-and-supplier management solution that delivers the data, tools, and intelligence required to give procurement the insight it needs to reduce cost, realize cooperative opportunities, improve contract compliance, and drive continuous improvements in spend-and-supplier management. NIGP's technology partner, Periscope Holdings, supports the ongoing development of the NIGP Code and the agencies that use it, a universal taxonomy for identifying commodities and services in their procurement systems. NIGP is a cofounding sponsor of U.S. Communities and its affiliate, Canadian Communities, demonstrating its conviction to fully support the practice of cooperative purchasing for the efficiencies it achieves for public entities and the tremendous savings cooperative programs realize for the taxpayer. It is also a cofounding supporter of the UPPCC and its two-level certification program for public procurement personnel. Established 1944.

Police Executive Research Forum (PERF)

1120 Connecticut Avenue, N.W., Suite 930
Washington, D.C. 20036
202-466-7820; fax: 202-466-7826

Website: policeforum.org

Executive director: Chuck Wexler

Major publication: *Subject to Debate* (bimonthly newsletter), Critical Issues in Policing series (several publications annually)

Purpose: To improve policing and advance professionalism through research and involvement in public policy debate. PERF is a national membership organization of progressive police executives from the largest city, county, and state law enforcement agencies. It conducts research and convenes national meetings of police executives and other stakeholders to identify best practices and policies on issues such as police use of force, crime reduction strategies, community and problem-oriented policing, and racial bias, as well as on organizational issues in policing. Incorporated 1977.

Police Foundation

1201 Connecticut Avenue, N.W.
Washington, D.C. 20036-2636
202-833-1460; fax: 202-659-9149

E-mail: pfinfo@policefoundation.org

Website: policefoundation.org

President: Jim Bueermann

Major publications: *Ideas in American Policing* series; research and technical reports on a wide range of law enforcement and public safety issues

Purpose: To improve policing through research, evaluation, field experimentation, training, technical assistance, technology, and information. Objective, nonpartisan, and nonprofit, the Police Foundation helps national, state, and local governments, both in the United States and abroad, to improve performance, service delivery, accountability, and community satisfaction with police services. The foundation offers a wide range of services and specializations, including research, evaluation, surveys, management and operational reviews, climate and culture assessment, training and technical assistance, early-warning and intervention systems, community police collaboration, accountability and ethics, community policing strategies, performance management, racial profiling/biased policing, professional and leadership development. Motivating all its efforts is the goal of efficient, effective, humane policing that operates within the framework of democratic principles. Established in 1970.

Public Risk Management Association (PRIMA)

700 South Washington Street, Suite 218
Alexandria, Virginia 22314-1516
703-528-7701; fax: 703-739-0200

E-mail: info@primacentral.org

Website: primacentral.org

Executive director: Marshall W. Davies, PhD

Major publications: *Public Risk Magazine;*

Purpose: To promote effective risk management in the public interest as an essential component of public administration. Established 1978.

Public Technology Institute (PTI)

1420 Prince Street, Suite 200
Alexandria, Virginia 22314
202-626-2400; fax: 202-626-2498

E-mail: dbowen@pti.org

Website: pti.org

Executive director: Alan R. Shark

Major publications: *CIO Leadership for Cities & Counties; Local Energy Assurance Planning Guide; Beyond e-Government & e-Democracy: A Global Perspective; Measuring Up 2.0; Performance Is the Best Politics; Roads Less Traveled: ITS for Sustainable Communities; Sustainable Building Technical Manual; Mission Possible: Strong Governance Structures for the Integration of Justice Information Systems; E-Government: Factors Affecting ROI; E-Government: A Strategic Planning Guide for Local Officials; Why Not Do It Ourselves? A Resource Guide for Local Government Officials and Citizens Regarding Public Ownership of Utility Systems; Online* magazine (www.prismonline.org); *Winning Solutions* (annual); case studies on energy and environmental technology development and sustainable management

Purpose: To identify and test technologies and management approaches that help all local governments provide the best possible services to citizens and business communities. With ICMA, NLC, and NACo, PTI works with progressive member cities and counties to (1) make communities "well-connected" by advancing communication capabilities; (2) develop tools and processes for wise decision making; and (3) promote sustainable approaches that ensure a balance between economic development and a clean, quality environment. PTI's member program engages cities and counties as laboratories for research, development, and public enterprise to advance technology applications in telecommunications, energy, the environment, transportation, and public safety. To disseminate member research, PTI provides print and electronic resources, and peer consultation and networking. Through partnerships with private vendors, PTI offers several technology products and services that help local governments save money by bypassing rigorist RFP requirements as they are competitively bid and chosen for superior quality and competitive pricing. PTI's research and development division continues to examine information and Internet technology, public safety, geographic information systems (GIS), energy-conserving technologies, sustainable management, and intelligent transportation systems. Established 1971.

Sister Cities International (SCI)

915 15th Street, N.W., 4th Floor
Washington DC 20005
202-347-8630; fax 202-393-6524

E-mail: info@sister-cities.org

Website: sister-cities.org

President and CEO: Mary Kane

Major publication: Sister Cities International Annual Membership Directory

Purpose: To build global cooperation at the municipal level, promote cultural understanding, and stimulate economic development. With its international headquarters in Washington, D.C., SCI, a nonprofit citizen diplomacy network, promotes youth involvement, cultural understanding, and humanitarian assistance. As an international membership organization representing nearly 2,000 partnerships in 140 countries, SCI officially certifies, represents, and supports partnerships between U.S. cities, counties, and states and similar jurisdictions in other countries to ensure their continued commitment and success to peace and prosperity. Established 1956.

Solid Waste Association of North America (SWANA)

1100 Wayne Avenue, Suite 650
Silver Spring, Maryland 20910
800-467-9262; fax: 301-589-7068

E-mail: info@swana.org

Website: swana.org

Executive director: John H. Skinner, PhD

Purpose: To advance the practice of environmentally and economically sound municipal solid-waste management in North America. Established 1961.

Special Libraries Association (SLA)

331 South Patrick Street
Alexandria, Virginia 22314-3501
703-647-4900; fax: 703-647-4901

E-mail: sla@sla.org

Website: sla.org

CEO: Janice R. Lachance

Major publication: *Information Outlook*

Purpose: To promote and strengthen its members through learning, advocacy, and networking initiatives. A nonprofit international organization for innovative information professionals and their strategic partners, SLA serves information professionals—including corporate, academic and government information specialists—in 75 countries. Established 1909.

State and Local Legal Center

Hall of States, 444 N Capitol Street, N.W., Suite 515
Washington, D.C. 20001
202-434-4845; fax: 202-737-1069

Website: statelocallc.org

Executive Director: Lisa Soronen

Publication list: Available on request

Purpose: The State and Local Legal Center files amicus briefs in the U.S. Supreme Court in support of states and local governments, conducts moot courts for attorneys arguing in the Supreme Court, and provides other assistance to states and local governments in connection with Supreme Court litigation. Established 1983.

Universal Public Procurement Certification Council (UPPCC)

151 Spring Street
Herndon, Virginia 20170
800-884-6073; fax: 703-796-9611

E-mail: certification@uppcc.org

Website: uppcc.org

Director: Ann Peshoff, CAE, CMP

Purpose: To identify and establish a standard of competency for the public procurement profession; establish and monitor eligibility requirements of those interested in achieving certification; and further the cause of certification in the public sector. The UPPCC certification programs have been established to meet the requirements of all public procurement personnel in federal, state, and local governments. Certification, which reflects established standards and competencies for those engaged in governmental procurement and attests to the purchaser's ability to obtain maximum value for the taxpayer's dollar, is applicable to all public and governmental organizations, regardless of size. The council offers two credentials: the Certified Professional Public Buyer (CPPB), which applies to individuals who have demonstrated prescribed levels of professional competency as buyers in governmental procurement, and the Certified Public Procurement Officer (CPPO), which applies to similar individuals who also assume managerial functions within their jurisdictions or agencies. As the trend in governmental procurement is for mandatory certification of procurement professionals, these credentials communicate to the taxpayer that the public employee who manages tax dollars has reached a level of education and practical experience within government procurement to be recognized by the UPPCC. Established 1978.

Urban Affairs Association (UAA)

University of Wisconsin–Milwaukee
P.O. Box 413
Milwaukee, Wisconsin 53201-0413
414-229-3025

Website: urbanaffairsassociation.org

Executive director: Dr. Margaret Wilder

Major publications: *Journal of Urban Affairs; Urban Affairs* (a newsletter)

Purpose: To encourage the dissemination of information and research findings about urbanism and urbanization; support the development of university education, research, and service programs in urban affairs; and foster the development of urban affairs as a professional and academic field. Established 1969.

Urban Institute (UI)

2100 M Street, N.W.
Washington, D.C. 20037
202-833-7200

Website: urban.org

President: Sarah Rosen Wartell

Publications: Research papers, policy briefs, events, podcasts, web modules, and books on social and economic issues, including health care, welfare reform, immigration policy, tax reform, prisoner reentry, housing policy, retirement, charitable giving, school accountability, economic development, and community revitalization; all publications available online except books

Purpose: To respond to needs for objective analyses and basic information on the social and economic challenges confronting the nation, and for nonpartisan evaluation of the government policies and programs designed to alleviate such problems. Established 1968.

Urban and Regional Information Systems Association (URISA)

701 Lee Street, Suite 680
Des Plaines, Illinois 60016
847-824-6300; fax: 847-824-6363

Website: urisa.org

Executive director: Wendy Nelson

Major publications: *URISA Journal; The GIS Professional;* Quick Studies, books and compendiums, salary surveys, conference proceedings, videos

Purpose: To provide exceptional educational experiences, a vibrant and connected community, and the essential resources that professionals in the spatial data community need to be successful in their careers. An independent, not-for-profit educational organization, URISA presents an abundance of educational programs, from webinars and workshops to multiday conferences; offers volunteer GIS expertise through its GISCorps program; and assists government agencies with benchmarking GIS maturity through its GIS Management Institute. Established 1966.

U.S. Conference of Mayors (USCM)

1620 Eye Street, N.W.
Washington, D.C. 20006
202-293-7330; fax: 202-293-2352

E-mail: info@usmayors.org

Website: usmayors.org

Executive director/CEO: Tom Cochran

Major publications: *U.S. Mayor; Mayors of America's Principal Cities*

Purpose: To act as the official nonpartisan organization of cities with populations of 30,000 or more; to aid the development of effective national urban policy; to ensure that federal policy meets urban needs; and to provide mayors with leadership and management tools. Each city is represented in the conference by its mayor. Established 1932.

Water Environment Federation (WEF)

601 Wythe Street
Alexandria, Virginia 22314-1994
571-830-1545; fax: 703-684-2492
800-666-0206

Websites: wef.org, weftec.org

Executive director: Jeff Eger

Major publications: *Water Environment Research; Water Environment and Technology; Water Environment Regulation Watch; The Stormwater Report;* series of Manuals of Practice

Purpose: To provide bold leadership, champion innovation, connect water professionals, and leverage knowledge to support clean and safe water worldwide. The WEF is a not-for-profit technical and educational organization of 36,000 individual members and 75 affiliated member associations representing water quality professionals around the world. Established 1928.

Authors and Contributors

Authors and Contributors

Ted A. Gaebler, who recently retired as the first city manager of Rancho Cordova, California, has been a city manager and/or chief executive officer of seven local government agencies. He is also a consultant, a lecturer, and the internationally known coauthor of *Reinventing Government.* Widely sought after to educate and inspire government officials to take a new approach to management, Mr. Gaebler has been acknowledged as a revolutionary "reinventor" and "public entrepreneur," changing governments peacefully from the inside out for over 40 years. He pioneered the Broker, Facilitator, Catalyst, and Educator philosophy to leverage the power, passion, and resources in the private and nonprofit sectors and among citizens. His methods continue to be innovative, imaginative, and entrepreneurial. In 2009 Mr. Gaebler received the L. P. Cookingham Award from ICMA for his lifelong work in training and mentoring young professionals entering the local government field. He graduated from Miami University in Ohio before earning his master's degree in government administration from the University of Pennsylvania's Wharton Graduate School of Business.

Cheryl Hilvert serves as the director of ICMA's Center for Management Strategies, which provides research, education, and technical assistance on leading management practices for local governments. A former local government manager with over 31 years of service in Ohio, she is also designated as a credentialed manager by ICMA. Ms. Hilvert has served as ICMA's Midwest regional vice president and as a board member and chair of the Alliance for Innovation, Ohio City/County Management Association,

Senior Executive Institute Advisory Committee, Cincinnati Area Local Government Management Association, and Greater Cincinnati Chapter of the American Society for Public Administration (ASPA). She has received numerous professional honors, including the 2010 Public Administrator of the Year from the Greater Cincinnati Chapter of ASPA and 2011 Program Excellence Award for Strategic Leadership and Governance from ICMA. She holds a bachelor's degree and a master of public administration degree from Eastern Kentucky University; she is also a graduate of the Senior Executive Institute at the University of Virginia and the Economic Development Institute at the University of Oklahoma.

Troy Holt serves as the director of communications and government relations for the city of Rancho Cordova, California. He has 25 years of public agency management experience in a range of departments, such as police, public works, transportation, and administrative services, as well as in the city manager's office. He is on the board of directors for the Sacramento chapter of the American Society for Public Administration and is a member of the ICMA Advisory Board on Graduate Education. A graduate of Harvard University's Kennedy School of Government Senior Executives in State and Local Government program, Mr. Holt holds a master of public administration degree with highest honors from Golden Gate University. He earned his bachelor of arts degree from the University of California–Irvine in social ecology with emphases in criminology; law and society; environmental health, science, and policy; psychology and social behavior; and planning, policy, and design.

George C. Homsy is an assistant professor in the Department of Public Administration at Binghamton University. His research revolves around local government sustainability and resilience, land use planning, and public service delivery. At Binghamton University, he is part of a team developing a new master's degree in the field of sustainable communities. He received both his master of regional planning degree and his PhD from Cornell University.

Elizabeth K. Kellar is president/CEO for the Center for State and Local Government Excellence and also serves as deputy executive director for ICMA. She is a Fellow in the National Academy of Public Administration and has served as chair of the Panel on the Federal System. She serves on the Advisory Council of the American University School of Public Affairs. She began her local government career with the City of Sunnyvale, California, and has a master's degree from the Ohio State University.

Tad McGalliard leads ICMA's research, outreach, member engagement, and technical assistance efforts offered by four program centers focused on sustainable communities, public safety, citizen engagement, high performance organizations, shared services, priority based budgeting, and performance measurement. He previously served as the director of ICMA's Center for Sustainable Communities. Prior to joining ICMA, he worked in research and development and extension services at Cornell University, and before that he was employed by the University of Tennessee's Energy, Environment and Resources Center (EERC). He received both his bachelor's and his master's degrees from the University of Tennessee.

Barbara H. Moore is the communications and marketing manager for ICMA International. This represents an "encore career" for Ms. Moore, who directed ICMA's publishing and information resources programs for many years before shifting to a new role with the organization in 2004. In the course of her career, she was a member of ICMA's senior management/leadership team and also served as the ICMA staff liaison to states in the Midwest Region and to the Advisory Board on Graduate Education, a group of managers who meet jointly with professors of public administration to explore ways to enhance the education of future local government professionals. Her responsibilities also included oversight of ICMA's Center for Performance Measurement and the Management Information Service, which was later superseded by the online Knowledge Network. She has a

bachelor's degree from Grinnell College in Grinnell, Iowa, and has enjoyed the educational benefits of editing numerous graduate-level public administration textbooks for ICMA.

Evelina R. Moulder, director of ICMA's survey research, is responsible for the development of survey instruments, design of the sample, design of logic checks, quality control, and analysis of survey results. Among the surveys conducted by ICMA under her supervision are economic development, e-government, financing infrastructure, homeland security, labor-management relations, parks and recreation, police and fire personnel and expenditures, service delivery, technology, and sustainability. She has also directed several survey projects funded by other organizations. With more than 25 years of experience in local government survey research, Ms. Moulder has collaborated extensively with government agencies, professors, the private sector, and other researchers in survey development, and she has played a key role in ICMA's homeland security and emergency response initiatives, including concept and proposal development.

Kimberly L. Nelson is associate professor of public administration and government at the School of Government at the University of North Carolina, Chapel Hill. Her research and teaching interests focus on local government management, local government form and structure, and innovation in local government. Her research on the effects of form of government on municipal performance and innovation has been published in leading journals, including *The American Review of Public Administration, Urban Affairs Review,* and *State and Local Government Review.* She is also the author of book chapters and a regular presenter and participant at the conferences of ICMA and the American Society for Public Administration. Dr. Nelson uses her research experience to inform her client work with local governments in strategic planning and improving local government–administrative relations, as well as to train local government leaders in promoting innovative practices. She received her PhD from North Carolina State University.

Robert J. O'Neill Jr. is executive director of ICMA. Prior to joining ICMA in November 2002, he served for two years as president of the National Academy of Public Administration (NAPA). From May through September of 2001, Mr. O'Neill was on temporary assignment at the Office of Management and Budget as counselor to the director and deputy director on management issues. Between 1997 and 2000, he served as Fairfax County executive, where he oversaw Virginia's largest general-purpose local government. His "reinvention" of the government of Hampton, Virginia, where he served as city manager between 1984 and 1997, was widely recognized by such organizations as the National League of Cities and Public Technology, Inc. He is a 1984 graduate of the Executive Program of the Colgate Darden Graduate School of Business at the University of Virginia. In 1996 Mr. O'Neill received the prestigious National Public Service Award presented by NAPA and the American Society for Public Administration; he was elected as a NAPA Academy Fellow in 1997 and was awarded an honorary doctorate of laws from Old Dominion University in 2000. He graduated summa cum laude from Old Dominion University with a bachelor's degree in political science in 1973; received his master of public administration degree from the Maxwell School of Citizenship and Public Affairs at Syracuse University in 1974; and in 2001 received that institution's highest honor, the Spirit of Public Service award.

James H. Svara is visiting professor at the School of Government, University of North Carolina at Chapel Hill, and research professor of public affairs at Arizona State University (ASU), specializing in local government leadership, innovation, and management. He is a Fellow of the National Academy of Public Administration, chair of the Code of Ethics Implementation Committee of the American Society for Public Administration, and an honorary member of ICMA. He is currently involved in an ICMA/ASU research project on social equity in sustainability programs in local government. He is author of *The Ethics Primer for Public Administrators in Government and Nonprofit Organizations,* 2nd edition.

David Swindell is director of the Center for Urban Innovation and an associate professor at Arizona State University (ASU), where he advocates the university metropolitan mission concept for developing new solutions to the challenges confronting municipalities. His publications, legislative testimonies, and teaching interests focus on community and economic development, especially public financing of sports facilities, the contribution of sports facilities to the economic development of urban space, the role of nonprofit community and neighborhood-based organizations as mechanisms for service delivery, and citizen satisfaction and performance measurement standards for public management and decision making. Before joining ASU, he served seven years as director of the interdisciplinary PhD in Public Policy at the University of North Carolina (UNC) at Charlotte. He was also director of the UNC-Charlotte MPA program and of the MPA program at Clemson University. He received his doctorate in public policy from Indiana University.

Karen Thoreson is president/chief operating officer for the Alliance for Innovation. Prior to working for the Alliance, she was economic development director for the city of Glendale, Arizona. She also served as assistant city manager of Tucson and as director of the community services department. Ms. Thoreson began her career in local government in Boulder, Colorado; since then, she has been a trainer and a speaker on public-private partnerships, community revitalization, innovation, and strategic planning. She has a bachelor's degree from the University of Minnesota and a master's degree in public administration from the University of Northern Colorado.

Mildred E. Warner is a professor in the City and Regional Planning Department at Cornell University, where her work focuses on the role of local government in community development. Her research addresses trends facing local government such as devolution, fiscal stress and privatization. She gives special attention to the local government response as regards economic development strategy, service delivery design and planning across generations. She publishes widely in the public administration, planning, and economic development literature. Dr. Warner received her BA from Oberlin College and her MA and PhD from Cornell.

Cumulative Index, 2010-2014

The cumulative index comprises the years 2010 through 2014 of *The Municipal Year Book*. Entries prior to 2010 are found in earlier editions.

How to Use This Index. Entries run in chronological order, starting with 2010. The **year** is in **boldface** numerals, followed by a colon (e.g., **10**:); the relevant page numbers follow. Years are separated by semicolons.

The Municipal Year Book 2014
Volume 81

Composition by
Erika Abrams
ICMA

Printing and binding by
United Book Press
Baltimore, MD